Peter Handke
Plays: 1

Offending the Audience, Self-Accusation, Kaspar, My Foot My Tutor, The Ride Across Lake Constance, They Are Dying Out

Offending the Audience: The subject is the audience. The actors speak to the audience and establish that there is no play, no story, no action, no hidden meaning, just themselves speaking to the audience. 'A dissection of our expectations about what ought to happen in the theatre.' *TLS*

Self-Accusation: 'A progressive (or maybe regressive) account of the development of the individual – from the buoyancy and responsiveness of childhood to the awareness of rules in society, to the eventual acceptance of guilt . . . valid and moving.' *Guardian*

'*Offending the Audience* and *Self-Accusation* are "Sprechstücke"; their subject is the language we use . . . Man is depicted as the product of language and becomes a montage of linguistic banalities: commands, definitions, prohibitions and all the familiar verbal restrictions of a repressive society. . . . With the "Sprechstücke" Handke created a special kind of verbal alienation, examining words on an empty stage, juggling with the same terms in various syntactical sequences and allowing the histrionics of presentation to make the familiar seem strange.' *TLS*

'*Kaspar* is based on the historical case of a sixteen-year-old boy who appeared from nowhere in Nuremberg in 1828 and who had to be taught to speak from scratch . . . Handke's play is a downright attack on the way language is used by a corrupt society to depersonalise the individual.' *Guardian*
'The play of the decade.' Max Frisch

My Foot My Tutor, a mime for two actors: 'Handke has here written an hour-long play without words that may at first look like a piece of audience-provocation, but that finishes up as sheer theatrical poetry.' *Guardian*

In *The Ride Across Lake Constance* a group of characters, known only by the names of the actors who perform the parts, talk and play games together, skating over the thin ice that separates them from unspoken danger. 'Intensely theatrical . . . An author for whom playwriting seems akin to tightrope walking.' *The Times*

'*They Are Dying Out* is a new departure for Handke as it appears to move out of his usual abstract parrying of language into the world of social encounter. Here he puts the pillars of the bourgeoisie under his microscope and, with his uncanny knack for making the familiar seem strange, shows us an alien race, suffocated by rationality, unable to cope with untamed subjective impulses.' *Plays and Players*

Peter Handke was born in Griffen, Austria, in 1942 and studied law at the University of Graz. In 1966 his first novel was published and his first play, *Offending the Audience*, was staged in Frankfurt. This was seen in London in 1971 and was followed by productions of *My Foot My Tutor* (1971), *Self Accusation*, *Prophecy* and *Calling for Help* (1972), *Kaspar* and *The Ride Across Lake Constance* (1972), the latter transferring successfully to the West End, *They Are* [...] Long Way Round (National Theatre, 19[...] Goalie's Anxiety at the Penalty Kick (sub[...] Short Letter, Long Farewell and the sem[...] which were published in Britain in 1977[...] drawn from his film of the same title, w[...] thematically connected novels, Slow Ho[...] Repetition (1988); Afternoon of a Writer ([...]

by the same author

PLAYS
The Long Way Round

NOVELS
The Goalie's Anxiety at the Penalty Kick
Short Letter, Long Farewell
A Sorrow Beyond Dreams
The Left-Handed Woman
Slow Homecoming
Across
Repetition
The Afternoon of a Writer
Absence

Plays: 1

Offending the Audience

Self-Accusation

Kaspar

My Foot My Tutor

The Ride Across Lake Constance

translated by Michael Roloff

They Are Dying Out

translated by Michael Roloff in collaboration with Karl Weber

with an introduction by Tom Kuhn

Methuen Drama

METHUEN CONTEMPORARY DRAMATISTS

This collection first published in Great Britain 1997
by Methuen Drama
Random House, 20 Vauxhall Bridge Road, London SW1V 2SA
and Australia, New Zealand and South Africa
Random House UK Limited Reg. No. 954009

CONTENTS

CHRONOLOGY

1942   Peter Handke born in Carinthia, Austria, where the family (mother, son and stepfather) then settle after the war; life of rural monotony.

1961–5   Law studies in Graz; first publications.

1965   The novel *Die Hornissen* (*The Hornets*) accepted by the renowned Suhrkamp publishing house and published the following year; Handke abandons his studies; begins his 'Sprechstücke' ('speak-ins'): *Weissagung* (*Prophecy*), *Selbstbezichtigung* (*Self-Accusation*) and *Hilferufe* (*Calling for Help*), as well as *Publikumsbeschimpfung* (see below).

He begins a period of restless moves, living briefly in various German cities and in Paris and the United States. Early travels in the old Yugoslavia and Romania, as well as, later, elsewhere in Europe, North America and Japan. Since 1991 he has lived near Paris.

1966   *Publikumsbeschimpfung* (*Offending the Audience*) and other 'Sprechstücke' published by Suhrkamp; first performance of *Publikumsbeschimpfung* at the Theater am Turm, Frankfurt, directed by Claus Peymann, 1966; first performance in Britain by The Other Company at the Oval House, London, 1970; *Selbstbezichtigung* first performed in Stockholm, 1967; the other 'Sprechstücke' first performed in Frankfurt and Oberhausen in 1966–7, and in Britain by the Almost Free Theatre, London, in 1972; *Self-Accusation* also broadcast on BBC Radio 3 in 1968.

1967   A second novel, *Der Hausierer* (*The Hawker*), is published. Handke receives the Gerhart Hauptmann Prize.

1968   *Kaspar* – first performances at both the Theater am Turm, Frankfurt, directed by Claus Peymann, and the Städtische Bühnen in Oberhausen, directed by Günter Büch; first performance in Britain by the Almost Free Theatre, London, 1973; broadcast in Germany in a radio version in 1981.

1969   *Das Mündel will Vormund sein* (*My Foot My Tutor*) – first performance at the Theater am Turm, Frankfurt, directed by Claus Peymann; first performance in Britain by the Open Space Theatre, London, 1971.

Die Innenwelt der Aussenwelt der Innenwelt (*The Innerworld of the Outerworld of the Innerworld*), poems, published.

1970   The story *Die Angst des Tormanns beim Elfmeter* (*The Goalie's Anxiety at the Penalty Kick*); later adapted as a television film (1972).

Der Ritt über den Bodensee (*The Ride Across Lake Constance*) – first performance in 1971 at the Schaubühne am Halleschen Ufer, Berlin, directed by Claus Peymann; first performance in Britain at the Hampstead Theatre, London, 1973.

INTRODUCTION

Peter Handke is an extraordinarily protean writer. For years now he has been challenging – sometimes baiting – his public with radical experiments and bold reinventions of his literary language and persona. His avant-garde creed is deceptively simple: that each aesthetic gesture may only be made once, for its effectiveness is immediately exhausted as it is reintegrated into the 'conventional'. Some critics, perhaps baffled by the contradictions of his at times esoteric œuvre, have been determined to trace Handke's literary expression to the dulling constrictions of his upbringing; they have labelled him 'Catholic', 'petty bourgeois', 'Austrian'. But Handke has become a much more varied and European phenomenon than this. His literary development might best be represented as a series of affronts: directed both at the public and, perhaps more significantly, against his own positions and most recent work. He has been a restless traveller, both literally and culturally: in Europe, in North America, and in the Far East; and he has lived for long periods in France and the United States. His plays have been performed in theatres all over the world, his books have been extensively translated, and since the 1980s he has enjoyed a rich partnership with the German film director Wim Wenders.

This volume presents the early and energetic dramatic forays with which this searchingly personal author shocked the European scene in the 1960s and 70s. The combination of qualities which keeps these works so lively – their intellectual rigour, biting irony and absurd playfulness – provides impressive testimony that, in the field of European theatre, Peter Handke is very definitely still one to be reckoned with.

The 1960s were a period of the politicisation of intellectual life, above all in Germany. The student movement was building up to its climax of protests and rebellions in 1968. Such leading writers of the older generation as Hans Magnus Enzensberger (b.1929) and Peter Weiss (b.1916) were edging close to a denial of the whole category of literature, preferring instead some form of direct political action. In the theatres, documentary drama was the new thing. The tone was set in 1963 by the premiere of Rolf Hochhuth's massive documentation of the complicity of the Holy See in the Nazi deportations of Jews, *The Representative*; that was followed by Peter Weiss's dramatisation of the Auschwitz trials, *The Investigation*, and his dense and untheatrical protest against US involvement in the Vietnam war, *Viet-Nam Discourse*. Against this background people found it hard to know what to make of Handke's *Offending the Audience* and the other 'Sprechstücke' (1965-7). There was protest there, that was clear enough, but it could seem a frightfully self-indulgent protest, obsessed with the forms of the theatre and denying the whole potential of literature to portray the world and to convey a message – capacities on which documentary drama appeared utterly dependent.

Handke followed up his plays with an aggressive attack on his fellow authors, delivered in Princeton in 1968, in which he taunted them with their 'Beschreibungsimpotenz' (impotent descriptivism). According to Handke, they were simply re-enacting the redundant rituals of various forms of representational realism which had been left far behind by his own avant-garde theory. For the left-wing cultural establishment in West Germany Handke soon became something of a hate-figure, while the more conservative critics tried to write him off as some deviant representative of the 'Beat-generation'. Handke responded with characteristic defiance: in a series of attacks on Brecht's political literature and Sartre's theory of 'engagement', and in essays, well-calculated to raise his public profile, with red-rag titles like 'I live in the ivory tower' and 'Literature is romantic'. To some extent Handke's positions were indeed simply a reprise of those moments of extreme aesthetic self-liberation which originate in early romantic theory and which had long since had their great twentieth-century day in Dadaism. In the context of the late 1960s, however, these were indecent propositions, thoughts one simply could not voice.

Handke's whole involvement in the theatre has its origins in a protest against received models. 'Modern drama', he wrote in 1965, 'is made up of attempts to break out' – of the constraints of genre and of the conventions of the theatre. One thing the student movement had brought to Handke, despite his disengaged individualism, was a sense of the possibility of alternative, more immediate and less institutionalised artforms, such as street-theatre. Despite the aggression with which he sometimes rounded on Brecht, Handke's embrace of these alternatives and his questioning of forms in fact brought him into quite close proximity with that unavoidable authority of twentieth-century German theatre. For Handke is where Brecht meets Ionesco. His insistence that the theatre is the site merely and solely of games, appearances and metaphors, not of the real, is reminiscent of French absurd theatre. But his determination to avoid realist illusionism and to involve the audience more directly in the theatre-event can also be seen in relation to Brecht's ideas.

Handke's theatre reveals its own theatricality, not in order that we may reflect directly on reality, but in order, in the first place, to demonstrate the theatre's own dependence on rules and conventions. He chooses the form of the 'Sprechstück' – 'spectacles without pictures' of the world, but with only words – to draw our attention back to the world of language. In his theatrical and linguistic games, which deny overt reference to the 'real' world, we perceive a kinship with another contemporary movement in German literature, namely with abstract or 'concrete' poetry. There are elements in early Handke of a pure and 'concrete' theatre (the relationship is acknowledged in the quotation of a poem by Ernst Jandl as an epigraph to *Kaspar*). Handke's purpose, however, is not merely an acoustic playfulness, but, on the contrary, a concerted critique of forms and of language. This critique is a central plank of Handke's aesthetic philosophy. Nevertheless, it would be a mistake to leave it at that. The idea of unmasking something apparently 'natural' and commonplace as an artificial construct brings us back once more to Brecht. Both Brecht and Handke employ a kind of disorienting 'estrangement' (Handke calls it 'Befremdung', rather than Brecht's social 'Verfremdung'), so that we may at least envisage that things could and should be otherwise. Handke does not see specifically social instruction as a possible task for art, and – unlike Brecht – he does not seek to promote a particular alternative: he calls Brecht's models 'arresting Christmas fairy-tales'. All the same, he does intend to arouse the sense of the possibility of alternatives. In unmasking the conventions of language and theatre

Handke reveals also how social life, and ultimately consciousness and perception too, are governed by an unconscious dramaturgy of convention.

Offending the Audience

Offending the Audience was initially conceived, not as a play, but as a polemical essay about the theatre; 'this piece is conducting an argument with the theatre', as the speakers say. Contrary to many accounts of the play (sometimes translated as *Insulting the Audience*) it is very far from simply an occasion for actors to stand at the front of the stage and abuse the public. In fact only a couple of the twenty-five pages, right at the beginning and right at the end, are given over to a brief torrent of inventive and neologistic invective. For the rest, the piece is indeed a confrontation with each and every one of the conventions of the usual theatre. Every possible expectation is categorically and explicitly denied by the four 'speakers': 'These boards don't signify a world. . . . This room does not make believe it is a room. . . . This is not another world. We are not pretending that you don't exist.' And so on. The point is to make the public conscious, not merely of the mechanisms and assumptions of the theatre, but also of the mechanisms and assumptions of *going to* the theatre. From the start, when the empty stage and peopled auditorium are both equally illuminated, it is clear that the public is not merely to be shocked by a spectacle, but to become themselves the subject of the play. They are invited to reflect – on their physical presence, their situation, and their whole role in the event: 'You were the heroes of this piece. . . . You were the find of the evening. You lived your roles.'

There is of course a glorious paradox in presenting a pamphlet against the theatre inside the theatre; and it is this paradox which any production of the play must exploit and enjoy. Claus Peymann's famous first production in Frankfurt helped to ensure a scandalous debut for Handke. However, the verbal and physical energy of Peymann's actors seemed to have turned *Offending the Audience* into a virtuoso piece of theatre. Handke's stark essay against a theatre of representation had become, in spite of itself, a wonderful spectacle. It had been reintegrated into just that institution of the theatre against which it was apparently directed. Later, when a volume of his collected plays was published, Handke himself reflected that it was perhaps time for a more straightforward production, with as few physical gestures as possible. After all, he had never wanted the public to *accept* his play, but rather to watch *all* plays with greater irritation, mistrust and awareness: 'This piece is a prologue. . . . the prologue to your future visits to the theatre.'

Offending the Audience was of course also an extreme statement of an aesthetic position, a position which, once stated, could only lose force as it was reiterated. The destruction of the experience of the theatre in the theatre could only ever succeed for a shocking utopian second of theatre-history. Thereafter, the dim-witted passivity and consumerism of the public were sure to reassert themselves; and a public that actually wanted to enjoy the rehearsal of its own disappointment and humiliation was no longer a worthy audience or subject for the play. Perhaps, in accordance with Handke's own theory of the avant-garde, *Offending the Audience* is a piece which might ideally have been performed only once.

Self-Accusation

Handke takes up the method of his first play in a further three short 'Sprechstücke': *Self-Accusation*, *Prophecy* and *Calling for Help*. In each of them there is no action, no stage, no characterisation, nothing to distract from the formal rehearsal, variation and denial of what he calls 'natural forms of expression'. They are all investigations of language and of the forms of the theatre, designed to serve, as Handke says in his 'Note', as 'autonomous prologues to the old plays' – as a means to sensitise the audience and to make them aware.

Self-Accusation is perhaps the most fascinatingly contradictory of the three. For here Handke permits himself just the slightest of hints of a plot and a personal history. The linguistic formulae on which the text is based are those of the Catholic confession and of the public self-vilification familiar from show-trials in totalitarian regimes. In a note on the play Handke insists that this is just a plagiaristic borrowing of the form, and that the 'I' who speaks is merely the first person of formal grammar, not a personalised 'I'. But he cannot obliterate the lingering sense of a personal guilt. Although the text is not formally divided between the speakers, this time there are explicitly two roles, male and female. The text begins with a dedication to Handke's real wife, Libgart, and ends with an apparently guilty self-revelation, 'I wrote this piece' (in early productions continuing, 'I shan't do it again'). Such indications are, however, thoroughly undermined by other features of the text. The first spoken words, 'I came into the world', establish the extremely generalised tone. They suggest that this is not a personal but a universal human lament; not personal guilt is the theme of the piece, but original sin, perhaps. Ultimately the 'I' has the capacity to flip over from the depersonalised speakers to the audience; as Handke remarked, the play is concerned with the spectator himself. However, all these interpretations soon begin to falter in the face of the random catalogue of real and imaginary misdemeanours and the almost sensuous crescendos of linguistic formulae: 'Which rules of love did I violate? . . . Which rules of cosmetics did I violate? . . . Which law of free fall did I violate?'

The 'Sprechstücke' present us with a condensed 'anti-dramaturgy'. Nevertheless, every gesture of denial and defiance remains dependent on the institutions of theatre and of literary language against which it pretends to rebel. Handke may play games against the traditional dramatic method, but he cannot play games entirely without it. *Antitheater* simply becomes the new theatre. What is more, despite the conviction that the theatre is no place for a serious discourse about the real world, despite the repeated assertions that in the theatre everything necessarily becomes a sort of formalised game, there is clearly also an educative potential lurking behind Handke's 'speak-ins'.

Kaspar

In *Kaspar*, Handke's next full-length play, this potential is realised more fully. What had seemed to have to do almost exclusively with the forms of the theatre, at most with the social experience of the theatre, now has to do explicitly with language, education and society. The first pages of *Self-Accusation* had already touched on the learning of language and of social identity; in *Kaspar*, those few paragraphs are extended and scrutinised over and over. Here also, by the creation of a named figure rather than just an anonymous voice, who is, moreover, enmeshed in a plot of sorts, Handke seems to have nudged at least a little closer to a drama for the real theatre. *Offending the Audience* was an important moment in twentieth-century theatre-history, but it is with *Kaspar* that Handke has created his own masterpiece of twentieth-century drama.

Kaspar Hauser, from whose story the play takes its title, was an adolescent foundling who turned up on the streets of Nuremberg in 1828. He appeared to have no language (but for a single sentence: 'I want to be someone like my father once was'), he had no knowledge of human society, and he could scarcely walk. When eventually he learnt to speak he could say only that he had lived, as long as he could remember, alone in a dark room. His case attracted enormous publicity. Soon Kaspar was surrounded by patrons and teachers, and in 1831 he was adopted by an English aristocrat, Lord Stanhope. Although his development remained uneven he acquired some skills and social graces and became for a time a social curiosity. In December 1833, apparently after other attacks and threats, he was found mysteriously murdered. The mystery surrounding Kaspar Hauser has never been cleared up. It is thought that he was perhaps an unwanted prince of the house of Baden, condemned to his inhuman fate by rivals within the family. In any event, he became a phenomenon of nineteenth-century intellectual inquiry, as, one by one, the anthropologists, linguistic philosophers, pedagogues, psychologists, and representatives of every other science and pseudo-science all had their say. Literary treatments abounded. Kaspar Hauser became the subject of a number of French and German novels and of poems by Paul Verlaine and Georg Trakl. More recently there have been at least three films about him, notably that by Werner Herzog in 1975.

Handke's *Kaspar* comes onto the stage as if he had never walked nor stood there, or anywhere else, before, and when he first speaks it is a version of the historical Kaspar Hauser's sentence that comes out: 'I want to be someone like somebody else once was.' Kaspar Hauser himself had been almost without prehistory, but for Handke's Kaspar even the notion of parentage is too much. Onto this extraordinary new beginning Handke now proceeds to project a terrible story of language learning and socialisation which has little or nothing to do with the historical model. 'The play *Kaspar* does not show how IT REALLY IS or REALLY WAS with Kaspar Hauser. It shows what IS POSSIBLE with someone. It shows how someone can be made to speak through speaking. The play could also be called *speech torture*.'

The world for Kaspar, at the outset of the play, is chaos; but it is a chaos into which he throws himself with some curiosity and enthusiasm. His sentence, however little sense it may seem to make, situates him between a past ('somebody once was') and a future ('I want to be'), and seems to offer him some security. It is his own sentence, and as such is perhaps already a sort of expression of identity. As the play proceeds, however, Kaspar is bombarded with linguistic material by disembodied 'prompters' until, first, his original sentence dissolves. Then he is guided systematically through a process of language acquisition. Language, it appears, is a necessary precondition for the proper differentiation of consciousness and the development of personality (this sort of determinism is familiar to linguistic theory as the Sapir-Whorf hypothesis). The language he learns does indeed organise the world for him, but it also closes it off from direct or 'natural' experience. Rather than an education, he receives a crippling deconstruction. He becomes a fluent speaker, but no longer of his own lines. Moreover, the new linguistic world which is created for him by the repetition of apparently innocent syntactic models is at times transparently tainted by a repressive social and political ideology: 'The rich man is rich but friendly. The poor man is poor but happy. . . . War is indeed a misfortune, but sometimes inescapable. . . . Force is indeed a dubious method, but it can be useful.' And so on. The examples can be both hilarious and at times deeply threatening. Just very occasionally the sentences that Kaspar articulates in reply suggest a deep comprehension of and resistance to the process: 'I was already awake. I was already kicking. I am whispering already. . . . I still don't believe it.' But it seems he has no choice. He ends section 27 of the play with a helpless tautology (albeit with biblical overtones) as his only expression of identity: 'I am the one I am.' Later, Kaspar's individual identity is so eroded that he becomes interchangeable with the other Kaspars who suddenly appear onstage from section 33 onwards. By the 'Intermission' he seems to have become 'self-confident'; in fact he has been utterly 'socialised' and robbed of the last remnants of a self which could have unsettled that confident world-view. By the very end of the play he is reduced once more to almost nonsensical babble – his final exclamation, 'Goats and monkeys', borrowed tellingly from Othello's anguished slide from social paragon to roaring beast. Originally the last line was a more explicit recognition: 'I: am: only: I: by chance.'

The criticism of language undertaken here is at the same time a criticism of social institutions and of what was known in the 1960s as the 'consciousness industry' of advertising and political sloganising. But it clearly goes beyond that too: speaking and language are thematised in their whole relation to order, authority, power and violence. Perhaps Handke is not even just saying that language *can* be used to manipulate and indoctrinate. Rather, in a typically radical gesture, he seems to be saying that language *has to* be a trap, that by language personality structures are necessarily deformed, if not destroyed. But the play remains ambivalent. It raises also the suggestion that poetry, in the Shakespeare quotation and in the anarchic associations and rhythms which lie beneath the controlled linguistic terror, may just conceal a capacity to resist these processes.

In *Kaspar* Handke has also gone a good step further than saying that the theatre cannot reproduce the world. On the contrary, now we can see how the world itself is little more than a reproduction of the theatre. Reading, watching, listening to this play we should learn that social conditions are themselves not 'given' or 'natural', but manipulated and staged. We should learn, as Handke puts it, 'to see through nature as dramaturgy', the dramaturgy, namely, of the repressive 'powers that be'.

My Foot My Tutor
Handke's short play, *My Foot My Tutor*, presents us with a more starkly simple and yet ultimately frustrating pantomime. As in *Kaspar*, we are ushered into a strange world of an apparently

autonomous theatre. At first Handke's ward and warden seem to bear even greater resemblance to the characters of traditional drama (their roles defined by their functional labels) than did Kaspar. Besides, whereas in *Kaspar* the stage and its props explicitly represented nothing more than themselves, here the stage-set presents us with a 'scene', an apparently familiar theatre-illusion: a field, a sunny day. But into this world of apparently secure symbolic representation Handke has introduced one utterly undermining presence: a cat. At first, having a live animal onstage seems to underpin the authentic present-tense feel of the scene. As the play progresses, however, the cat – who, according to the occasional stage 'direction', simply 'does what it does' – emerges as an ironically powerful image of resistance to images, and to all authorial, dramaturgical or directorial control (so much so that it was omitted from the first performance). As for the 'characters', they are locked in an austere, mute drama, for this is a play without even the distractions of a spoken text. Instead of a plot, or developing characters, or a significant relationship, Handke offers us a bizarre focus on apparently trivial gestures: eating an apple, sitting at a table, reading a newspaper. The set and figures soon cease to imply any familiar or specific reference to a real world. Instead, the obsessive attention to details of insignificant behaviour serve to catch our imagination and provoke our frustrated will to interpret in perhaps quite random and unforeseen ways.

What we most certainly do discover – and in this the play is an extension of *Kaspar* – is that even a world without language is very far from free. The German title, *Das Mündel will Vormund sein* (the ward/minor wants to be warden/guardian), suggests perhaps yet another narrative of processes of education and training and of social power relationships gone awry. The fragmentary episodes appear to illustrate a relationship of almost total subjugation of ward to warden: the warden's pencil is much bigger than the ward's, the warden's pumpkin absurdly trumps the ward's apple-eating. The ward's dependence leads in turn to clumsy attempts to emulate his guardian, or to provoke a different relationship. There are signs of a ridiculous and probably utterly harmless protest. By the end, the simple agricultural scene of slicing the tops of beets has taken on an unmistakable air of subdued violence (the German for beet, 'Rübe', is also slang for head).

Critics and theatre-practitioners alike have discovered that they can treat this play either as a sequence of almost Brechtian practice scenes, rehearsing the bare gestics of social attitudes, or else as a despairing dumb-play, closer in inspiration to Beckett than anything else Handke has written. Elsewhere, Handke has suggested, in flat contradiction of Brecht, that phenomena, gestures and objects may all have a kind of language of their own which remains essentially untranslatable into speech. *My Foot My Tutor* has not been Handke's only silent play. In 1992 he followed it up with a *tour de force* of endlessly interpretable fragments of actions, encounters, plots and relationships, *The Hour We Knew Nothing of Each Other*.

The Ride Across Lake Constance

The Ride Across Lake Constance is to some extent a résumé of the theatrical and antitheatrical gestures which have preceded it. In formal terms it is a combination of a 'Sprechstück' and a dumb-play, combining speech and gesture in that rigorous abstraction now familiar from *Self-Accusation* and *My Foot My Tutor* (which Handke himself has described as a prelude to *The Ride*). Thematically, where *Offending the Audience* attacked the assumptions of the theatre and *Kaspar* those of language, *The Ride Across Lake Constance* declares war on the whole notion of a semiotic scheme or system of categorisation. Our very organs of perception, maybe even the phenomena of nature themselves (to which we have no certain access) have run aground on the silted immobility of the systems.

This time Handke's stage-set is an exaggerated image of a stage-set, with its staircase and doors and carefully positioned furniture. Through it and over it Handke's over-theatrical figures (who in production are to bear the names of the actors themselves) rehearse a dream-like choreography, of alternating elegance and brutality, derived from a familiar repertoire of gestures, poses, clichés and dialogues. Handke gives us 60 meticulous pages of hollow social (and theatrical) comedy: of conversations about flambéed kidneys and cigars, and meandering pantomimes with rings and sticking drawers, all dislocated by misunderstandings and stumbling ineptitude. The actors play with the props as if they were props, and with each other as if they were just bodies, or puppets. The fragmentary citation of dramatic forms – of slapstick, farce, baroque tragedy – entails the citation too of human relationships: of masters and servants (again), of flirtation and love, and of exchange and commerce. But there is again no plot, and no purpose. The helpless figures are locked in generalised rituals of utter alienation, which admit no individual impulse or human life. The play is carried forward, it seems, only by a chaotic and comic process of (false) association.

The title of the play refers to the legend of a romantic ballad (see Translator's Note) in which a rider, unknowing, crosses the frozen surface of a lake. For Handke this becomes a metaphor for our relationship with language and with all sorts of social communication, the thin and slippery ice-sheet of convention above unspeakable and murky depths. But unlike the horseman, Handke, and to a certain extent his figures too, recognise the peril. Moments in which the rituals are performed with all the certainty of sleepwalkers alternate with those in which the 'actors' fleetingly and disablingly become aware. Their consciousness of their fragile situation destroys the sanity and security of their world.

The denial of symbolic meaning has been a feature of all Handke's plays from *Offending the Audience* on; now in *The Ride Across Lake Constance* the interpretation of words and gestures has become the central theme and problem. All unequivocal meanings for the action (even the direct metaphorical relationship between title and content) are dissolved in play. What remains is a powerful yearning for a world which is not mediated like this; but that, it seems, cannot be.

They Are Dying Out

The motifs and techniques of the final play in this collection, *They Are Dying Out*, which followed the others after a short but significant break from drama, are already familiar. The material, however, the portrayal of a capitalist big businessman, opens up a completely new perspective. It is sometimes taken to reveal retrospectively the social impetus in all of Handke's writing. Certainly the play does contain quite unmistakable satirical jabs at aspects of capitalist society, at business and advertising practices, and at a world in which 'rationality' has been reduced to the 'rationalisation' of market economics. Even here, however, the social critique may not be all that central. In the middle of the play there is an extended and scornful attack on the sort of politically 'responsible' drama in which the bourgeoisie can 'enjoy' 'the other class, as crude and unadorned as possible' (a drama represented in these years for Handke by the work of Franz Xaver Kroetz). We should be wary of assuming that Handke himself might have fallen into the trap of easy social didacticism.

As well as almost conventional seeming characters (another master and servant) and an unashamedly 'illusionist' set, the 'plot', for once, is clear and simple. It unfolds, however, only in the background. In the foreground we witness the gradual crisis of Hermann Quitt, a long and hopeless struggle to assert his individual ego against all the demands of his social role. It is this agony of selfhood which is Handke's central theme. The play is static, rather than dynamic, but then perhaps so too is the crisis it reflects. It proceeds by monologue, rather than by dramatic dialogue – even in the second scene, where the other characters speak a great deal, but it is Quitt's silence that impresses both them and us. In Quitt himself we observe an almost tragi-comic conflict between the desiring subject and his constructed identity. He tries to anchor himself in memory, but he can only summon up vague and fragmentary details of human feeling, which manifest themselves above all as cultural quotation. His opening statement of his 'sadness' carries echoes of Antonio's opening speech in *The Merchant of Venice*, that first great social drama of capitalism (and much else besides), and of Leonce's expression of *ennui* in Georg Büchner's classic social comedy *Leonce und Lena*. But the familiar models are only cited. The characters 'act as if they were tragic figures', Handke remarked, 'but they remain under the shadow of a parody'. Quitt's last speech resembles some Hamletesque monologue with every last morsel of nobility or greatness removed. What makes it all the more painful is that the character is himself aware of his belated repetitions, as Handke is aware of his (post)modernist dilemma: 'What slips out of me is only the raw sewage of previous centuries.'

The drama sets up a self-conscious relationship between 'play' and 'reality'. When Koerber-Kent remarks, 'In reality you are conscious of your position, like all of us', Quitt replies, 'But only in reality'. To Quitt the world of capitalist economic competition appears as a game, which may contain no serious reality at all. Indeed, 'Spiel' (game or play) becomes the all-embracing category. Quitt's own mental state and his inability to maintain his proper 'role' are themselves artificial. His suffering lacks serious substance, even though it will have fatal consequences. To comfort him, his servant Hans reads aloud from a novel by the nineteenth-century writer Adalbert Stifter. In this text too there is an agony of self-doubt; but for Stifter it is enacted in a secure context of real feeling, of human respect, of nobility of expression, and of the eternal truths of nature. In Handke's play all of these values have been subverted; nature has become an industrial wasteland. And in still one further ironic twist, Stifter's own claim to 'authenticity' is swiftly undermined. Quitt redefines his noble gestures as poses, and establishes his place in cultural history as one of the sad initiators of a meaningless modern 'Weltschmerz'. There is no refuge. In this 'play-world' the individual cannot hope to retreat into inwardness, for there is no coherent and feeling individual ('Sensitive is a word I only associate with condoms') and there is no 'inwardness' – only 'the innerworld of the outerworld of the innerworld' (as Handke had already entitled a collection of his poems), an endless succession of carefully moulded Russian doll-like masks.

After this ambivalently nihilistic burlesque, it is perhaps unsurprising that it would be some years before Handke was ready to return to writing for the theatre.

Handke once wrote: 'I have only one theme, to achieve clarity, or to achieve greater clarity, about myself, to know myself or not to know myself, to learn what I do wrong, what I think wrong, what I think unthinkingly, what I say unthinkingly, what I say automatically, what others too do, think and say unthinkingly: to become attentive and to make others attentive: to become and to make others more sensible, more sensitive, more precise, so that I and others too may exist more precisely and more sensitively, so that I may communicate better and consort better with others.' In the first place this seems to be a statement of an unrelenting introversion. To a degree it may account for the indigestibility of some of Handke's writing. What the text may lose as entertainment, it must gain as a medium for experiencing the self. But the sentence goes on. It is, Handke suggests, only through the experience of making oneself more aware, and by changing oneself through literature, that one can hope to begin to make others more aware. The accusations of solipsism which were at one time commonly directed at this writer begin to appear unjustified. There is a window out of Handke's ivory tower.

In the works of the early years there are certainly still suspicions of an ambiguous self-indulgence. We may uncover, here and there, elements of a socially specific criticism; but for the most part we are overwhelmed by an extreme and general epistemological scepticism. At his worst, Handke can appear simply to be lamenting the necessary consensus (of language and so on) which makes human society possible – as well as, perhaps, unbearable – and to be retreating into lonely resignation. At his best, he seems to be proclaiming the urgent necessity of breaking open the reifications and frozen categories of our conceptual world, in order to reassert the individual. In this case, the subjectivism becomes a brave and essential reflection on the first term of any epistemology.

Handke started his literary career by shocking and offending the West German literary establishment. Today it is hard to imagine the history of post-war German literature without his stingingly provocative and yet deeply reflective presence. He is introduced here as a dramatist, but he is also a poet and translator and he has made an important contribution to European film. He is, moreover, the author of a number of important prose works: short novels, stories, notebooks and semi-autobiographical narratives, for the most part of extreme and devastating alienation.

In the mid-1970s, in a series of short prose works of extraordinary intensity and linguistic virtuosity (*Short Letter, Long Farewell, A Sorrow Beyond Dreams, A Moment of True Feeling, The*

Left-Handed Woman) Handke perhaps achieved the perilous move from his obsessive critiques of language and epistemology, turning from the problems of perception and categorisation to those of existence. It is not a progress that is easily summarised. Handke's individualism has itself effectively resisted categorisation. Single works and his development as a whole have both been riven by contradiction. The ruptures with the past, which I mentioned at the outset, have always involved a return to the past. The attempts to escape literature (by protest, denial, insistent subjectivism) have all led back in the end to literature. And Handke has tripped comparatively lightly, with humour and humanity, around the intellectual aporias in which his critics have so often become bogged down. Paradoxically enough, in the more recent works, it is perhaps literary culture itself which begins to emerge as the essential human nourishment, which permits a more authentic communication and opens a possible path to a redemption out of this mediated world. But that is to point far beyond the scope of this volume, beyond the isolated fragments of *Kaspar*, beyond the hesitant denials of *They Are Dying Out*, to the later prose and to dramas such as *The Long Way Round* of 1981. It has certainly been a very long way round by which Handke has edged towards the tentative utopianism of such a parable of being as *Wings of Desire*.

Tom Kuhn
St Hugh's College, Oxford
December 1996

OFFENDING THE AUDIENCE

Publikumsbeschimpfung

translated by Michael Roloff

for Karlheinz Braun, Claus Peymann,
Basch Peymann, Wolfgang Wiens, Peter Steinbach,
Michael Gruner, Ulrich Hass, Claus Dieter Reents,
Rüdiger Vogler, John Lennon

Offending the Audience was first produced in Britain at the Oval House, London, in December 1970 by The Other Company. The cast were: Jane Bond, Judy Monahan, Andrew Norton and Robert Walker; directed by Naftali Yavin.

TRANSLATOR'S NOTE

In translating the invective at the end of *Offending the Audience*, I translated the principle according to which they are arranged – that is, I sought to create new acoustic patterns in English – rather than translate each epithet literally, which would only have resulted in completely discordant patterns. In nearly every other respect these are translations and not adaptations.

M.R.

Rules for the actors

Listen to the litanies in the Catholic churches.

Listen to football teams being cheered on and booed.

Listen to the rhythmic chanting at demonstrations.

Listen to the wheels of a bicycle upturned on its seat spinning until the spokes have come to rest and watch the spokes until they have reached their resting point.

Listen to the gradually increasing noise a concrete mixer makes after the motor has been started.

Listen to debaters cutting each other off.

Listen to 'Tell Me' by the Rolling Stones.

Listen to the simultaneous arrival and departure of trains.

Listen to the hit parade on Radio Luxembourg.

Listen in on the simultaneous interpreters at the United Nations.

Listen to the dialogue between the gangster (Lee J. Cobb) and the pretty girl in 'The Trap', when the girl asks the gangster how many more people he intends to kill; whereupon the gangster asks, as he leans back, How many are left? and watch the gangster as he says it.

See the Beatles' movies.

In 'A Hard Day's Night' watch Ringo's smile at the moment when, after having been teased by the others, he sits down at his drums and begins to play.

Watch Gary Cooper's face in 'The Man From the West'. In the same movie watch the death of the mute as he runs down the deserted street of the lifeless town with a bullet in him, hopping and jumping and emitting those shrill screams.

Watch monkeys aping people and llamas spitting in the zoo.

Watch the behaviour of tramps and idlers as they amble on the street and play the machines in the penny arcades.

When the theatregoers enter the room into which they are meant to go, they are greeted by the usual pre-performance atmosphere. One might let them hear noises from behind the curtain, noises that make believe that scenery is being shifted about. For example, a table is dragged across the stage, or several chairs are noisily set up and then removed. One might let the spectators in the first few rows hear directions whispered by make-believe stage managers and the whispered interchanges between make-believe stagehands behind the curtain. Or, even better, use tape recordings of other performances in which, before the curtain rises, objects are really shifted about. These noises should be amplified to make them more audible, and perhaps should be stylized and arranged so as to produce their own order and uniformity.

The usual theatre atmosphere should prevail. The ushers should be more assiduous than usual, even more formal and ceremonious, should subdue their usual whispering with even more style, so that their behaviour becomes infectious. The programmes should be elegant. The bell signals should not be forgotten; the signals are repeated at successively briefer intervals. The gradual dimming of the lights should be even more gradual if possible; perhaps the lights can be dimmed in successive stages. As the ushers proceed to close the doors, their gestures should become particularly solemn and noticeable. Yet, they are only ushers. Their actions should not appear symbolic. Latecomers should not be admitted. Inappropriately dressed ticket holders should not be admitted. The concept of what is sartorially inappropriate should be strictly applied. None of the spectators should call attention to himself or offend the eye by his attire. The men should be dressed in dark jackets, with white shirts and inconspicuous ties. The women should shun bright colours.

There is no standing-room. Once the doors are closed and the lights *dim, it gradually becomes quiet behind the curtain too. The silence behind the curtain and the silence in the auditorium are alike. The spectators stare a while longer at the almost imperceptibly fluttering curtain, which may perhaps billow once or twice as though someone had hurriedly crossed the stage. Then the curtain grows still. There is a short pause. The curtain slowly rises, allowing an unobstructed view. Once the stage is completely open to view, the four speakers step forward from upstage. Nothing impedes their progress. The stage is empty. As they walk forward non-committally, dressed casually, it becomes light on stage as well as in the audience. The light on stage and in the auditorium is of the same intensity as at the end of a performance and there is no glare to hurt the eyes. The stage and the auditorium remain lighted throughout the performance. Even as they approach, the speakers don't look at the audience. They don't direct the words they are speaking at the audience. Under no circumstance should the audience get the impression that the words are directed at them. As far as the speakers are concerned, the audience does not yet exist. As they approach, they move their lips. Gradually their words became intelligible and finally they become loud. The invectives they deliver overlap one another. The speakers speak pell-mell. They pick up each other's words. They take words out of each other's mouths. They speak in unison, each uttering different words. They repeat. They grow louder. They scream. They pass rehearsed words from mouth to mouth. Finally, they rehearse one word in unison. The words they use in this prologue are the following (their order is immaterial):* You chuckle-heads, you small-timers, you nervous nellies, you fuddy-duddies, you windbags, you sitting ducks, you milksops. *The speakers should strive for a certain acoustic uniformity. However, except for the acoustic pattern, no other picture should be produced. The invectives are not directed at anyone in particular. The manner of their delivery should not induce a meaning. The speakers reach the front of the stage before they finish rehearsing their invectives. They stand at ease but form a sort of pattern. They are not completely fixed in their positions but move according to the movement which the words they speak lend them. They now look at the public, but at no one person in particular. They are silent for a while. They collect themselves. Then they begin to speak. The order in which they speak is immaterial. The speakers have roughly the same amount of work to do.*

You are welcome.

This piece is a prologue.

You will hear nothing you have not heard here before.
You will see nothing you have not seen here before.
You will see nothing of what you have always seen here.
You will hear nothing of what you have always heard here.

You will hear what you usually see.
You will hear what you usually don't see.
You will see no spectacle.
Your curiosity will not be satisfied.
You will see no play.
There will be no playing here tonight.
You will see a spectacle without pictures.

You expected something.
You expected something else perhaps.
You expected objects.
You expected no objects.
You expected an atmosphere.
You expected a different world.
You expected no different world.
In any case, you expected something.
It may be the case that you expected what you are hearing now.
But even in that case you expected something different.

You are sitting in rows. You form a pattern. You are sitting in a certain order. You are facing in a certain direction. You are sitting equidistant from one another. You are an audience. You form a unit. You are auditors and spectators in an auditorium. Your thoughts are free. You can still make up your own mind. You see us speaking and you hear us speaking. You are beginning to breathe in one and the same rhythm. You are beginning to breathe in one and the same rhythm in which we are speaking. You are breathing the way we are speaking. We and you gradually form a unit.

You are not thinking. You don't think of anything. You are thinking along. You are not thinking along. You feel uninhibited. Your thoughts are free. Even as we say that, we insinuate ourselves into your thoughts. You have thoughts in the back of your mind. Even as we say that, we insinuate ourselves into the thoughts in the back of your mind. You are thinking along. You are hearing. Your thoughts are following in the track of our thoughts. Your thoughts are not following in the track of our thoughts. You are not thinking. Your thoughts are not free. You feel inhibited.

You are looking at us when we speak to you. You are not watching us. You are looking at us. You are being looked at. You are unprotected. You no longer have the advantage of looking from the shelter of darkness into the light. We no longer have the disadvantage of looking through the blinding light into the dark. You are not watching. You are looking at and you are being looked at. In this way, we and you gradually form a unit. Under certain conditions, therefore, we, instead of saying *you*, could say *we*. We are under one and the same roof. We are a closed society.

You are not listening to us. You heed us. You are no longer eavesdropping from behind a wall. We are speaking directly to you. Our dialogue no longer moves at right angles to your glance. Your glance no longer pierces our dialogue. Our words and your glances no longer form an angle. You are not disregarded. You are not treated as mere hecklers. You need not form an opinion from a bird's or a frog's perspective of anything that happens here. You need not play referee. You are no longer treated as spectators to whom we can speak in asides. This is no play. There are no asides here. Nothing that takes place here is intended as an appeal to you. This is no play. We don't step out of the play to address you. We have no need of illusions to disillusion you. We show you nothing. We are playing no destinies. We are playing no dreams. This is not a factual report. This is no documentary play. This is no slice of life. We don't tell you a story. We don't perform any actions. We don't simulate any actions. We don't represent anything. We don't put anything on for you. We only speak. We play by addressing you. When we say we, we may also mean you. We are not acting out your situation. You cannot recognize yourselves in us. We are playing no situation. You need not feel that we mean you. You cannot feel that we mean you. No mirror is being held up to you. We don't mean you. We are addressing you. You are being addressed. You will be addressed. You will be bored if you don't want to be addressed.

You are sharing no experience. You are not sharing. You are not following suit. You are experiencing no intrigues here. You are experiencing nothing. You are not imagining anything. You don't have to imagine anything. You need no prerequisites. You don't need to know that this is a stage. You need no expectations. You need not lean back expectantly. You don't need to know that this is only playing. We make up no stories. You are not following an event. You are not playing along. You are being played with here. That is a wordplay.

What is the theatre's is not rendered unto the theatre here. Here you don't receive your due. Your curiosity is not satisfied. No spark will leap across from us to you. You will not be electrified. These boards don't signify a world. They are part of the world. These boards exist for us to stand on. This world is no different from yours. You are no longer eavesdroppers. You are the subject matter. The focus is on you. You are in the crossfire of our words.

This is no mirage. You don't see walls that tremble. You don't hear the spurious sounds of doors snapping shut. You hear no sofas squeaking. You see no apparitions. You have no visions. You see no picture of something. Nor do you see the suggestion of a picture. You see no picture puzzle. Nor do you see an empty picture. The emptiness of this stage is no picture of another emptiness. The emptiness of this stage signifies nothing. This stage is empty because objects would be in our way. It is empty because we don't need objects. This stage represents nothing. It represents no other emptiness. This stage *is* empty. You don't see any objects that pretend to be other objects. You don't see a darkness that pretends to be another darkness. You don't see a brightness that pretends to be another brightness. You don't see any light that pretends to be another light. You don't hear any noise that pretends to be another noise. You don't see a room that pretends to be another room. Here you are not experiencing a time that pretends to be another time. The time on stage is no different from the time off stage. We have the same local time here. We are in the same location. We are breathing the same air. The front of the stage is not a line of demarcation. It is not only sometimes no demarcation line. It is no demarcation line as long as we are speaking to you. There is no invisible circle here. There is no magic circle. There is no room for play here. We are not playing. We are all in the same room. The demarcation line has not been penetrated, it is not pervious, it doesn't even exist. There is no radiation belt between you and us. We are not self-propelled stage props. We are no pictures of something. We are no representatives. We represent nothing. We demonstrate nothing. We have no pseudonyms. Our heartbeat does not pretend to be another's heartbeat. Our bloodcurdling screams don't pretend to be another's bloodcurdling screams. We don't step out of our roles. We have no roles. We are ourselves. We are the mouthpiece of the author. You cannot make yourself a picture of us. You don't need to make yourself a picture of us. We are ourselves. Our opinion and the author's opinion are not necessarily the same.

The light that illuminates us signifies nothing. Neither do the clothes we wear signify anything. They indicate nothing, they are not unusual in any way, they signify nothing. They signify no other time to you, no other climate, no other season, no other degree of latitude, no other reason to wear them. They have no function. Nor do our gestures have a function, that is, to signify something to you. This is not the world as a stage.

We are no slapstick comedians. There are no objects here that we might trip over. Insidious objects are not on the programme. Insidious objects are not part of the play because we are not playing with them. The objects are not intended to be insidious; they are insidious. If we happen to trip, we trip unwittingly. Unwitting as well are mistakes in dress; unwitting, too, are our perhaps foolish faces. Slips of the tongue, which amuse you, are not intended. If we stutter, we stutter without meaning to. We cannot make dropping a handkerchief part of the play. We are not playing. We cannot make the insidiousness of objects part of the play. We cannot camouflage the insidiousness of objects. We cannot be of two minds. We cannot be of many minds. We are no clowns. We are not in the ring. You don't have the pleasure of encircling us. You are not enjoying the comedy of having a rear view of us. You are not enjoying the comedy of insidious objects. You are enjoying the comedy of words.

The possibilities of the theatre are not exploited here. The realm of possibilities is not exhausted. The theatre is not unbounded. The theatre is bound. Fate is meant ironically here. We are not theatrical. Our comedy is not overwhelming. Your laughter cannot be liberating. We are not playful. We are not playing a world for you. This is not half of one world. We and you do not constitute two halves.

You are the subject matter. You are the centre of interest. No actions are performed here, you are being acted upon. That is no wordplay. You are not treated as individuals here. You don't become individuals here. You have no individual traits. You have no distinctive physiognomies. You are not individuals here. You have no characteristics. You have no destiny. You have no history. You have no past. You are on no wanted list. You have no experience of life. You have the experience of the theatre here. You have that certain something. You are playgoers. You are of no interest because of your capacities. You are of interest solely in your capacity as playgoers. As playgoers you form a pattern here. You are no personalities. You are not singular. You are a plurality of persons. Your faces point in one direction. You are an event. You are *the* event.

You are under review by us. But you form no picture. You are not symbolic. You are an ornament. You are a pattern. You have features that everyone here has. You have general features. You are a species. You form a pattern. You are doing and you are not doing the same thing: you are looking in one direction. You don't stand up and look in different directions. You are a standard pattern and you have a pattern as a standard. You have a standard with which you came to the theatre. You have the standard idea that where we are is up and where you are is down. You have the standard idea of two worlds. You have the standard idea of the world of the theatre.

You don't need this standard now. You are not attending a piece for the theatre. You are not attending. You are the focal point. You are in the crossfire. You are being inflamed. You can catch fire. You don't need a standard. You are the standard. You have been discovered. You are the discovery of the evening. You inflame us. Our words catch fire on you. From you a spark leaps across to us.

This room does not make believe it is a room. The side that is open to you is not the fourth wall of a house. The world does not have to be cut open here. You don't see any doors here. You don't see the two doors of the old dramas. You don't see the back door through which he who shouldn't be seen can slip out. You don't see the front door through which he who wants to see him who shouldn't be seen enters. There is no back door. Neither is there a non-existent door as in modern drama. The non-existent door does not represent a non-existent door. This is not another world. We are not pretending that you don't exist. You are not thin air for us. You are of crucial importance to us because you exist. We are speaking to you because you exist. If you did not exist, we would be speaking to thin air. Your existence is not simply taken for granted. You don't watch us through a keyhole. We don't pretend that we are alone in the world. We don't explain ourselves to ourselves only in order to put you in the know. We are not conducting an exhibition purely for the benefit of your enlightenment. We need no artifice to enlighten you. We need no tricks. We don't have to be theatrically effective. We have no entrances, we have no exits, we don't talk to you in asides. We are putting nothing over on you. We are not about to enter into a dialogue. We are not in a dialogue. Nor are we in a dialogue with you. We have no wish to enter into a dialogue with you. You are not in collusion with us. You are not eyewitnesses to an event. We are not taunting you. You don't have to be apathetic any more. You don't have to watch inactively any more. No actions take place here. You feel the discomfort of being watched and addressed, since you came prepared to watch and make yourselves comfortable in the shelter of the dark. Your presence is every moment explicitly acknowledged with every one of our words. Your presence is the topic we deal with from one breath to the next, from one moment to the next, from one word to the next. Your standard idea of the theatre is no longer presupposed as the basis of our actions. You are neither condemned to watch nor free to watch. You are the subject. You are the play-makers. You are the counterplotters. You are being aimed at. You are the target of our words. You serve as targets. That is a metaphor. You serve as the target of our metaphors. You serve as metaphors.

Of the two poles here, you are the pole at rest. You are in an arrested state. You find yourselves in a state of expectation. You are no subjects. You are objects here. You are the objects of our words. Still, you are subjects too.

There are no intervals here. The intervals between words lack significance. Here the unspoken word lacks significance. There are no unspoken words here. Our silences say nothing. There is no deafening silence. There is no silent silence. There is no deathly quiet. Speech is not used to create silence here. This play includes no direction telling us to be silent. We make no artificial pauses. Our pauses are natural pauses. Our pauses are not eloquent like speech. We say nothing with our silence. No abyss opens up between words. You cannot read anything between our lines. You cannot read anything in our faces. Our gestures express nothing of consequence to anything. What is inexpressible is not said through silences here. Glances and gestures are not eloquent here. Becoming silent and being silent is no artifice here. There are no silent letters here. There's only the mute *h*. That is a pun.

You have made up your minds now. You have recognized that we negate something. You have recognized that we repeat ourselves. You have recognized that we contradict ourselves. You have recognized that this piece is conducting an argument with the theatre. You have recognized the dialectical structure of the piece. You have recognized a certain spirit of contrariness. The intention of the piece has become clear to you. You have recognized that we primarily negate. You have recognized that we repeat ourselves. You recognize. You see through. You have not made up your minds. You have not seen through the dialectical structure of the piece. Now you are seeing through. Your thoughts were one thought too slow. Now you have thoughts in the back of your mind.

You look charming. You look enchanting. You look dazzling. You look breathtaking. You look unique.

But you don't make an evening. You're not a brilliant idea. You are tiresome. You are not a rewarding subject. You are a theatrical blunder. You are not true to life. You are not theatrically effective. You don't send us. You don't enchant us. You don't dazzle us. You don't entertain us fabulously. You are not playful. You are not sprightly. You have no tricks up your sleeve. You have no flair for the theatre. You have nothing to say. Your début is unconvincing. You are not with it. You don't help us pass the time. You are not addressing the human quality in us. You leave us cold.

This is no drama. No action that has occurred elsewhere is re-enacted here. Only a now and a now and a now exist here. This is no make-believe which re-enacts an action that really happened once upon a time. Time plays no role here. We are not acting out a plot. Therefore we are not playing time. Time is for real here, it expires from one word to the next. Time flies in the words here. It is not alleged that time can be repeated here. No play can be repeated here and play at the same time it did once upon a time. The time here is *your* time. Space time here is your space time. Here you can compare your time with our time. Time is no noose. That is no make-believe. It is not alleged here that time can be repeated. The umbilical cord connecting you to your time is not severed here. Time is not at play here. We mean business with time here. It is admitted here that time expires from one word to the next. It is admitted that this is *your* time here. You can check the time here on your watches. No other time governs here. The time that governs here is measured against your breath. Time conforms to your wishes here. We measure time by your breath, by the batting of your eyelashes, by your pulsebeats, by the growth of your cells. Time expires here from moment to moment. Time is measured in moments. Time is measured in your moments. Time goes through your stomach. Time here is not repeatable as in the make-believe of a theatre performance. This is no performance: you have not to imagine anything. Time is no noose here. Time is not cut off from the outside world here. There are no two levels of time here. There are no two worlds here. While we are here, the earth continues to turn. Our time up here is your time down there. It expires from one word to the next. It expires while we, we and you, are breathing, while our hair is growing, while we are sweating, while we are smelling, while we are hearing. Time is not repeatable even if we repeat our words, even if we mention again that our time is your time, that it expires from one word to the next, while we, we and you, are breathing, while our hair is growing, while we sweat, while we smell, while we hear. We cannot repeat anything, time is expiring. It is unrepeatable. Each moment is historical. Each of your moments is a historical moment. We cannot say our words twice. This is no make-believe. We cannot do the same thing once again. We cannot repeat the same gestures. We cannot speak the same way. Time expires on our lips. Time is unrepeatable. Time is no noose. That is no make-believe. The past is not made contemporaneous. The past is dead and buried. We need no puppet to embody a dead time. This is no puppet show. This is no nonsense. This is no play. This is no sense. You recognize the contradiction. Time here serves the wordplay.

This is no manœuvre. This is no exercise for the emergency. No one has to play dead here. No one has to pretend he is alive. Nothing is posited here. The number of wounded is not prescribed. The result is not predetermined on paper. There is no result here. No one has to present himself here. We don't represent except what we are. We don't represent ourselves in a state other than the one we are in now and here. This is no manœuvre. We are not playing ourselves in different situations. We are not thinking of the emergency. We don't have to represent our death. We don't have to represent our life. We don't play ahead of time what and how we will be. We make no future contemporaneous in our play. We don't represent another time. We don't represent the emergency. We are speaking while time expires. We speak of the expiration of time. We are not acting as if. We are not acting as if we could repeat time or as if we could anticipate time. This is neither make-believe nor a manœuvre. On the other hand we do act as if. We act as if we could repeat words. We appear to repeat ourselves. Here is the world of appearances. Here appearance is appearance. Appearance is here appearance.

You represent something. You are someone. You are something. You are not someone here but something. You are a society that represents an order. You are a theatre society of sorts. You are an order because of your kind of dress, the position of your bodies, the direction of your glances. The colour of your clothes clashes with the colour of your seating arrangement. You also form an order with the seating arrangement. You are dressed up. With your dress you observe an order. You dress up. By dressing up, you demonstrate that you are doing something that you don't do every day. You are putting on a masquerade so as to partake of a masquerade. You partake. You watch. You stare. By watching, you become rigid. The seating arrangement favours this development. You are something that watches. You need room for your eyes. If the curtain comes down, you gradually become claustrophobic. You have no vantage point. You feel encircled. You feel inhibited. The rising of the curtain merely relieves your claustrophobia. Thus it relieves you. You can watch. Your view is unobstructed. You become uninhibited. You can partake. You are not in dead centre as when the curtain is closed. You are no longer someone. You become something. You are no longer alone with yourselves. You are no longer left to your own devices. Now you are with it. You are an audience. That is a relief. You can partake.

Up here there is no order now. There are no objects that demonstrate an order to you. The world here is neither sound nor unsound. This is no world. Stage props are out of place here. Their positions are not chalked out on the stage. Since they are not chalked out, there is no order here. There are no chalk marks for the standpoint of things. There are no memory props for the standpoint of persons. In contrast to you and your seating arrangement, nothing is in its place here. Things here have no fixed places like the places of your seating arrangements down there. This stage is no world, just as the world is no stage.

Nor does each thing have its own time here. No thing has its own time here. No thing has its fixed time here when it serves as a prop or when it becomes an obstacle. We don't act as if things were really used. Here things *are* useful.

You are not standing. You are using the seating arrangements. You are sitting. Since your seating arrangements form a pattern, you form a pattern as well. There is no standing-room. People enjoy art more effectively when they sit than if they stand. That is why you are sitting. You are friendlier when you sit. You are more receptive. You are more open-minded. You are more long-suffering. Sitting, you are more relaxed. You are more democratic. You are less bored. Time seems less long and boring to you. You allow more to happen to you. You are more clairvoyant. You are less distracted. It is easier for you to forget your surroundings. The world around you disappears more easily. You begin to resemble one another more. You begin to lose your personal qualities. You begin to lose the characteristics that distinguish you from each other. You become a unit. You become a pattern. You become one. You lose your self-consciousness. You become spectators.

You become auditors. You become apathetic. You become all eyes and ears. You forget to look at your watch. You forget yourself.

Standing, you would be more effective hecklers. In view of the anatomy of the human body, your heckling would be louder if you stood. You would be better able to clench your fists. You could show your opposition better. You would have greater mobility. You would not need to be as well-behaved. You could shift your weight from one foot to the other. You could more easily become conscious of your body. Your enjoyment of art would be diminished. You would no longer form a pattern. You would no longer be rigid. You would lose your geometry. You would be better able to smell the sweat of the bodies near you. You would be better able to express agreement by nudging each other. If you stood, the sluggishness of your bodies would not keep you from walking. Standing, you would be more individual. You would oppose the theatre more resolutely. You would give in to fewer illusions. You would suffer more from absentmindedness. You would stand more on the outside. You would be better able to leave yourself to your own devices. You would be less able to imagine represented events as real. The events here would seem less true to life to you. Standing, for example, you would be less able to imagine a death represented on this stage as real. You would be less rigid. You wouldn't let yourself be put under as much of a spell. You wouldn't let as much be put over on you. You wouldn't be satisfied to be mere spectators. It would be easier for you to be of two minds. You could be at two places at once with your thoughts. You could live in two space-time continuums.

We don't want to infect you. We don't want to goad you into a show of feelings. We don't play feelings. We don't embody feelings. We neither laugh nor weep. We don't want to infect you with laughter by laughing or with weeping by laughing or with laughter by weeping or with weeping by weeping. Although laughter is more infectious than weeping, we don't infect you with laughter by laughing. And so forth. We are not playing. We play nothing. We don't modulate. We don't gesticulate. We express ourselves by no means but words. We only speak. We express. We don't express ourselves but the opinion of the author. We express ourselves by speaking. Our speaking is our acting. By speaking, we become theatrical. We are theatrical because we are speaking in a theatre. By always speaking directly to you and by speaking to you of time, of now and of now and of now, we observe the unity of time, place and action. But we observe this unity not only here on stage. Since the stage is no world unto itself, we also observe the unity down where you are. We and you form a unity because we speak directly to you without interruption. Therefore, under certain conditions, we, instead of saying you, could say we. That signifies the unity of action. The stage up here and the auditorium constitute a unity in that they no longer constitute two levels. There is no radiation belt between us. There are no two places here. Here is only one place. That signifies the unity of place. Your time, the time of the spectators and auditors, and our time, the time of the speakers, form a unity in that no other time passes here than your time. Time is not bisected here into played time and play time. Time is not played here. Only real time exists here. Only the time that we, we and you, experience ourselves in our own bodies exists here. Only one time exists here. That signifies the unity of time. All three cited circumstances, taken together, signify the unity of time, place and action. Therefore this piece is classical.

Because we speak to you, you can become conscious of yourself. Because we speak to you, your self-awareness increases. You become aware that you are sitting. You become aware that you are sitting in the theatre. You become aware of the size of your limbs. You become aware of how your limbs are situated. You become aware of your fingers. You become aware of your tongue. You become aware of your throat. You become aware how heavy your head is. You become aware of your sex organs. You become aware of batting your eyelids. You become aware of the muscles with which you swallow. You become aware of the flow of your saliva. You become aware of the beating of your heart. You become aware of raising your eyebrows. You become aware of a prickling sensation on your scalp. You become aware of the impulse to scratch yourself. You become aware of sweating under your armpits. You become aware of your sweaty hands. You become aware of your parched hands. You become aware of the air you are inhaling and exhaling through your mouth and nose. You become aware of our words entering your ears. You acquire presence of mind.

Try not to blink your eyelids. Try not to swallow any more. Try not to move your tongue. Try not to hear anything. Try not to smell anything. Try not to salivate. Try not to sweat. Try not to shift in your seat. Try not to breathe.

Why, you are breathing. Why, you are salivating. Why, you are listening. Why, you are smelling. Why, you are swallowing. Why, you are blinking your eyelids. Why, you are belching. Why, you are sweating. Why, how terribly self-conscious you are.

Don't blink. Don't salivate. Don't bat your eyelashes. Don't inhale. Don't exhale. Don't shift in your seat. Don't listen to us. Don't smell. Don't swallow. Hold your breath.

Swallow. Salivate. Blink. Listen. Breathe.

You are now aware of your presence. You know that it is *your* time that you are spending here. *You* are the topic. You tie the knot. You untie the knot. You are the centre. You are the occasion. You are the reasons why. You provide the initial impulse. You provide us with words here. You are the playmakers and the counterplotters. You are the young comedians. You are the enchanted lovers, you are the ingénues, you are the sentimentalists. You are the grandes dames, you are the character actors, you are the bon vivants and the heroes. You are the heroes and the villains of this piece.

Before you came here, you made certain preparations. You came here with certain preconceptions. You went to the theatre. You prepared yourself to go to the theatre. You had certain expectations. Your thoughts were one step ahead of time. You imagined something. You prepared yourself for something. You prepared yourself to partake in something. You prepared yourself to be seated, to sit on the rented seat and to attend something. Perhaps you had heard of this piece. So you made preparations, you prepared yourself for something. You let events come toward you. You were prepared to sit and have something shown to you.

The rhythm you breathed in was different from ours. You went about dressing yourself in a different manner. You got started in a different way. You approached this location from different directions. You used the public transport system. You came on foot. You came by cab. You used your own means of transport. Before you got under way, you looked at your watch. You expected a telephone call, you picked up the receiver, you turned on the lights, you turned out the lights, you closed doors, you turned keys, you stepped out into the open. You propelled your legs. You let your arms swing up and down as you walked. You walked. You walked from different directions all in the same direction. You found your way here with the help of your sense of direction.

Because of your intention you distinguished yourselves from others who were on their way to other locations. Simply because of your intention, you instantly formed a unit with the others who were on their way to this location. You had the same objective.

You planned to spend a part of your future together with others at a definite time.

You crossed traffic lanes. You looked left and right. You observed traffic signals. You nodded to others. You stopped. You informed others of your destination. You told of your expectations. You communicated your speculations about this piece. You expressed your opinion of this piece. You shook hands. You had others wish you a pleasant evening. You took off your shoes. You held doors open. You had doors held open for you. You met other theatre-goers. You felt like conspirators. You observed the rules of good behaviour. You helped out of coats. You let yourselves be helped out of coats. You stood around. You walked around. You heard the bells. You grew restless. You looked in the mirror. You checked your make-up. You threw sidelong glances. You noticed sidelong glances. You walked. You paced. Your movements became more formal. You heard the bell. You looked at your watch. You became conspirators. You took your seat. You took a look around. You made yourself comfortable. You heard the bell. You stopped chatting. You aligned your glances. You raised your heads. You took a deep breath. You saw the lights dim. You became silent. You heard the doors closing. You stared at the curtain. You waited. You became rigid. You did not move any more. Instead, the curtain moved. You heard the curtain rustling. You were offered an unobstructed view of the stage. Everything was as it always is. Your expectations were not disappointed. You were ready. You leaned back in your seat. The play could begin.

At other times you were also ready. You were on to the game that was being played. You leaned back in your seats. You perceived. You followed. You pursued. You let happen. You let something happen up here that had happened long ago. You watched the past which by means of dialogue and monologue made believe it was contemporaneous. You let yourselves be captivated. You let your-selves become spellbound. You forgot where you were. You forgot the time. You became rigid and remained rigid. You did not move. You did not act. You did not even come up front to see better. You followed no natural impulses. You watched as you watch a beam of light that was produced long before you began to watch. You looked into dead space. You looked at dead points. You experienced a dead time. You heard a dead language. You yourselves were in a dead room in a dead time. It was dead calm. No breath of air moved. You did not move. You stared. The distance between you and us was infinite. We were infinitely far away from you. We moved at an infinite distance from you. We had lived infinitely long before you. We lived up here on the stage before the beginning of time. Your glances and our glances met in infinity. An infinite space was between us. We played. But we did not play with you. You were always posterity here.

Plays were played here. Sense was played here. Nonsense with meaning was played here. The plays here had a background and an underground. They had a false bottom. They were not what they were. They were not what they seemed. There was something behind them. The things and the plot seemed to be, but they were not. They seemed to be as they seemed, but they were different. They did not seem to seem as in a pure play, they seemed to be. They seemed to be reality. The plays here did not pass the time, or they did not only pass the time. They had meaning. They were not timeless like the pure plays, an unreal time passed in them. The conspicuous meaninglessness of some plays was precisely what represented their hidden meaning. Even the pranks of pranksters acquired meaning on these boards. Always something lay in wait. Always something lay in ambush between the words, gestures and props and sought to mean something to you. Always something had two or more meanings. Something was always happening. Something happened in the play that you were supposed to think was real. Stories always happened. A played and unreal time happened. What you saw and heard was supposed to be not only what you saw and heard. It was supposed to be what you did not see and did not hear. Everything was meant. Everything expressed. Even what pretended to express nothing expressed something because something that happens in the theatre expresses something. Everything that was played expressed something real. The play was not played for the play's sake but for the sake of reality. You were to discover a played reality behind the play. You were supposed to fathom the play. Not a play, reality was played. Time was played. Since time was played, reality was played. The theatre played tribunal. The theatre played circus ring. The theatre played moral institution. The theatre played dreams. The theatre played tribal rites. The theatre played mirrors for you. The play exceeded the play. It hinted at reality. It became impure. It meant. Instead of time staying out of play, an unreal and uneffective time transpired. With the unreal time an unreal reality was played. It was not there, it was only signified to you, it was performed. Neither reality nor play transpired here. If a pure play had been played here, time could have been left out of play. A pure play has no time. But since a reality was played, the corresponding time was also played. If a pure play had been played here, there would have been only the time of the spectators here. But since reality was part of the play here, there were always two times: your time, the time of the spectators, and the played time, which seemed to be the real time. But time cannot be played. It cannot be repeated in any play. Time is irretrievable. Time is irresistible. Time is unplayable. Time is real. It cannot be played as real. Since time cannot be played, reality cannot be played either. Only a play where time is left out of play is a play. A play in which time plays a role is no play. Only a timeless play is without meaning. Only a timeless play is self-sufficient. Only a timeless play does not need to *play* time. Only for a timeless play is time without meaning. All other plays are impure plays. There are only plays without time, or plays in which time is real time, like the sixty minutes of a football game, which has only one time because the time of the players is the same time as that of the spectators. All other plays are sham plays. All other plays mirror meretricious facts for you. A timeless play mirrors no facts.

We could do a play within a play for you. We could act out happenings for you that are taking place outside this room during these moments while you are swallowing, while you are batting your eyelashes. We could illustrate the statistics. We could represent what is statistically taking place at other places while you are at this place. By representing what is happening, we could make you imagine these happenings. We could bring them closer to you. We would not need to represent anything that is past. We could play a pure play. For example, we could act out the very process of dying that is statistically happening somewhere at this moment. We could become full of pathos. We could declare that death is the pathos of time, of which we speak all the time. Death could be the pathos of this real time which you are wasting here. At the very least, this play within a play would help bring this piece to a dramatic climax.

But we are not putting anything over on you. We don't imitate. We don't represent any other persons and any other events, even if they statistically exist. We can do without a play of features and a play of gestures. There are no persons who are part of the plot and therefore no impersonators. The plot is not freely invented, for there is no plot. Since there is no plot, accidents are impossible. Similarity with still living or scarcely dead or long-dead persons is not accidental but impossible. For we don't represent anything and are no others than we are. We don't even play ourselves. We are speaking. Nothing is invented here. Nothing is imitated. Nothing is fact. Nothing is left to your imagination.

Owing to the fact that we are not playing and not acting playfully, this piece is half as funny and half as tragic. Owing to the fact that we only speak and don't fall outside time, we cannot depict anything for you and demonstrate nothing for you. We illustrate nothing. We conjure up nothing out of the past. We are not in conflict with the past. We are not in conflict with the present. We don't anticipate the future. In the present, the past, and the future, we speak of time.

That is why, for example, we cannot represent the now and now of dying that is statistically happening now. We cannot represent the gasping for breath that is happening now and now, or the tumbling and falling now, or the death throes, or the grinding of teeth now, or the last words, or the last sigh now, that is statistically happening now this very second, or the last exhalation, or the last ejaculation that is happening now, or the breathlessness that is statistically commencing now, and now, and now, and now, and so on, or the motionlessness now, or the statistically ascertainable rigor mortis, or the lying absolutely quiet now. We cannot represent it. We only speak of it. We are speaking of it *now*.

Owing to the fact that we only speak and owing to the fact that we don't speak of anything invented, we cannot be equivocal or ambiguous. Owing to the fact that we play nothing, there cannot exist two or more levels here or a play within a play. Owing to the fact that we don't gesticulate and don't tell you any stories and don't represent anything, we cannot be poetical. Owing to the fact that we only speak to you, we lose the poetry of ambiguity. For example, we cannot use the gestures and expressions of dying that we mentioned to represent the gestures and expressions of a simultaneously transpiring instance of sexual intercourse that is statistically transpiring now. We can't be equivocal. We cannot play on a false bottom. We cannot remove ourselves from the world. We don't need to be poetic. We don't need to hypnotize you. We don't need to hoodwink you. We don't need to cast an evil eye on you. We don't need a second nature. This is no hypnosis. You don't have to imagine anything. You don't have to dream with open eyes. With the illogic of your dreams you are not dependent on the logic of the stage. The impossibilities of your dreams do not have to confine themselves to the possibilities of the stage. The absurdity of your dreams does not have to obey the authentic laws of the theatre. Therefore we represent neither dreams nor reality. We make claims neither for life nor for dying, neither for society nor for the individual, neither for what is natural nor for what is supernatural, neither for lust nor for grief, neither for reality nor for the play. Time elicits no elegies from us.

This piece is a prologue. It is not the prologue to another piece but the prologue to what you did, what you are doing, and what you will do. You are the topic. This piece is the prologue to the topic. It is the prologue to your practices and customs. It is the prologue to your actions. It is the prologue to your inactivity. It is the prologue to your lying down, to your sitting, to your standing, to your walking. It is the prologue to the plays and to the seriousness of your life. It is also the prologue to your future visits to the theatre. It is also the prologue to all other prologues. This piece is world theatre.

Soon you will move. You will make preparations. You will prepare yourself to applaud. You will prepare yourself not to applaud. When you prepare to do the former, you will clap one hand against the other, that is to say, you will clap one palm to the other palm and repeat these claps in rapid succession. Meanwhile, you will be able to watch your hands clapping or not clapping. You will hear the sound of yourself clapping and the sound of clapping next to you and you will see next to you and in front of you the clapping hands bobbing back and forth or you will not hear the expected clapping and not see the hands bobbing back and forth. Instead, you will perhaps hear other sounds and will yourself produce other sounds. You will prepare to get up. You will hear the seats folding up behind you. You will see us taking our bows. You will see the curtain fall. You will be able to designate the noises the curtain makes during this process. You will pocket your programmes. You will exchange glances. You will exchange words. You will get moving. You will make comments and hear comments. You will suppress comments. You will smile meaningfully. You will smile meaninglessly. You will push in an orderly fashion into the foyer. You will show your cloakroom tickets to redeem your hats and coats. You will stand around. You will see yourselves in mirrors. You will help each other into coats. You will hold doors open for each other. You will say your good-byes. You will accompany. You will be accompanied. You will step into the open. You will return into the everyday. You will go in different directions. If you remain together, you will be a theatre party. You will go to a restaurant. You will think of tomorrow. You will gradually find your way back into reality. You will be able to call reality harsh again. You will be sobered up. You will lead your own lives again. You will no longer be a unit. You will go from one place to different places.

But before you leave you will be insulted.

We will insult you because insulting you is also one way of speaking to you. By insulting you, we can be straight with you. We can switch you on. We can eliminate the free play. We can tear down a wall. We can observe you.

While we are insulting you, you won't just hear us, you will listen to us. The distance between us will no longer be infinite. Due to the fact that we're insulting you, your motionlessness and your rigidity will finally become overt. But we won't insult *you*, we will merely use insulting words which you yourselves use. We will contradict ourselves with our insults. We will mean no one in particular. We will only create an acoustic pattern. You won't have to feel offended. You were warned in advance, so you can feel quite unoffended while we're insulting you. Since you are probably thoroughly offended already, we will waste no more time before thoroughly offending you, you chuckleheads.

You let the impossible become possible. You were the heroes of this piece. You were sparing with your gestures. Your parts were well rounded. Your scenes were unforgettable. You did not play, you *were* the part. You were a happening. You were the find of the evening. You lived your roles. You had the lion's share of the success. You saved the piece. You were a sight. You were a sight to have seen, you bum-lickers.

You were always with it. Your honest toiling didn't help the piece a bit. You contributed only the cues. The best you created was the little you left out. Your silences said everything, you small-timers.

You were thoroughbred actors. You began promisingly. You were true to life. You were realistic. You put everything under your spell. You played us off the stage. You reached Shakespearean heights, you jerks, you skinheads, you scum of the melting pot.

Not one wrong note crossed your lips. You had control of every scene. Your playing was exquisite nobility. Your countenances were of rare exquisiteness. You were a smashing cast. You were a dream cast. You were inimitable, your faces unforgettable. Your sense of humour left us gasping. Your tragedy was of antique grandeur. You gave your best, you spoilsports, you gatecrashers, you fuddy-duddies, you bubbleheads, you powder puffs, you sitting ducks.

You were one of a kind. You had one of your better days tonight. You played ensemble. You were imitations of life, you drips, you diddlers, you atheists, you double-dealers, you fence-sitters, you dirty Jews.

You showed us brand-new vistas. You were well advised to do this piece. You outdid yourselves. You played yourselves loose. You turned yourselves inside out, you lonely crowd, you culture vultures, you nervous nellies, you bronco busters, you moneybags, you potheads, you washouts, you wet blankets, you fire eaters, you generation of freaks, you hopped-up sons and daughters of the revolution, you napalm specialists.

You were priceless. You were a hurricane. You drove shudders up our spines. You swept everything before you, you Colonial hangmen, you savages, you rednecks, you hatchet men, you sub-humans, you fiends, you beasts in human shape, you killer pigs.

You were the right ones. You were breathtaking. You did not disappoint our wildest hopes. You were born actors. Play-acting was in your blood, you butchers, you buggers, you bullshitters, you bullies, you rabbits, you fuck-offs, you farts.

You had perfect breath-control, you windbags, you waspish wasps, you wags, you gargoyles, you tackheads, you milksops, you mickey-mices, you chicken-shits, you cheap skates, you wrong numbers, you zeros, you back numbers, you one-shots, you centipedes, you supernumeraries, you superfluous lives, you crumbs, you cardboard figures, you *pain* in the mouth.

You are accomplished actors, you hucksters, you traitors to your country, you embezzlers, you would-be revolutionaries, you re-actionaries, you conshies, you ivory-tower artists, you defeatists, you massive retaliators, you white-rabbit pacifists, you nihilists, you individualists, you Communists, you vigilantes, you socialists, you minute men, you whizz-kids, you turtledoves, you crazy hawks, you stool pigeons, you worms, you antediluvian monstrosities, you claqueurs, you clique of babbits, you rabble, you blubber, you quivering reeds, you wretches, you ofays, you oafs, you spooks, you blackbaiters, you cooky pushers, you abortions, you bitches and bastards, you nothings, you thingamajigs.

O you cancer victims, O you haemorrhoid sufferers, O you multiple sclerotics, O you syphilitics, O you cardiac conditions, O you para-plegics, O you catatonics, O you schizoids, O you paranoids, O you hypochondriacs, O you carriers of causes of death, O you suicide candidates, O you potential peacetime casualties, O you potential war dead, O you potential accident victims, O you poten-tial increase in the mortality rate, O you potential dead.

You wax figures. You impersonators. You bad-hats. You troupers. You tear-jerkers. You potboilers. You foul mouths. You sell-outs. You deadbeats. You phonies. You milestones in the history of the theatre. You historic moments. You immortal souls. You positive heroes. You abortionists. You anti-heroes. You everyday heroes. You luminaries of science. You beacons in the dark. You educated gasbags. You cultivated classes. You befuddled aristocrats. You rotten middle class. You lowbrows. You people of our time. You children of the world. You sadsacks. You church and lay digni-taries. You wretches. You congressmen. You commissioners. You scoundrels. You generals. You lobbyists. You Chiefs of Staff. You chairmen of this and that. You tax evaders. You presidential advisers. You U-2 pilots. You agents. You corporate-military establishment. You entrepreneurs. You Eminencies. You Excell-encies. You Holiness. Mr President. You crowned heads. You pushers. You architects of the future. You builders of a better world. You mafiosos. You wiseacres. You smart-alecs. You who embrace life. You who detest life. You who have no feeling about life. You ladies and gents you, you celebrities of public and cultural life you, you who are present you, you brothers and sisters you, you comrades you, you worthy listeners you, you fellow humans you.

You were welcome here. We thank you. Good night.

The curtain falls at once. However, it does not remain closed but rises again immediately regardless of the behaviour of the public. The speakers stand and look at the public without looking at anyone in particular. Roaring applause and wild whistling is piped in through the loudspeakers; to this, one might add taped audience reactions to pop-music concerts. The deafening howling and yelling lasts until the public begins to leave. Only then does the curtain descend once and for all.

SELF-ACCUSATION

Selbstbezichtigung

translated by Michael Roloff

for Libgart

This piece is a *Sprechstück* for one male and one female speaker. It has no roles. Female and male speaker, whose voices are attuned to each other, alternate or speak together, quiet and loud, with abrupt transitions, thus producing an acoustic order. The stage is empty. The two speakers use microphones and loudspeakers. The auditorium and the stage are lighted throughout. The curtain is not used at any time, not even at the end of the piece.

I came into the world.

I became. I was begotten. I originated. I grew. I was born. I was entered in the birth register. I grew older.

I moved. I moved parts of my body. I moved my body. I moved on one and the same spot. I moved from the spot. I moved from one spot to another. I had to move. I was able to move.

I moved my mouth. I came to my senses. I made myself notice-able. I screamed. I spoke. I heard noises. I distinguished between noises. I produced noises. I produced sounds. I produced tones. I was able to produce tones, noises and sounds. I was able to speak. I was able to scream. I was able to remain silent.

I saw. I saw what I had seen before. I became conscious. I recognized what I had seen before. I recognized what I had recognized before. I perceived. I perceived what I had perceived before. I became conscious. I recognized what I had perceived before.

I looked. I saw objects. I looked at indicated objects. I indicated indicated objects. I learned the designation of indicated objects. I designated indicated objects. I learned the designation of objects that cannot be indicated. I learned. I remembered. I remembered the signs I learned. I saw designated forms. I designated similar forms with the same name. I designated differences between dissimilar forms. I designated absent forms. I learned to fear absent forms. I learned to wish for the presence of absent forms. I learned the words 'to wish' and 'to fear'.

I learned. I learned the words. I learned the verbs. I learned the difference between being and having been. I learned the nouns. I learned the difference between singular and plural. I learned the adverbs. I learned the difference between here and there. I learned the demonstrative pronouns. I learned the difference between this and that. I learned the adjectives. I learned the difference between good and evil. I learned the possessives. I learned the difference between mine and yours. I acquired a vocabulary.

I became the object of sentences. I became the attribute of sentences. I became the object and the attribute of main and subordinate clauses. I became the movement of a mouth. I became a sequence of letters of the alphabet.

I said my name. I said I. I crawled on all fours. I ran. I ran toward something. I ran away from something. I stood up. I stepped out of the passive mode. I became active. I walked at approximately a right angle to the earth. I leapt. I defied the force of gravity. I learned to relieve myself outside my clothes. I learned to bring my body under my control. I learned to control myself.

I learned to be able. I was able. I was able to want. I was able to walk on two legs. I was able to walk on my hands. I was able to remain. I was able to remain upright. I was able to remain prone. I was able to crawl on my stomach. I was able to play dead. I was able to hold my breath. I was able to kill myself. I was able to spit. I was able to nod. I was able to say no. I was able to perform gestures. I was able to question. I was able to answer questions. I was able to imitate. I was able to follow an example. I was able to play. I was able to do something. I was able to fail to do something. I was able to destroy objects. I was able to picture objects to myself. I was able to value objects. I was able to speak objects. I was able to speak about objects. I was able to remember objects.

I lived in time. I thought of beginning and end. I thought of myself. I thought of others. I stepped out of nature. I became. I became unnatural. I came to my history. I recognized that I am not you. I was able to tell my history. I was able to conceal my history.

I was able to want something. I was able not to want something.

I made myself. I made myself what I am. I changed myself. I became someone else. I became responsible for my history. I became co-responsible for the histories of the others. I became one history among others. I made the world into my own. I became sensible.

I no longer had to obey only nature. I was supposed to comply with rules. I was supposed to. I was supposed to comply with mankind's historic rules. I was supposed to act. I was supposed to fail to act. I was supposed to let happen. I learned rules. I learned as a metaphor for rules 'the snares of rules'. I learned rules for behaviour and for thoughts. I learned rules for inside and outside. I learned rules for things and people. I learned general and specific rules. I learned rules for this world and the afterworld. I learned rules for air, water, fire and earth. I learned the rules and the exceptions to the rules. I learned the basic rules and the derivative rules. I learned to pretend. I became fit for society.

I became: I was supposed to. I became capable of eating with my hands: I was supposed to avoid soiling myself. I became capable of adopting other people's practices: I was supposed to avoid my own malpractices. I became capable of distinguishing between hot and cold: I was supposed to avoid playing with fire. I became capable of separating good and evil: I was supposed to eschew evil. I became capable of playing according to the rules: I was supposed to avoid an infraction of the rules of the game. I became capable of realizing the unlawfulness of my actions and of acting in accordance with this realization: I was supposed to eschew criminal acts. I became capable of using my sexual powers: I was supposed to avoid misusing my sexual powers.

*   *   *

I was included in all the rules. With my personal data I became part of the record. With my soul I became tainted by original sin. With my lottery number I was inscribed in the lottery lists. With my illnesses I was filed in the hospital ledger. With my firm I was entered in the commercial register. With my distinguishing marks I was retained in the personnel records.

I came of age. I became fit to act. I became fit to sign a contract. I became fit to have a last will and testament.

As of a moment in time I could commit sins. As of another moment I became liable to prosecution. As of another moment I could lose my honour. As of another moment I could oblige myself contractually to do or to abstain from doing something.

I became duty-bound to atone. I became duty-bound to have an address. I became duty-bound to make restitution. I became duty-bound to pay taxes. I became duty-bound to do military service. I became duty-bound to do my duty. I became duty-bound to go to school. I became duty-bound to be vaccinated. I became duty-bound to care. I became duty-bound to pay my bills. I became duty-bound to be investigated. I became duty-bound to be educated. I became duty-bound to give proof. I became duty-bound to be insured. I became duty-bound to have an identity. I became duty-bound to be registered. I became duty-bound to pay maintenance. I became duty-bound to execute. I became duty-bound to testify.

I became. I became responsible. I became guilty. I became pardonable. I had to atone for my history. I had to atone for my past. I had to atone for the past. I had to atone for my time. I came into the world only with time.

Which demands of time did I violate? Which demands of practical reason did I violate? Which secret paragraphs did I violate?

Which programmes did I violate? Which eternal laws of the universe did I violate? Which laws of the underworld did I violate? Which of the most primitive rules of common decency did I violate? Which and whose party lines did I violate? Which laws of the theatre did I violate? Which vital interests did I violate? Which unspoken law did I violate? Which unwritten law did I violate? Which command of the hour did I violate? Which rules of life did I violate? Which common-sense rules did I violate? Which rules of love did I violate? Which rules of the game did I violate? Which rules of cosmetics did I violate? Which laws of aesthetics did I violate? Which laws of the stronger did I violate? Which commands of piety did I violate? Which law of the outlaws did I violate? Which desire for change did I violate? Which law of the world and the afterworld did I violate? Which rule of orthography did I violate? Which right of the past did I violate? Which law of free fall did I violate? Did I violate the rules, plans, ideas, postulates, basic principles, etiquettes, general propositions, opinions and formulas of the whole world?

I did. I failed to do. I let do. I expressed myself. I expressed myself through ideas. I expressed myself through expressions. I expressed myself before myself. I expressed myself before myself and others. I expressed myself before the impersonal power of the law and of good conduct. I expressed myself before the personal power of God.

I expressed myself in movements. I expressed myself in actions. I expressed myself in motionlessness. I expressed myself in inaction.

I signified. I signified with each of my expressions. With each of my expressions I signified the fulfilment or disregard of rules.

I expressed myself by spitting. I expressed myself by showing disapproval. I expressed myself by showing approval. I expressed

myself by relieving nature. I expressed myself by discarding
useless and used objects. I expressed myself by killing live beings.
I expressed myself by destroying objects. I expressed myself by
breathing. I expressed myself by sweating. I expressed myself by
secreting snot and tears.

I spat. I spat out. I spat with an aim. I spat at. I spat on the floor
in places where it was improper to spit on the floor. I spat on the
floor in places where spitting was a violation of health regulations.
I spat in the face of people whom it was a personal insult of God
to spit at. I spat on objects which it was a personal insult of
human beings to spit upon. I did not spit in front of people when
spitting out before them allegedly brought good luck. I did not
spit in front of cripples. I did not spit at actors before their performance. I did not use the spittoon. I expectorated in waiting
rooms. I spat against the wind.

I expressed approval in places where the expression of approval
was prohibited. I expressed disapproval at times when the expression of disapproval was not desired. I expressed disapproval and
approval in places and at times when the expression of disapproval
and the expression of approval were intolerable. I failed to express
approval at times when the expression of approval was called for. I
expressed approval during a difficult trapeze act in the circus. I
expressed approval inopportunely.

I discarded used and useless objects in places where discarding
objects was prohibited. I deposited objects in places where de-
positing objects was punishable. I stored objects in places where
storing objects was reprehensible. I failed to deliver objects I was
legally obligated to deliver. I threw objects out the window of a
moving train. I failed to throw litter into litter baskets. I left litter
lying in the woods. I threw burning cigarettes into hay. I failed to
hand over pamphlets dropped by enemy planes.

*   *   *

I expressed myself by speaking. I expressed myself by appropriating objects. I expressed myself by reproducing live beings. I expressed myself by producing objects. I expressed myself by looking. I expressed myself by playing. I expressed myself by walking.

I walked. I walked purposelessly. I walked purposefully. I walked on paths. I walked on paths on which it was prohibited to walk. I failed to walk on paths when it was imperative to do so. I walked on paths on which it was sinful to walk purposelessly. I walked purposefully when it was imperative to walk purposelessly. I walked on paths on which it was prohibited to walk with an objective. I walked. I walked even when walking was prohibited and against custom. I walked through passages through which it was an act of conformity to pass. I stepped on property on which it was a disgrace to step. I stepped on to property without my identity papers when it was prohibited to step on it without identity papers. I left buildings which it was a lack of solidarity to leave. I entered buildings which it was unseemly to enter without a covered head. I stepped on territory which it was prohibited to step upon. I visited the territory of a state which it was prohibited to visit. I left the territory of a state which it was a hostile act to leave. I drove into streets in a direction it was undisciplined to enter. I walked in directions it was illegal to walk in. I went so far that it was inadvisable to go farther. I stopped when it was impolite to stop. I walked on the right of persons when it was thoughtless to walk on their right. I sat down on seats that were reserved for others to sit on. I failed to walk on when ordered to walk on. I walked slowly when it was imperative to walk quickly. I failed to get on my feet when it was imperative to get on my feet. I lay down in places where it was forbidden to lie down. I stopped at demonstrations. I walked on by when it was imperative to offer help. I entered no-man's-land. I lay down on the floor when there was an R in the month. I delayed people's flight by walking slowly in narrow hallways. I jumped off moving buses. I opened the carriage door before the train had come to a complete stop.

I spoke. I spoke out. I spoke out what others thought. I only thought what others spoke out. I gave expression to public opinion. I falsified public opinion. I spoke at places where it was impious to speak. I spoke loudly at places where it was inconsiderate to speak loudly. I whispered when it was required to speak up. I remained silent at times when silence was a disgrace. I spoke as a public speaker when it was imperative to speak as a private person. I spoke with persons with whom it was dishonourable to speak. I greeted people whom it was a betrayal of principle to greet. I spoke in a language which it was a hostile act to use. I spoke about objects of which it was tactless to speak. I suppressed my knowledge of a crime. I failed to speak well of the dead. I spoke ill of absent persons. I spoke without being asked to. I spoke to soldiers on duty. I spoke to the driver during the trip.

I failed to observe the rules of the language. I committed linguistic blunders. I used words thoughtlessly. I blindly attributed qualities to the objects in the world. I blindly attributed to the words for the objects words for the qualities of the objects. I regarded the world blindly with the words for the qualities of the objects. I called objects dead. I called complexity lively. I called melancholy black. I called madness bright. I called passion hot. I called anger red. I called the ultimate questions unanswerable. I called the milieu genuine. I called nature free. I called horror frightful. I called laughter liberating. I called freedom inalienable. I called loyalty proverbial. I called fog milky, I called the surface smooth. I called severity Old Testament-like. I called the sinner poor. I called dignity inborn. I called the bomb menacing. I called the doctrine salutary. I called darkness impenetrable. I called morality hypocritical. I called lines of demarcation vague. I called the raised forefinger moralistic. I called mistrust creative. I called trust blind. I called the atmosphere sober. I called conflict productive. I called conclusions futuristic. I called integrity intellectual. I called capitalism corrupt. I called emotions murky. I called the picture of the world distorted. I called ideology false. I called the view of the world fuzzy. I called criticism constructive. I called science unbiased. I called precision scientific. I called eyes sparkling. I called results easily obtainable. I called the dialogue useful. I called dogma rigid. I called the discussion necessary. I called opinion subjective. I called pathos hollow. I called mysticism obscure. I called thoughts unripe. I called horseplay foolish. I called monotony oppressive. I called results obvious. I called being true. I called truth profound. I called lies shallow. I called life rich. I called money of no account. I called reality vulgar. I called the moment delicious. I called war just. I called peace lazy. I called weight dead. I called conflicts irreconcilable. I called the fronts fixed. I called the universe curved. I called snow white. I called ice cold. I called spheres round. I called a something certain. I called the measure full.

I appropriated objects. I acquired objects as property and possessions. I appropriated objects at places where the appropriation of objects was prohibited on principle. I appropriated objects which it was an act hostile to society to appropriate. I claimed objects as private property when it was inopportune to claim I owned them. I declared objects to be public property when it was unethical to remove them from private hands. I treated objects without care when it was prescribed to treat them with care. I touched objects which it was unaesthetic and sinful to touch. I separated objects from objects which it was inadvisable to separate. I failed to keep the required distance from objects from which it was imperative to keep the required distance. I treated persons like objects. I treated animals like persons. I took up contact with living beings with whom it was immoral to take up contact. I touched objects with objects which it was useless to bring into touch with each other. I traded with living beings and objects with which it was inhuman to trade. I treated fragile goods without care. I connected the positive pole to the positive pole. I used externally applicable medicine internally. I touched exhibited objects. I tore scabs off half-healed wounds. I touched electric wires. I failed to register letters that had to be sent registered. I failed to affix a stamp to applications that required a stamp. I failed to wear mourning clothes upon a death in the family. I failed to use skin cream to protect my skin from the sun. I dealt in slaves. I dealt in uninspected meat. I climbed mountains with shoes unfit for mountain climbing. I failed to wash fresh fruit. I failed to disinfect the clothes of plague victims. I failed to shake the hair lotion before use.

I looked and listened. I looked at. I looked at objects which it was shameless to look at. I failed to look at objects which it was a dereliction of duty to fail to look at. I failed to watch events which it was philistine to fail to watch. I failed to watch events in the position prescribed to watch them I failed to avert my eyes during events it was treasonable to watch. I looked back when looking back was proof of a bad upbringing. I looked away when it was cowardly to look away. I listened to persons whom it was unprincipled to listen to. I inspected forbidden areas. I inspected buildings in danger of collapse. I failed to look at persons who were speaking to me. I failed to look at persons with whom I was speaking. I watched unadvisable and objectionable movies. I heard information in the mass media that was hostile to the state. I watched games without a ticket. I stared at strangers. I looked without dark glasses into the sun. I kept my eyes open during sexual intercourse.

I ate. I ate more than I could stomach. I drank more than my bladder could hold. I consumed food and drink. I ingested the four elements. I inhaled and exhaled the four elements. I ate at moments when it was undisciplined to eat. I failed to breathe in the prescribed manner. I breathed air which it was below my station to breathe. I inhaled when it was harmful to inhale. I ate meat during the fast days. I breathed without a gas mask. I ate on the street. I inhaled exhaust gases. I ate without knife and fork. I failed to leave myself time to breathe. I ate the Host with my teeth. I failed to breathe through my nose.

I played. I played wrong. I played according to rules which, according to existing rules, were against convention. I played at times and places where it was asocial and ingenuous to play. I played with persons with whom it was dishonourable to play. I played with objects with which it was unceremonious to play. I failed to play at times and places where it was unsociable to fail to play. I played according to the rules when it was individualistic not to play according to the rules. I played with myself when it would have been humane to play with others. I played with powers with whom it was presumptuous to play. I failed to play seriously. I played too seriously. I played with fire. I played with lighters. I played with marked cards. I played with human lives. I played with spray cans. I played with life. I played with feelings. I played myself. I played without chips. I failed to play during playtime. I played with the inclination to evil. I played with my thoughts. I played with the thought of suicide. I played on a thin sheet of ice. I played and trespassed at one and the same time. I played despair. I played with my despair. I played with my sex organ. I played with words. I played with my fingers.

I came into the world afflicted with original sin. My very nature inclined toward evil. My innate viciousness expressed itself at once in envy of my fellow suckling. One day in the world, I was no longer free of sin. Bawling, I craved my mother's breasts. All I knew was to suck. All I knew was to gratify my desires. With my reason I refused to recognize the laws that were placed in the universe and in myself. I was conceived in malice. I was begotten in malice. I expressed my malice by destroying things. I expressed my malice by trampling live beings to death. I was disobedient out of love of play. What I loved in playing was the sense of winning. I loved in fantastic stories the itch in my ear. I idolized people. I took greater delight in the trivia of poets than in useful knowledge. I feared a solecism more than the eternal laws. I let myself be governed solely by my palate. I only trusted my senses. I failed to prove that I had a sense of reality. I not only loved crimes, I loved committing crimes. I preferred to do evil in company. I loved accomplices. I loved complicity. I loved sin for its danger. I did not search for truth. The pleasure I took in art was in my pain and my compassion. I pandered to the desires of my eyes. I failed to recognize the purpose of history. I was godforsaken. I was forsaken by the world. I did not designate the world as *this* world. I also included the heavenly bodies in the world. I was sufficient for myself. I cared only for worldly things. I took no cold bath against melancholy. I took no hot bath against passion. I used my body for wrong ends. I failed to take notice of the facts. I failed to subordinate my physical nature to my spiritual nature. I denied my nature. I ran up against the nature of things. I indiscriminately sought power. I indiscriminately sought money. I failed to teach myself to regard money as a means. I lived in excess of my means. I failed to have the means to put up with the state of affairs. I myself determined how I would fashion my life. I did not overcome myself. I did not toe the line. I disturbed the eternal order. I failed to recognize that evil is only the absence of good. I failed to recognize that evil is only an abuse. I gave birth to death in my sins. I made myself, with my sins, one with the cattle that is to be slaughtered in the slaughterhouse but snuffles at the very iron designed to slaughter it. I failed to resist the beginnings. I failed to find the moment to stop. I made myself an image of the highest being. I sought not to make myself an image of the highest being. I refused to divulge the name of the highest being. I only believed in the three persons of grammar. I told myself that there is no higher being so as not to have to fear it. I looked for the opportunity. I did not use the chance. I did not submit to necessity. I did not count on the possibility. I did not learn from bad examples. I did not learn from the past. I abandoned myself to the free play of forces. I mistook freedom for license. I mistook honesty for self-exposure. I mistook obscenity for originality. I mistook the dream for reality. I mistook life for the cliché. I mistook coercion for necessary guidance. I mistook love for instinct. I mistook the cause for the effect. I failed to observe the unity of thought and action. I failed to see things as they really are. I succumbed to the magic of the moment. I failed to regard existence as a provisional gift. I broke my word. I did not have command of the language. I did not reject the world. I did not affirm authority. I was a naïve believer in authority. I did not husband my sexual powers. I sought lust as an end in itself. I was not sure of myself. I became a puzzle to myself. I wasted my time. I overslept my time. I wanted to stop time. I wanted to speed up time. I was in conflict with time. I did not want to grow older. I did not want to die. I did not let things come toward me. I could not limit myself. I was impatient. I could not wait for it. I did not think of the future. I did not think of *my* future. I lived from one moment to the next. I was domineering. I behaved as though I was alone in the world. I proved ill-bred. I was self-willed. I lacked a will of my own. I did not work on myself. I failed to make work the basis of my existence. I failed to see God in every beggar. I did not eradicate evil at its roots. I irresponsibly thrust children into the world. I failed to adapt my pleasures to my social circumstances. I sought for bad company. I always wanted to be at the centre. I was too much alone. I was not enough alone. I led my own life too much. I failed to grasp the meaning of the word 'too'. I failed to regard the happiness of all mankind as my ultimate aim. I did not place the common interest before the individual interest. I did not face the music. I disregarded orders. I failed to disobey unjustifiable orders. I did not know my limits. I failed to see things in their relationship with one another. I made no virtue of necessity. I switched convictions. I was incorrigible. I failed to put myself at the service of the cause. I was satisfied with the status quo. I saw no one but myself. I yielded to insinuations. I decided neither for one nor for the other. I took no stand. I disturbed the balance of power. I violated generally acknowledged principles. I did not fulfil the quota. I fell behind the goal that had been set. I was one and everything to myself. I did not take enough fresh air. I woke up too late. I did not clean the pavement. I left doors unlocked. I stepped too near the cage. I failed to keep entrances free. I failed to keep exits free. I pulled the communication cord without a proper reason. I leaned bicycles against forbidden walls. I solicited and peddled. I did not keep the streets clean. I did not take off my shoes. I leaned out the window of a moving train. I handled open fires in rooms that were fire-traps. I paid unannounced visits. I did not get up for invalids. I lay down in a hotel bed with a lighted cigarette. I failed to turn off taps. I spent nights on park benches. I failed to keep dogs on a lead. I failed to muzzle dogs that bit. I failed to leave umbrellas and coats in the cloakroom. I touched goods before I bought them. I failed to close containers immediately after use. I tossed pressurized containers into the fire. I crossed on the red. I walked on motorways. I walked along the railway track. I failed to walk on the pavement. I failed to pass right down inside buses. I did not hold on to the straps. I used the toilet while the train was standing in the station. I did not follow the instructions of the staff. I started motor vehicles where it was prohibited to do so. I failed to push buttons. I crossed the rails in railway stations. I failed to step back when trains were coming in. I exceeded the load limit in lifts. I disturbed the quiet of the night. I affixed posters to forbidden walls. I tried to open doors by pushing when they could only be pulled open. I tried to open doors by pulling when they could only be pushed open. I roamed the streets after dark. I lit lights during blackouts. I did not remain calm in accidents. I left the house during curfew. I did not remain at my post during catastrophes. I thought of myself first. I indiscriminately rushed out of rooms. I activated alarm signals without authorization. I destroyed alarm signals without authorization. I failed to use emergency exits. I pushed. I trampled. I failed to break the window with the hammer. I blocked the way. I put up unauthorized resistance. I did not stop when challenged. I did not raise my hands above my head. I did not aim at the legs. I played with the trigger of a cocked gun. I failed to save women and children first. I approached the drowning from behind. I kept my hands in my pockets. I took no evasive action. I did not let myself be blindfolded. I did not look for cover. I offered an easy target. I was too slow. I was too fast. I *moved*.

I did not regard the movement of my shadow as proof of the movement of the earth. I did not regard my fear of the dark as proof of my existence. I did not regard the demands of reason for immortality as proof of life after death. I did not regard my nausea at the thought of the future as proof of my non-existence after death. I did not regard subsiding pain as proof of the passage of time. I did not regard my lust for life as proof that time stands still.

I am not what I was. I was not what I should have been. I did not become what I should have become. I did not keep what I should have kept.

I went to the theatre. I heard this piece. I spoke this piece. I wrote this piece.

KASPAR

translated by Michael Roloff

thixtheen years
thoutheast station
whath thould
whath thould
he do
thoutheast station
thixtheen years
whath thould
the fellow
whath thould
he do
thixtheen years
thoutheast station
what thould
he do
the fellow
with hith
thixtheen years

Ernst Jandl

The play *Kaspar* does not show how IT REALLY IS or REALLY WAS with Kaspar Hauser. It shows what IS POSSIBLE with someone. It shows how someone can be made to speak through speaking. The play could also be called *speech torture*. To formalize this torture it is suggested that a kind of magic eye be constructed above the ramp. This eye, without however diverting the audience's attention from the events on stage, indicates, by blinking, the degree of vehemence with which the PROTAGONIST is addressed. The more vehemently he defends himself, the more vehemently he is addressed, the more vehemently the magic eye blinks. (Or one might employ a jerking indicator of the kind used on scales for tests of strength in amusement parks.) Although the sense of what the voices addressing the protagonist say should always be completely comprehensible, their manner of speaking should be that of voices which in reality have a technical medium interposed between themselves and the listeners: telephone voices, radio or television announcers' voices, the voice that tells the time on the phone, the voices of automatic answering services of all kinds, the speech mannerisms of sports commentators, of stadium announcers, of narrators in the more endearing cartoons, of announcers of train arrivals and departures, of interviewers, of gym teachers who by the way they speak make their directions correspond to the sequence of the gymnastic movements, of language course records, of policemen as they speak through megaphones at demonstrations, etc., etc. These manners of speaking may all be applied to the text, but only in such a way that they clarify the SENSE or NONSENSE of what is being said. The audience need not be aware which manner of speaking is being used at any given moment, but, etc. At the same time, the miniature scenes should be projected, enlarged, on the back of the stage.

Kaspar (Kasper means clown in German) does not resemble any other comedian; rather, when he comes on stage he resembles Frankenstein's monster (or King Kong).

The front curtain is already drawn. The audience does not see the stage as a representation of a room that exists somewhere, but as a representation of a stage. The stage represents the stage. At first glance, the objects on the stage look theatrical: not because they imitate other objects, but because the way they are situated with respect to one another does not correspond to their usual arrangement in reality. The objects, although genuine (made of wood, steel, cloth, etc), are instantly recognizable as props. They are play objects. They have no history. The audience cannot imagine that, before they came in and saw the stage, some tale had already taken place on it. At most they can imagine that the stage hands have moved objects hither and thither. Nor should the audience be able to imagine that the props on stage will be part of a play that pretends to take place anywhere except on stage: they should recognize at once that they will witness an event that plays only on stage and not in some other reality. They will not experience a story but watch a theatrical event. This event will last until the curtain falls at the end of the piece: because no story will take place, the audience will not be in a position to imagine that there is a sequel to the story. The stage should look something like this: the backdrop of the stage consists of a curtain of the same size and fabric as the front curtain. The folds of the curtain are vertical and plentiful, so the audience has difficulty distinguishing the place where the curtain parts. The wings are bare. The props are in front of the backdrop: they are obviously actors' props. They look new, so the audience won't think they are seeing the representation of a junk shop; and to avoid this possibility, the objects are in their normal positions: the chairs are straight up, the broom is leaning, the cushions lie flat, the drawer is where it belongs in the table. However, so the audience won't think it is seeing the representation of a home-furnishing exhibition, the objects are situated without any obvious relationship to each other; they stand there tastelessly, so the audience recognizes a stage in the objects on display. The chairs stand far from the table, as though they had nothing to do with it; they do not stand at the usual angle to the table or at a normal angle towards each other (they should not, however, give a picture of disorder). The table and its drawer face the audience. Elsewhere on stage there is another table, smaller, lower, with only three legs. Centre stage is empty. Two chairs stand elsewhere, each with a different backrest, one with a cushion, one without. Somewhere else is a sofa with room for almost five persons. Half the sofa (from the vantage point of those sitting in the centre of the auditorium) should be behind the wings, thus indicating backstage. Elsewhere there is a rocking chair. Somewhere else, a broom and shovel, one of them bearing the clearly discernible word STAGE or the name of the theatre. Somewhere else, a waste-paper basket with the same inscription. On the large table, but not in the middle, stands a broad-necked bottle with water in it, and next to it a glass. At the back of the stage is a stylish wardrobe with a large key in the lock. None of the props has any particularly unusual characteristic that might puzzle the beholder. In front, in the centre of the apron, is a microphone.

The first person in the audience to enter the theatre should find the stage lighted softly. Nothing moves on stage. Every theatregoer should have sufficient time to observe each object and grow sick of it or come to want more of it. Finally, the lights are slowly dimmed as usual, an occurrence that might be accompanied by, for example, a continuous muted violin tone ('The tone of the violin is more ample than that of the guitar' – Kaspar). The theatre is dark throughout the play. (While the audience comes in and as they wait for the play to begin, this text might be read softly over the microphones, and repeated over and over.)

1

Behind the backdrop, something stirs. The audience detects this in the movement of the curtain. The movement begins on the left or right of the curtain and continues towards the centre, gradually becoming more vehement and more rapid. The closer the person behind the curtain comes to the centre, the greater the bulge in the curtain. What at first was only a grazing of the curtain becomes, now that the material is obviously pliable, an attempt to break through. The audience realizes more and more clearly that someone wants to get through the curtain on to the stage but has not discovered the slit in the curtain. After several futile tries at the wrong spots – the audience can hear the curtain being thrashed – the person finds the slit that he had not even been looking for. A hand is all one sees at first; the rest of the body slowly follows. The other hand holds on to a hat, so the curtain won't knock it off. With a slight movement, the figure comes on stage, the curtain slipping off it and then falling shut behind it. Kaspar stands on stage.

2

The audience has the opportunity to observe Kaspar's face and makeup: he simply stands there. His makeup is theatrical. For example, he has on a round, wide-brimmed hat with a band; a light-coloured shirt with a closed collar; a colourful jacket with many (roughly seven) metal buttons; wide trousers; clumsy shoes; on one shoe, for instance, the very long laces have become untied. He looks droll. The colours of his outfit clash with the colours on stage. Only at the second or third glance should the audience realize that his face is a mask; it is a pale colour; it is life-like; it may have been fashioned to fit the face of the actor. It expresses astonishment and confusion. The mask-face is round because the expression of astonishment is more theatrical on round, wide faces. Kaspar need not be tall. He stands there and does not move from the spot. He is the incarnation of astonishment.

3

He begins to move. One hand still holds the hat. His way of moving is highly mechanical and artificial. However, he does not move like a puppet. His peculiar way of moving results from his constantly changing from one way of moving to another. For example, he takes the first step with one leg straight out, the other following timorously and 'shaking'. He might take the next step in the same manner but reverse the order. With the next step, he throws one leg high in the air and drags the other leg heavily behind him; the next step, he has both feet flat on the ground; the next he takes with the wrong foot first, so that with the subsequent step he must put the other leg far forward to catch up with the first leg; he takes the next two steps (his pace quickens and he comes close to toppling over) by placing the right leg on the left and the left leg on the right, and he almost falls; on the next step, he is unable to get one leg past the other and steps on it; again, he barely avoids falling; the next step he takes is so long he almost slips into a split, consequently he must drag the other leg laboriously after him; in the meantime he has tried to move the right leg farther forward, but in another direction, so once more he almost loses his balance; on the next step, which is even more hurried, he places one foot toe-forward, the other toe-backwards, whereupon he attempts to align the toe on one foot with the toe on the other, becomes discombobulated, turns on his axis, and, as the audience has feared all along, finally falls to the ground. Before this occurs, however, he has not been walking towards the audience; his walk consists of spirals back and forth across the stage; it is not so much walking as something between an imminent fall and convoluted progress, with one hand holding on to the hat, a hand which remains on his head when he does fall. At the end of his fall, the audience sees Kaspar sitting on the stage floor in something like a disorderly lotus-position. He does not move; only the hand holding the hat becomes autonomous: it gradually lets go of the hat, slips down along his body, dangling awhile before it too stops. Kaspar just sits there.

4

He begins to speak. He utters a single sentence over and over: I want to be someone like somebody else was once. *He utters the sentence so that it is obvious that he has no concept of what it means, without expressing anything but that he lacks awareness of the meaning of the sentence. He repeats the sentence several times at regular intervals.*

5

In the same position on the floor, the lotus position, Kaspar repeats the sentence, now giving it almost every possible kind of expression. He utters it with an expression of perseverance, utters it as a question, exclaims it, scans it as though it were verse. He utters it with an expression of happiness, of relief. He hyphenates the sentence. He utters it in anger and with impatience; with extreme fear. He utters it as a greeting, as an invocation in a litany, as an answer to a question, as an order, as an imprecation. Then, in monotone, he sings the sentence. Finally he screams it.

6

When this does not get him anywhere, he gets up. First he tries getting up all at once. He fails. Half-way up, he falls down again. On the second attempt he gets almost all the way up, only to fall once more. Now he laboriously draws his legs out from under him, during which process, his toes get caught on the back of his knees. Finally he pries his legs apart with his hands. He stretches out his legs. He looks at his legs. At the same time he bends his knees, drawing them towards himself. Suddenly he is squatting. He watches as the floor leaves him. He points with his hand at the floor which is becoming more remote. He utters his sentence with an air of wonderment. Now he is standing upright, turns his head this way and that, towards the objects on stage, and repeats the sentence: I want to be someone like somebody else was once.

7

He begins to walk again, still in an artificial manner, but now more regularly: for example, the feet are turned inward, the knees stiff; the arms hang slack, as do the fingers. He directs his sentence, not tonelessly yet without expressing anything, at a chair. He directs the sentence, expressing with it that the first chair has not heard him, at the next chair. Walking on, he directs the sentence at the table, expressing with it that neither chair heard him. Still walking, he directs the sentence at the wardrobe, expressing with it that the wardrobe does not hear him. He

*utters the sentence once more in front of the wardrobe, but without express-
ing anything : I want to be someone like somebody else was once. As
though by accident, he kicks the wardrobe. Once again he kicks the
wardrobe, as though intentionally. He kicks the wardrobe once more :
whereupon all the wardrobe doors open, gradually. The audience sees that
the wardrobe contains several colourful theatrical costumes. Kaspar does
not react to the movement of the wardrobe doors. He has only let himself
be pushed back a bit. Now he stands still until the wardrobe doors have
stopped moving. He reacts to the open doors with the sentence :* I want to
be someone like somebody else was once.

8

*The tri-sectioning of events now sets in : first, Kaspar moves across the
stage, now no longer avoiding each object but touching it (and more) ;
second, after having done something to each object, Kaspar says his
sentence ; third, the prompters now begin to speak from all sides, they
make Kaspar speak by speaking. The prompters – three persons, say –
remain invisible (their voices are perhaps pre-recorded) and speak
without undertones or overtones ; that is, they speak neither with the
usual irony, humour, helpfulness, human warmth, nor with the usual
ominousness, dread, incorporeality or supernaturalness – they speak
comprehensibly. Over a good amplifying system they speak a text that is
not theirs. They do not speak to make sense but to show that they are
playing at speaking, and do so with great exertion of their voices even
when they speak softly. The following events ensue : the audience sees
Kaspar walking from the wardrobe to the sofa and simultaneously hears
speaking from all sides.*

*Kaspar goes to the sofa. He
discovers the gaps between the
cushions. He puts one hand into a
gap. He can't extract his hand. To
help extract it, he puts his other
hand into the gap. He can't
extract either hand. He tugs at
the sofa. With one tug he gets
both hands free but also flings one
sofa cushion on to the floor,*

Already you have a sentence
with which you can make
yourself noticeable. With this
sentence you can make yourself
noticeable in the dark, so no
one will think you are an
animal. You have a sentence
with which you can tell yourself
everything that you *can't* tell
others. You can tell yourself

whereupon, after a moment of looking, he utters the sentence: I want to be someone like somebody else was once.

how it goes with you. You have a sentence with which you can already contradict the same sentence.

The prompters stop speaking at about the time Kaspar does something to whatever object he happens to be touching: the sofa cushion falls on the floor at the moment the prompters stop speaking; this functions like a full stop. Kaspar's sentence after each encounter with an object is preceded by a brief pause.

9

Kaspar walks to the table. He notices the drawer in the table. He tries to turn the knob on the drawer but is unable to. He pulls on the drawer. It comes out a little. He tugs once more at the drawer. The drawer is now askew. He tugs at it once more. The drawer loses hold and falls to the floor. Several objects, such as silverware, a box of matches, and coins, fall out of the drawer. After regarding them for a moment Kaspar says: I want to be someone like somebody else was once.

The sentence is more useful to you than a word. You can speak a sentence to the end. You can make yourself comfortable with a sentence. You can occupy yourself with a sentence and have gotten several steps further ahead in the meantime. You can make pauses with the sentence. Play off one word against the other. With the sentence you can compare one word with the other. Only with a sentence, not with a word, can you ask leave to speak.

10

Kaspar walks towards a chair. He tries to walk straight ahead even though the chair is in his way. While walking, he shoves the chair ahead in front of him. Still walking, he becomes entangled in the chair. Still

You can play dumb with the sentence. Assert yourself with the sentence against other sentences. Name everything that gets in your way and move it out of your way. Familiarize yourself with all objects. Make

*walking, he tries to disentangle
himself from the chair. At first he
becomes more and more
dangerously entwined in it, but
then, as he is about to surrender
to the chair, he becomes free of it
just because he was about to give
in. He gives the chair a kick, so
that it flies off and falls over.
After regarding it for a moment:*
I want to be someone like
somebody else was once.

all objects into a sentence with
the sentence. You can make all
objects into *your* sentence.
With this sentence, all objects
belong to you. With this
sentence, all objects are yours.

11

*Kaspar walks towards the small
table. The table has three legs.
Kaspar lifts the table with one
hand and yanks with the other
hand on one leg but is unable to
pull it out. He turns the leg, first
in the wrong direction. He turns
it in the right direction and
unscrews the leg. He is still
holding the table with the other
hand. He slowly withdraws the
hand. The table rests on his
fingertips. He withdraws his
fingertips. The table
topples over. After regarding it
for a moment:* I want to be
someone like somebody else was
once.

To put up resistance. A
sentence to divert you. A
sentence with which you can
tell yourself a story. You have
a sentence which gives you
something to chew on when
you are hungry. A sentence
with which you can pretend you
are crazy: with which you can
go crazy. A sentence to be
crazy with: for remaining crazy.
You have a sentence with which
you can begin to take notice of
yourself: with which you can
divert attention from yourself.
A sentence to take a walk with.
To stumble over. To come to a
halt with in mid-sentence. To
count steps with.

12

*Kaspar walks towards the
rocking chair. He walks around*

You have a sentence you can
speak from beginning to end

it. *He touches it as though
unintentionally. The chair begins
to rock, Kaspar takes a step back.
The chair continues to rock.
Kaspar takes one step farther
back. The rocking chair stops
moving. Kaspar takes two steps
towards the chair and nudges it
with his foot, making it move
slightly. When the chair is
rocking, he uses his hand to make
it rock more. When the chair is
rocking more strongly, he uses his
foot to make it rock even more.
When the rocking chair is
rocking even more strongly, he
gives it an even stronger shove
with his hand, so the rocking
chair is now rocking dangerously.
He gives it one more kick with
his foot. Then, as the rocking
chair is about to tip over, though
it is still not quite certain
whether it will fall or go on
rocking, he gives it a little shove
with his hand which suffices to tip
it over. Kaspar runs off from the
turned-over chair. Then he
returns, step by step. After
regarding it for a moment :* I
want to be someone like
somebody else was once.

and from end to beginning.
You have a sentence to say yea
and say nay with. You have a
sentence to deny with. You
have a sentence with which you
can make yourself tired or
awake. You have a sentence to
blindfold yourself with. You
have a sentence to bring order
into every disorder: with which
you can designate every
disorder in comparison to
another disorder as a
comparative order: with which
you can declare every disorder
an order: can bring yourself
into order: with which you can
talk away every disorder. You
have a sentence you can take as
a model. You have a sentence
you can place between yourself
and everything else. You are
the lucky owner of a sentence
which will make every
impossible order possible for
you and make every possible
and real disorder impossible
for you: which will exorcize
every disorder from you.

13

*Kaspar takes a look around. A
broom is standing there. He walks
to the broom. He draws the broom
towards himself with his hand or*

You can no longer visualize
anything without the sentence.
You are unable to see an object
without the sentence. Without

*foot, so that it now leans at a
wider angle. He tugs once more at
the broom, again increasing the
angle. Once more, just a little.
The broom begins to slip, and
falls. After regarding it for a
moment :* I want to be someone
like somebody else was once.

the sentence, you cannot put
one foot in front of the other.
You can remind yourself with
the sentence because you
uttered the sentence while
taking your last step, and you
can recall the last step you took
because you uttered the
sentence.

14

*Kaspar walks towards the one
chair that is still upright. He
stops in front of it. He remains
standing in front of it for the
duration of the sentence.
Suddenly he sits down. After
looking for a moment :* I want to
be someone like. *He has
obviously been interrupted in
mid-sentence.*

You can hear yourself. You
become aware. You become
aware of yourself with the
sentence. You become aware of
yourself. You stumble
something which interrupts the
sentence which makes you
aware that you have stumbled
upon something. You become
aware: you can become aware:
you are aware.

15

Kaspar sits there. He is quiet.

You learn to stammer with the
sentence and with the sentence
you learn that you are
stammering, and you learn to
hear with the sentence and you
learn with the sentence that you
are hearing, and with the
sentence you learn to divide
time into time before and time
after uttering the sentence, and
you learn with the sentence
that you are dividing time, just
as you learn with the sentence

that you were elsewhere the
last time you uttered the
sentence, just as you learn with
the sentence that you are
elsewhere now, and learn to
speak with the sentence and
learn with the sentence that you
are speaking; and you learn
with the sentence that you are
speaking a sentence, and you
learn with the sentence to speak
another sentence, just as you
learn that there are other
sentences, just as you learn
other sentences, and learn to
learn; and you learn with the
sentence that there is an order
and you learn with the sentence
to learn order.

16

The stage is blacked out.
You can still crawl off behind
the sentence: hide: contest it.
The sentence can still mean
anything.

17
*The stage becomes bright. Kaspar
sits there quietly. Nothing
indicates that he is listening. He
is being taught to speak. He
would like to keep his sentence.
His sentence is slowly but surely
exorcized through the speaking of
other sentences. He becomes
confused.*

The sentence doesn't hurt you
yet, not one word. Does hurt
you. Every word does. Hurt,
but you don't know that that
which hurts you is a sentence
that. Sentence hurts you
because you don't know that it
is a sentence. Speaking hurts
you but the speaking does not.

Hurt nothing hurts you because
you don't know yet what.
Hurting is everything hurts you
but nothing. Really hurts you
the sentence does. Not hurt you
yet because you don't know
yet that it is. A sentence
although you don't know that
it is a sentence, it hurts you,
because you don't know that it
is a sentence that hurts. You.

I want to be someone like
somebody else was once.

*Kaspar defends himself with his
sentence:*
I want.
I want to be like once.
I want to be someone like once.
Somebody else.
Like a person else.
Somebody.

He still maintains his sentence:
I want to be someone like
somebody else was once.

You begin, with yourself, you,
are a, sentence you, could form,
of yourself, innumerable,
sentences, you sit, there but,
you don't, know that, you sit
there. You don't sit, there
because you, don't know that,
you sit there you, can form, a
sentence, of yourself, you sit in,
your coat, is buttoned, the belt,
on your, trousers is, too loose,
you have, no shoelace you, have
no, belt your coat, is
unbuttoned, you are not even,
there you, are an un, loosed
shoe, lace. You cannot defend
yourself against any sentence:

He defends himself again:
Was I.
Somebody else like else.
Somebody else someone.
Be like I.
I be I.

The shoelace hurts you. It
does not hurt you because it is
a shoelace but because you lack
the word for it, and the
difference between the tight
and the loose shoelace hurts

Somebody was.
Be one.
I a person.
I want to be else.
Like somebody else somebody.
Once like somebody.
Was somebody.
Like once.
I want to be somebody like.

you because you don't know
the difference between the tight
and the loose shoelace. The
coat hurts you, and the hair
hurts you. You, although you
don't hurt yourself, hurt
yourself. You hurt yourself
because you don't know what is
you. The table hurts you, and
the curtain hurts you. The words
that you hear and the words
that you speak hurt you.
Nothing hurts you because you
don't know what hurting is,
and everything hurts, you don't
know what anything means.
Because you don't know the
name of anything, everything
hurts you even if you don't
know that it hurts you because
you don't know what the word
hurt means:

The first divergence:
I want to be like somebody else
like somebody else once was
somebody else.

*He resists more vehemently but
with less success:*
One.
Be.
Somebody.
Was.
Want.
Somebody else.

You hear sentences: something
like your sentence: You
compare something comparable.
You can play off your sentence
against other sentences and
already accomplish something:
such as becoming used to the
open shoelace. You are
becoming used to other
sentences, so that you cannot
do without them any more. You

can no longer imagine your sentence all alone by itself: it is no longer your sentence alone: you are already looking for other sentences. Something has become impossible: something else has become possible:

Somebody else like I like once I want to be.

He resists even more vehemently, but even less successfully:
Waswant!
Somelike!
Someonce!
Somel!
Besome!
Likeonce!
Elsh!

Where are you sitting? You are sitting quietly. What are you speaking? You are speaking slowly. What are you breathing? You are breathing regularly. Where are you speaking? You are speaking quickly. What are you breathing? You are breathing in and out. When are you sitting? You are sitting more quietly. Where are you breathing? You are breathing more rapidly. When are you speaking? You are speaking louder. What are you sitting? You are breathing. What are you breathing? You are speaking. What are you speaking? You are sitting. Where are you sitting? You are speaking in and out:

Olce ime kwas askwike lein.

The prompters address Kaspar very vehemently:

Kaspar utters a very long e.	Order. Put. Lie. Sit.
Kaspar utters an n *for not quite as long a duration as the* e.	Put. Order. Lie. Sit. Lie. Put. Order. Sit.
Kaspar utters a shorter s.	Sit. Lie. Put. Order.
Kaspar utters a brief, formally difficult, r.	Order. Put. Lie. Sit.
Kaspar utters a p, *and tries to stretch the* p *like the other letters, an endeavour in which he of course fails utterly.*	Put. Order. Sit. Lie. Sit. Lie. Order. Stand.
With great formal difficulties, Kaspar utters a t.	Stand. Sit. Lie. Order.
With great effort, Kaspar utters a d.	Lies. Stands. Sits. In order:
Kaspar seeks to produce some kind of sound by means of movements such as stomping his feet, scraping, shoving a chair back and forth, and finally perhaps by scratching on his clothes.	*The prompters are now speaking calmly, already sure of their success:* Listening? Staying? Opening up? Hear! Remain!! Open up!!!
Kaspar tries with all his strength to produce a single sound. He tries it with his hands and feet. He cannot do it. His strenuous movements become weaker and weaker. Finally he stops moving altogether. Kaspar has finally been silenced. His sentence has	*The prompters let him mutely exert himself.*

been exorcized. Several moments
of quiet.

18
Kaspar is made to speak. He is
gradually needled into speaking
through the use of speech
material.

The table stands. The table fell
over? The chair fell over! The
chair stands? The chair fell
over and stands? The chair fell
over but the table stands. The
table stands or fell over!
Neither the chair fell over nor
the table stands nor the chair
stands nor the table fell over?!
You are sitting on a chair that
fell over:

Kaspar is still mute.

The table is a horror for you.
But the chair is no horror
because it is no table. But your
shoelace is a horror because the
broom is no chair. But the
broom is no horror because it
is a table. But the chair is no
horror because it is the table as
well as the shoelace. But the
shoelace is no horror because it
is neither a chair nor a table
nor a broom. But the table is a
horror because it is a table. But
the table, chair, broom, and
shoelace are a horror because
they are called table, chair,
broom, and shoelace. They are
a horror to you because you
don't know what they are
called:

Kaspar begins to speak:
Fallen down.
He begins to speak a little:
Because.
Often.
Me.
Never.
Least.
Into.
Let.
Me.
Nothing.
Although.
How.
Because me here at least already.

He comes closer and closer to uttering a regular sentence:
Into the hands.
Far and wide.
Or there.
Fell out.
Beat eyes.
No is.
Goes neither home.
To the hole.
Goat eyes.
Rain barrel.
How dark.
Pronounced dead.
If I myself already here at least tell.

Eels. Running.
Boiled. From behind.

They continue to stuff him with enervating words: For a wardrobe on which you sit is a chair, or not? Or a chair on which you sit is a wardrobe when it stands on the place of the wardrobe, or not? Or a table which stands on the place of the wardrobe is a chair when you sit on it, or not? Or a chair on which you sit is a wardrobe as soon as it can be opened with a key and clothes hang in it, even if it stands on the place of the table and you can sweep the floor with it; or not?

A table is a word you can apply to the wardrobe, and you have a real wardrobe and a possible table in place of the table, and? And a chair is a word you can apply to the broom, so that you have a real broom and a possible chair in place of the chair, and? And a broom is a word you can apply to the shoelace, and you have a real shoelace and a possible broom in place of the shoelace, and? And a shoelace is a word you can apply to the table, so that you suddenly have neither a table nor a shoelace in place of the table, and?

The chair still hurts you, but the word chair already pleases

Right. Later. Horse.
Never stood. Screams.
Faster. Puss. Thrashing.
Whimpers. The knee.
Back. Crawls.
Hut. At once.
Candle. Hoarfrost. Stretch.
Awaits. Struggles.
Rats. Unique. Worse.
Walked. Living. Farther.
Jumped. Yes. Should.

Entered am chair without rags
on the shoelace, which
meantime talked to death struck
the feet, without broom on the
table, which are standing turned
over some distance from the
wardrobe, scarcely two saving
drops from the curtain.

you. The table still hurts you
but the word table already
pleases you. The wardrobe still
hurts you a little, but the word
wardrobe already pleases you
more. The word shoelace is
beginning to hurt you less
because the word shoelace
pleases you more and more.
The broom hurts you less the
more the word broom pleases
you. Words no longer hurt you
when the word words pleases
you. The sentences please you
more the more the word
sentence pleases you:

Words and things. Chair and
shoelace. Words without things.
Chair without broom. Things
without words. Table without
thing. Wardrobe without
shoelace. Words without table.
Neither words nor things.
Neither words nor shoelace.
Neither words nor table. Table
and words. Words and chair
without things. Chair without
shoelace without words and
wardrobe. Words and things.

Things without words. Neither
word nor things. Words and
sentences. Sentences:
Sentences: Sentences:

Kaspar utters a normal sentence:
That time, when I was still
there, my head never ached as
much, and I was not tormented
the way I am now that I am
here.

It becomes dark.

19
*It becomes light, Kaspar slowly
begins to speak:*
After I came in, as I see only
now, I put, as I see only now,
the sofa into disorder,
whereupon, as I see only now,
the wardrobe door with which
I, as I see only now, played, as
I see only now, with my foot,
was left open, whereupon I, as
I see only now, ripped, as I see
only now, the drawer out of the
table, whereupon, as I see only
now, I threw over another
table, thereupon a rocking
chair, as I see only now, also
turned over, as well as a further
chair and broom, as I see only
now, whereupon I walked
towards, as I see only now, the
only chair still standing (as I
see only now) and sat down. I
neither saw anything nor heard
anything, and I felt good. *He*

gets up. Now I have got up and
noticed at once, not just now,
that my shoelace was untied.
Because I can speak now I can
put the shoelace in order. Ever
since I can speak I can bend
down to the shoelace in normal
fashion. Ever since I can speak
I can put everything in order.
He bends down towards the
shoelace. He moves one leg
forward so as to be able to bend
down better towards the shoelace.
But because he was standing
with the other leg on the shoelace,
he stumbles as he moves the leg
forward and falls after making a
futile attempt to remain upright
– for a moment it looks as
though he might stop himself, but
he doesn't. In the process he also
overturns the chair he had been
sitting on. After a moment of
silence:
Ever since I can speak I can
stand up in an orderly manner;
but falling only hurts ever since
I can speak; but the pain when
I fall is half as bad ever since
I know that I can speak about
the pain; but falling is twice as
bad ever since I know that one
can speak about my falling; but
falling doesn't hurt at all any
more ever since I know that I
can forget the pain; but the
pain never stops at all any more
ever since I know that I can
feel ashamed of falling.

20

*Kaspar sets in. He speaks
slowly:*

Do remember that and don't
forget it!

Do remember that and don't
forget it!

Do remember that and don't
forget it!

Do remember that and don't
forget it!

Do remember that and don't
forget it!

Do remember that and don't
forget it!

Do remember that and don't
forget it!

Do remember that and don't
forget it!

Do remember that and don't
forget it!

Do remember that and don't
forget it!

Do remember that and don't
forget it!

Do remember that and don't
forget it!

Ever since you can speak an
orderly sentence you are
beginning to compare
everything that you perceive
with this orderly sentence, so
that the sentence becomes a
model. Each object you perceive
is that much simpler, the
simpler the sentence with which
you can describe it: that object
is an orderly object about which
no further questions remain to
be asked after a short simple
sentence: an orderly object is
one which is entirely clarified
with a short simple sentence:
all you require for an orderly
object is a sentence of three
words: an object is orderly
when you don't first have to
tell a story about it. For an
orderly object you don't even
require a sentence: for a normal
object the word for the object
suffices. Stories only begin with
abnormal objects. You yourself
are normal once you need to
tell no more stories about
yourself: you are normal once
your story is no longer
distinguishable from any other
story: when no thesis about you
provokes an anti-thesis. You
should not be able to hide
behind a single sentence any
more. The sentence about your

shoelace and the sentence about
you must be alike except for
one word: in the end they must
be alike to the word.

21

*A spotlight follows Kaspar's hand
which is slowly approaching the
loose shoelace. It follows Kaspar's
other hand, which is also
approaching the shoelace. He
slowly crosses one shoelace over
the other. He holds the crossed
ends up. He winds one end
precisely around the other. He
holds up both ends, crossed. He
draws the shoelaces together,
slowly and deliberately. He
elaborately makes a noose with
one lace. He places the other lace
around the noose. He pulls it
through underneath. He draws
the noose tight. The first order
has been created. The spotlight is
extinguished.*

The table stands. With the
word table you think of a table
which stands: a sentence is not
needed any more. The scarf is
lying. When the scarf is lying,
something is not in order. Why
is the scarf lying? The scarf
already requires other sentences.
Already the scarf has a story:
does the scarf have a knot tied
at one end, or has someone
thrown the scarf on the floor?
Was the knot ripped off the
scarf? Was someone choked to
death with the scarf? The
curtain is falling just now: at
the word curtain you think of
a curtain that is falling just
now: a sentence is not needed
any more. What is worth
striving for is a curtain that is
just falling.

22

*The spotlight follows Kaspar's
hand, which, by pushing up the
jacket, approaches the belt, which
may be very wide. The spotlight
follows Kaspar's other hand,
which also moves towards the
belt. One hand slips the belt end*

A sentence which demands a
question is uncomfortable: you
cannot feel at home with such
a sentence. What matters is
that you form sentences that
you can at least feel at ease
with. A sentence which

out of very many belt loops. One hand holds the prong of the buckle while the other draws the belt away from the prong. This hand pulls the belt tight while the other hand puts the prong through the next hole. The belt end, which has become even longer through the tightening of the belt, is again passed carefully through the many loops until the trousers fit as they should obviously fit. The spotlight darkens.

demands another sentence is unpretty and uncomfortable. You need homely sentences: sentences as furnishings: sentences which you could actually save yourself: sentences which are a luxury. All objects about which there are still questions to be asked are disorderly, unpretty, and uncomfortable. Every second sentence (*the words are timed to coincide with the loops through which Kaspar is passing the belt*) is disorderly, unpretty, uncomfortable, irksome, ruthless, irresponsible, in bad taste.

23

The spotlight follows Kaspar's hand which is buttoning his jacket from top to bottom. One button is left over at the bottom. The spot points to the leftover button, as does Kaspar's hand. Then it follows the hand as it unbuttons the jacket from bottom to top, but more rapidly than it buttoned it. Then it follows Kaspar's hand as it buttons the jacket once more, even more quickly. This time he succeeds. The spot and Kaspar's hands both point to the bottommost button. Then the hands release the button. The spot reveals that everything is in order. Then it goes out.

Every object must be the picture of an object: every proper table is the picture of a table. Every house must be the picture of a house. Every proper table is (*the words are timed to coincide with the buttoning*) orderly, pretty, comfortable, peaceful, inconspicuous, useful, in good taste. Each house (*the words coincide with the unbuttoning*) that tumbles, trembles, smells, burns, is vacant, is haunted is not a true house. Every sentence (*the words again coincide with the buttoning*) which doesn't disturb, doesn't

threaten, doesn't aim, doesn't
question, doesn't choke,
doesn't want,
doesn't
assert is a
picture of a sentence.

24

*The spot shines on Kaspar. It is
obvious that his jacket does not
match his trousers, either in
colour or in style. Kaspar just
stands there.*

A table is a true table when the
picture of the table matches the
table: it is not yet a genuine
table if the picture of the table
alone coincides with the table
whereas the picture of the table
and chair together do not
coincide with the table and
chair. The table is not yet a
true, actual, genuine, right,
correct, orderly, normal, pretty,
even prettier, spectacularly
beautiful table if you yourself
do not fit the table. If the table
is already a picture of a table,
you cannot change it: if you
can't change the table, you
must change yourself: you must
become a picture of yourself
just as you must make the table
into a picture of a table and
every possible sentence into a
picture of a possible sentence.

25

*Kaspar puts the stage in order.
While the spotlight follows him
and everything he does, he moves
from one object to the other and*

*His actions are accompanied by
sentences from the prompters. At
first these sentences are adjusted
to Kaspar's movements, until*

corrects whatever harm he has done to it. Moreover, he puts the objects into their normal relationships towards each other, so that the stage gradually begins to look inhabitable. Kaspar creates his own (three) walls for himself. Each of his steps and movements is something new to which the spotlight calls attention. Occasionally he accompanies his actions with sentences. Every interruption of the action produces an interruption of the sentence. Every repetition of an action produces a repetition of the sentence. As he nears the completion of his task, his actions more and more obey the sentences of the prompters, whereas in the beginning the prompters' sentences adjusted themselves to his actions. First of all, Kaspar rights the chair on which he had been sitting, saying, for example: I am righting the chair and the chair is standing. *He goes to the second chair and raises it, this time with one hand. The spot shines on the hand, which holds on to a vertical rod on the backrest:* I am putting up the second chair: I can count. The first chair has two rods. The second chair has three rods: I can compare. *He squats down behind the chair and embraces the rods with both hands. He shakes them:* everything that is

Kaspar's movements gradually begin to adjust to the movement of the sentences. The sentences clarify events on the stage, of course without describing them. There is a choice among the following sentences.

Everyone is born with a wealth of talents.

Everyone is responsible for his own progress.

Everything that does harm is made harmless.

Everyone puts himself at the service of the cause. Everyone says yes to himself.

Work develops an awareness of duty in everyone.

Each new order creates disorder.

Everyone feels responsible for the smallest mote of dust on the floor.

Whoever possesses nothing replaces his poverty with work.

All suffering is natural.

Every working man must be given leisure time in accordance with his need to replenish the energy expended while working.

Everyone must build his own world.

barred with rods is a chair. *One rod breaks in half. He quickly puts the two halves together again :* Everything that breaks is only a rod in a chair. Everything that can be covered up is only a rod in a chair. *He walks to the large table. This time, before he kneels down, he pulls his trousers up over his knees :* I pull my trousers up over my knees so they won't get dirty. *He quickly picks up what had fallen out of the drawer :* Everything that cuts is only a table knife. Everything that lies face up is a playing card. *He tries picking up a match with his whole hand. He fails. He tries with two fingers and succeeds :* Everything I can't pick up with my whole hand is a match. *He quietly pushes the drawer into the table. He still has the match in his hand. He sees another match on the floor. He picks it up, whereupon the match in his hand drops. He picks it up, whereupon the second match falls out of his hand (the movements are very precise, the spot follows). For the first time he uses his other hand to pick up the match. He holds the two matches in his two fists. He no longer has a hand free to open the drawer. He stands before the drawer. Finally he gives the match from one hand to the other*

Example is a lesson that all men can read.

A foolish consistency is the hobgoblin of little minds.

Good order is the foundation of all things.

A fanatical desire for order does not have to lead to a *coup d'etat*.

Every step extends one's perspective.

That table is a meeting place.

The room informs you about its inhabitant.

An apartment is a prerequisite for an orderly life.

Flowers should stand there as though they had a common centre.

Don't stand if you can sit.

Bending down expends more energy than anything else.

A burden is lighter the closer it is held to the body.

Put only things you don't use often into the top shelves.

Saving means saving energy.

Balance the weight on both arms.

The table won't run away from you.

hand : I can hold one hand free.
Everything that can move
freely is a hand. *He opens the
drawer wide, with one hand. He
puts the matches in the drawer,
pushing the drawer shut with the
other hand, whereupon the first
hand gets caught in the drawer.
He pulls on the caught hand
while pushing in with the other
hand, exerting himself more and
more in both endeavours. Finally
he is able to free his hand with
one violent pull while the other
hand, with one violent push,
pushes in the drawer. He does
not rub his hand but moves on
immediately, righting the rocking
chair, which had fallen near the
table, almost in one movement
with the bang of the drawer as it
is shut. Immediately afterward
he leans the broom against the
wall. Almost before the audience
has time to realize it, he is
kneeling before the three-legged
table replacing the leg, all his
movements being rapidly followed
by the spotlight. As he moves, he
says, also very rapidly :*
Everything that bangs is only a
table drawer: everything that
burns is only a chapped lip:
everything that puts up
resistance is only a fallen
broom: everything that gets in
the way is only a snowdrift:
everything that rocks is only a
rocking horse: everything that

Always take a fresh look at
your work.

Only if you're healthy can you
achieve a lot.

Disorder outrages all decent-
thinking men.

One of the most beautiful
things in life is a well-set table.

The furnishings should
complement you.

Apportion your time correctly.

A place for everything and
everything in its place.

Happy are those who have
steered a middle course.

Nothing is given to you in life.

The fingernails are a special
index of order and cleanliness.

Suggest with a friendly smile
that you like your work.

What has always been the way
you find it, you won't be able
to change at once.

Everyone must be able to do
everything.

Everyone should be completely
absorbed in his work.

Everything that appears to harm
you is only in your best interest.

You should feel responsible for
the furniture.

dangles is only a punching ball: everything that can't move is only a wardrobe door. *In the meantime he has marched to the wardrobe door and banged it shut. But it won't stay shut. He slams it shut again. It slowly opens again. He pushes it shut. As soon as he lets go of it, it opens up again:* Everything that doesn't close is a wardrobe door. Everything that frightens me is only a wardrobe door. Everything that hits me in the face is only a wardrobe door. Everything that bites me is only a wardrobe door. (*Each of these sentences coincides with Kaspar's attempts to slam or push the door shut.*) *Finally he leaves the wardrobe open. He goes to the sofa, puts it back in order, at the same time shoving it completely on stage. The spotlight precedes him, designating the place where the sofa should stand. Two other spots precede him, showing where the two chairs should stand. He puts the chairs there. (The spotlights are of different colours.) Another spot designates the place for the rocking chair. He follows it and places the rocking chair in its appointed spot. Another light already indicates the place for the little table. He puts it there. Another spot appears, designating the appropriate place for broom and shovel. He wants to put*

Sweep the floor in the direction of the boards.

When you clink glasses, they should ring clearly.

Every step must become completely natural to you.

You must be able to
act
independently.

Outside show is a poor substitute for
inner worth.

The merit of originality is not novelty; it is sincerity.

The golden rule in life is moderation in all things.

There's nothing in this world constant but inconstancy.

A bad beginning makes a bad ending.

Circumstances are beyond the control of man; but his conduct is in his own hands.

In an orderly room the soul also becomes orderly.

Every object you see for the second time you can already call your own.

The relativeness
of means
is your basic principle.

Running water

*them there but the spot moves on
and he follows it. It goes
backstage and he follows it there
with shovel and broom in hand.
The spot returns without him and
is already fixed on a place on the
stage when Kaspar returns. In
his arms he holds a large vase
with flowers. He puts the vase in
the designated place. Another
spot indicates a place on the little
table. Kaspar leaves the stage
and returns with a plateful of
decorative fruit. He puts it on
the little table. Another spot
designates an empty place in the
corner of the stage. He leaves the
stage and returns with a small
stool. He puts it in its appointed
place. Another spot indicates an
empty area on the backdrop. He
gives a sign to the stage-rigging
loft and a painting is lowered
on to the empty area. (What the
painting represents is of no
importance as long as it goes
with the furnishings.) Kaspar
directs it until it hangs perfectly.
He stands there. Another spot
walks ahead of him to the open
wardrobe. It lights up the clothes.
Kaspar goes to the wardrobe.
Quickly he takes off his jacket,
but finds no place to put it. The
spotlight goes backstage and he
follows it with the jacket over his
arm. He returns with a clothes
tree and hangs the jacket up on
it. He walks to the wardrobe and*

does not
become stagnant.

A room
should be
like a picture book.

Sitting all your life
is unhealthy.

A room
should have
a timeless character.

You must show
confidence
in your work.

There is no woodworm
in the door hinges.

You must be able to be proud
of what you have achieved.

Your well-being is determined
by your achievement.

The floor makes a decisive
difference in the overall
impression of the room.

What matters
is to be with it.

Doors lock, but also constitute
connections to the outside
world.

The objects
must supplement
your image.

All work is
what you
make of it.

*picks out another jacket, puts it
on, buttons it. He stands there.
He takes off his hat. He hangs
the hat up on the clothes tree.
The stage becomes increasingly
more colourful. He has now
begun to move in rhythm to the
sentences from the prompters. A
continuous sound has set in softly.
It now becomes louder. It is
apparent that the jacket goes
with the trousers and the other
objects. Everything on stage goes
with everything else. For a
moment Kaspar looks like a
dummy at an interior-decoration
exhibition. Only the open
wardrobe disrupts the harmony
of the picture. The continuous
tone becomes even louder. Kaspar
stands there and lets people look
him over. The stage is festively
lit.*

The order
should not be
a soul-less order.

You are
what you have.

Living in dark rooms
only makes for unnecessary
thoughts.

The order
of the objects
creates
all

prerequisites
for
happiness.

What is a nightmare in the dark
is
joyous certainty
in the light.

Every order
eventually looses its
terror.

You're not in the world for fun.

26

*The light on stage is very
gradually extinguished, the tone
adjusting itself to the light.
Kaspar is speaking as the light
goes out. He begins to speak in a
deep, well-modulated voice, but
raises it as the light and the
continuous sound subside. The
darker the stage and the softer*

the tone, the more shrill and ill-sounding Kaspar's voice becomes. Finally, with the onset of complete darkness and the ceasing of the continuous sound, he is whimpering in the highest registers: Everything that is bright is peaceful: everything that is quiet is peaceful: everything that is in its place is peaceful: everything peaceful is friendly: everything friendly is inhabitable: everything inhabitable is comfortable: everything comfortable is no longer ominous: everything I can name is no longer ominous: everything that is no longer ominous belongs to me: I am at ease with everything that belongs to me: everything I am at ease with strengthens my self-confidence: everything that belongs to me is familiar to me: everything I am familiar with strengthens my self-confidence: everything that is familiar to me lets me breathe a sigh of relief: everything I am familiar with is orderly: everything that is orderly is beautiful: everything that is beautiful is good for my eyes: everything that is good for my eyes is good for me: everything that is good for me makes me good: everything that makes me good makes me good for something. *It is now completely dark. As it again*

The prompters speak while Kaspar is speaking, however without making him incomprehensible, whereas they themselves are only barely comprehensible because they speak too softly, their words overlap, they leave out syllables, reverse the order of the words, or put the wrong emphasis on them. In regular sequence they speak something like the following text: Struck the table. Sat between chairs. Rolled up the sleeves. Stayed on the floor. Looked behind curtains. Spat into hands. Struck the table. Stayed on the floor. Rolled up sleeves. Sat down between chairs. Sat down at the table together. Struck the table. Sat down in the nettles. Slammed the door. Rolled up sleeves. Struck the chairs. Beaten to a pulp. Struck the table. Sat down in the nettles. Knocked down. Spit in front of feet. Struck between the eyes. Broke the chain. Stayed tough. Sat down in the nettles. Knocked out. Beat down the request. Showed the fists. Beaten to a pulp. Struck a low blow. Exterminated from

*becomes bright very gradually,
Kaspar begins to speak again, at
first with a pleasant-sounding
voice, but the brighter it becomes,
the higher and shriller his voice
gets:* Everything that is in order
is in order because I say to
myself that it is in order, just
as everything that lies on the
floor is a dead fly because I say
to myself that everything that
lies on the floor is only a dead
fly, just as everything that lies
on the floor lies there only for
a short while because I say to
myself that it lies there only for
a short while, just as everything
that lies gets up again because
I say to myself that it gets up
again, just as everything that I
say to myself is in order
because I say to myself that
everything that I say to myself
is in order.

head to toe. Smashed the floor.
Spat in front of the feet. Struck
between the eyes. Broke the
china. Pushed into the nettles.
Smashed the table. Struck a
low blow. Smashed the
communal table. Struck down.
Smashed the set. Smashed the
door. Struck down the heckler.
Stayed tough. Smashed all
prejudices.

27
*Kaspar is now taught the model
sentences with which an orderly
person struggles through life.
While he was uttering his last
sentences, he sat down in the
rocking chair. During the
following course of instruction he
continues to sit in the chair, but
begins to rock only gradually. At
first he drawls his words,
although speaking with intensity,
without punctuation marks; then*

*While Kaspar is sitting in the
rocking chair, the words the
prompters uttered just now,
which anticipate the aphorisms,
are repeated: now, because
Kaspar is silent, they are more
comprehensible and become
completely comprehensible
towards the end, and then turn
into the following model
sentences:* Every sentence helps
you along: you get over every

he begins to speak with full stops,
finally with hyphens, finally
he makes exaggerated sense, and
ultimately he utters model
sentences.

object with a sentence: a
sentence helps you get over an
object when you can't really get
over it, so that you really get
over it: a sentence helps you to
get over every other sentence
by letting itself take the place
of the other sentence: the door
has two sides: truth has two
sides: if the door had three
sides, truth would have three
sides: the door has many sides:
truth has many sides: the door:
the truth: no truth without a
door. You beat the dust off
your trousers: you beat the
thought out of your head: if
you couldn't beat the dust off
your trousers, you couldn't beat
the thought out of your head.
You finish speaking: you finish
thinking: if you couldn't finish
speaking, you couldn't say the
sentence: I finish thinking. You
look again: you think again: if
you couldn't look again, you
couldn't say the sentence: I
think again: if you couldn't
look again, you couldn't think
again.

The pupil of the eye is round
fear is round had the pupil
perished fear would have
perished but the pupil is there
and fear is there if the pupil
weren't honest I couldn't say
fear is honest if the pupil were
not permitted fear wouldn't be

permitted no fear without pupil
if the pupil weren't moderate
I couldn't say fear only arises
at room temperature fear is less
honest than is permitted fear is
drenched warm as a hand on
the contrary

You are standing. The table is
standing. The table is not
standing, it was placed there.
You are lying. The corpse is
lying. The corpse is not lying,
it was placed there. If you
couldn't stand and if you
couldn't lie, you couldn't say:
the table is standing, and the
corpse is lying: if you couldn't
lie and stand, you couldn't
say: I can neither lie nor stand.

A fat man is true to life cold
sweat is commonplace if a fat
man weren't true to life and if
his cold sweat weren't
commonplace a fat man
couldn't become afraid and if a
fat man couldn't lie on his
stomach I couldn't say he
neither stands up nor can he
sing

The room is small but mine.
The stool is low but
comfortable. The sentence is
harsh but just. The rich man is
rich but friendly. The poor man
is poor but happy. The old man
is old but sturdy. The star is

famous but modest. The
madman is mad but harmless.
The criminal is scum but a
human being none the less. The
cripple is pitiable but also a
human being. The stranger is
different, but it doesn't matter:

But the snow falls contentedly.
The fly runs over the water but
not excessively. The soldier
crawls through the mud but
pleasurably. The whip cracks
on the back but aware of its
limits. The fool runs into the
trap but at peace with the
world. The condemned man
leaps into the air but
judiciously. The factory gate
squeaks but that passes away.

The ring is decorative as well
as an object of value. The
community is not only a burden
but also a joy. War is indeed a
misfortune, but sometimes
inescapable. The future is
obscure but it also belongs to
the enterprising. Playing is not
only a diversion, but is also a
preparation for reality. Force is
indeed a dubious method, but
it can be useful. A harsh youth
is indeed unjust, but it makes
you hard. Hunger is bad
indeed, but there are worse
things. Whipping is
reprehensible indeed, but one
also has to see the positive side:

The sunflowers are not only abundant, but also summer and winter. The corners are glowing indeed, but for dying of thirst they are not only made to order but also spend a meditative old age observed by daylight. The better solutions are not only not worth striving for, but indeed eat right out of my hand, yet will also decisively and emphatically reject any and all interference.

The more lovingly the table has been laid, the more you love to come home. The greater the want of space, the more dangerous the thoughts. The more happily you work, the more quickly you find a way to yourself. The more self-assured you are, the easier it is for you to get ahead. The greater the mutual trust, the more bearable the living together. The more the hand perspires, the less sure of himself the man is. The cleaner the flat, the cleaner the tenant. The farther south you go, the lazier the people:

The more wood on the roof, the more mildew in the bread oven. The more cities with cellars, the more machinations on the slag heaps. The brighter the clotheslines, the more suicides in the trade department. The more emphatic the demand for reason in the mountains, the more ingratiating the dog-eat-dog laws of free nature.

It goes without saying that a large vase stands on the floor, just as it goes without saying that a smaller vase stands on a stool, while it goes without saying that an even smaller vase stands on a chair, just as it goes without saying that an even smaller vase stands on the table, while it goes without saying that creepers stand even higher. It goes without saying that well-being is determined by achievement. It goes without saying that despair is out of place here:

It goes without saying that the flour sack strikes the rat dead. It goes without saying that hot bread lets children come prematurely into the world. It goes without saying that discarded matches introduce a demonstration of confidence.

You gain something new from each object. No one stands on the sidelines. Every day the sun rises. No one is irreplaceable. Every new building means peace. No one is an island. Every industrious person is liked everywhere. No one is

Every split straw is a vote for the progressive forces. No country fair means security for all. Each dripping tap is an example of a healthy life. No sensible arm is lifted for the burning department store. Every pneumatic-drill operator who comes upon a corpse corresponds to a rapid-firing mechanism that can deliver six thousand rounds per minute.

allowed to shirk his task. Each new shoe hurts in the beginning. No one has the right to exploit another. Every courteous person is punctual. No one who has a high opinion of himself lets others do his work for him. Every sensible person will bear the whole situation in mind with every step he takes. No one points the finger at others. Every person deserves respect, even a cleaning woman.

A cat is no getting on. A stone is not a completely satisfied need. A straw man is no body count. Running away is no equality of rights. To stretch a rope across the path is no permanent value.

Poverty is no disgrace. War is not a game. A state is not a gangster organization. A flat is no sanctuary. Work is no picnic. Freedom is no licence. Silence is no excuse. A conversation is no interrogation.

The appendix bursts. The grenade bursts. If the appendix couldn't burst, you couldn't say: the grenade bursts.

The dog barks. The commander barks.

The water is rising. The fever is rising. If the water couldn't rise, the fever couldn't rise.

The avalanche roars. The angry man roars.

The angry man thunders. Thunder thunders. Without the angry man, thunder couldn't thunder.

The flags flutter. The eyelids flutter.

The balloon swells. The jubilation swells. Without the balloon, the jubilation couldn't swell.

The laughing man gurgles. The swamp gurgles.

The nervous nelly jerks. The hanged man jerks. If it weren't for the nervous nelly, the hanged man couldn't jerk.

The firewood cracks. The bones crack.

The blood screams to high heaven. The injustice screams to high heaven. Without the blood, injustice could not scream to high heaven.

The door springs open. The skin springs open. The match burns. The slap burns. The grass trembles. The fearful girl trembles. The slap in the face

smacks. The body smacks. The
tongue licks. The flame licks.
The saw screeches. The torture
victim screeches. The lark trills.
The policeman trills. The
blood stops. The breath stops.

It is not true that the conditions
are as they are represented; on
the contrary, it is true that the
conditions are different from
their representation.

It is untrue that the
representation of the
conditions is the only possible
representation of the conditions:
on the contrary, it is true that
there exist other possibilities of
the representation of the
conditions. *Kaspar speaks along
with the prompters to the end of
this sequence.*

It is untrue that the
representation of the conditions
is the only possible
representation of the conditions:
on the contrary, it is true that
there exist other possibilities of
the representation of the
conditions. It does not
correspond to the facts to
represent the conditions at all;
on the contrary, it corresponds
to the facts not to represent
them at all. That the
conditions correspond to the
facts is untrue.

You bend down; someone sees
you, you rise; you see yourself.
You move yourself; someone
reminds you; you set yourself
down; you remember yourself.
You are afraid of yourself;
someone quiets you; someone
explains you; you rush
yourself; you explain yourself;
you disquiet yourself:

I am quieting myself.

You were already making a fist.

I was still screaming.

You still took a deep breath.

I was already there.

The chair still stands in its place.

I was still standing.

Nothing has changed yet.

I was already awake.

The door is already shut tight.

I was already kicking.

Some were still sleeping.

I am whispering already.

One can still hear knocking on the wall.

I still wasn't hearing anything.

Some never learn.

I am outside already.

Here and there someone is still moving.

I still don't believe it.

Many are already placing their hands on the head.

I am already running.

Some are still breathing.

I am pulling in my head already.

Someone still objected.

I am already hearing.

A single person is still
whispering.

I already understand.

Single shots are still being fired.

I know already.

you

passed

you

living weight

you

light and easy

you

within reach

you

nothing to look for

you

a better life

you

good laugh

you

master everything

you

will win everywhere

you

lowered the mother mortality

you

was leading

you

more and more comprehensively

you

free of

you

is peace and future

you

a relationship to the world

you

which moved things closer

you

peaceful purposes

you

constant growing

you

in case of emergency to

you

only for protection

you

irresistibly

you

reached

you

trampled

you

called

you

was and is

you

recognized myself.

You know what you are saying.
You say what you are thinking.
You think like you feel. You
feel what it depends on.

You know on what it depends.
You know what you want. You
can if you want to. You can if
you only want to. You can if
you must.

You only want what everyone
wants. You want because you
feel pressed. You feel you can
do it. You must because you
can.

Say what you think. You can't
say except what you think. You
can't say anything except what
you are also thinking. Say what
you think. When you want to
say what you don't think you
must begin to think it that very
moment. Say what you think.
You can begin to speak. You
must begin to speak. When you
begin to speak you will begin
to think what you speak even

when you want to think
something different. Say what
you think. Say what you don't
think. When you have begun
to speak you will think what
you are saying. You think what
you are saying, that means you
can think what you are saying,
that means it is good that you
think what you are saying, that
means you ought to think what
you are saying, that means, on
the one hand, that you may
think what you are saying, and
on the other hand, that you
must think what you are saying,
because you are not allowed to
think anything *different* from
what you are saying. Think
what you are saying:

When I am, I was. When I
was, I am. When I am, I will
be. When I will be, I was.
Although I was, I will be.
Although I will be, I am. As
often as I am, I have been. As
often as I have been, I was.
While I was, I have been.
While I have been, I will be.
Since I will be, I will have
been. Since I have been, I am.
Due to the fact that I am, I
have been. Due to the fact that
I have been, I was. Without
having been, I was. Without
having been, I will be. So that I
will be, I have been. So that I
will have been, I have been.

Before I was, I was. Before I
had become, I am. I am so that
I will have become. I will have
become so that I was. I was as
soon as I will have become. I
will have become as soon as I
will be. I will be while I will
have become. I will have
become while I had become. I
became because I will have
become. I will have become
because I became. I became
because I will have become. I
will have become because I am.
I am the one I am.
I am the one I am.
I am the one I am.

Kaspar stops rocking.

Why are there so many black
worms flying about?

The stage becomes black.

28

*As it grows light again after
several moments of quiet, the
prompters speak once more :* You
have model sentences with
which you can get through life:
by applying these models to
your sentences, you can impose
order on everything that
appears disorderly: you can
declare it ordered: every object
can be what you designate it to
be: if you *see* the object
differently from the way you

speak of it, you must be
mistaken: you must say to
yourself that you are mistaken
and you *will* see the object: if
you don't *want* to say that to
yourself, then it is obvious that
you want to be forced, and
really want to say it after all.

*It has now become very bright.
Kaspar is quiet.*

29

You can learn and make
yourself useful. Even if there
are no limits: you can draw
them. You can perceive: notice:
become aware in all innocence:
every object becomes a
valuable. You can develop in
an orderly fashion.

*It becomes even brighter. Kaspar
is even quieter.*

30

You can quiet yourself with
sentences: you can be nice and
quiet.

*It is very bright. Kaspar is very
quiet.*

31

You've been cracked open.

32

*The stage becomes dark suddenly.
After a moment :* You become
sensitive to dirt.

33
*It becomes bright, but not very.
Kaspar is sitting in the rocking
chair. A second Kaspar with the
same kind of face-like mask, the
same costume, comes on stage
from the wings. He enters,
sweeping with a broom. He
quickly cleans the stage, each
movement being made distinctly
visible, for example, by the spot.
In passing he gives the wardrobe
door a shove, but it won't stay
shut. He cleans carefully under
the sofa. He sweeps the dirt into
a pile at the edge on the side of
the stage. He walks across the
stage to fetch the shovel. He
walks back to the pile of dirt and
sweeps the dirt on to the shovel.
He does not succeed in sweeping
the dirt on to the shovel with a
single swipe of the broom, nor
quite with the second swipe. By
zigzagging backwards across the
stage, between objects, without
however bothering the first
Kaspar, he continues to try to
sweep the rest of the dirt on to the
shovel. He sweeps and sweeps
until he disappears backstage. At
that moment the stage darkens.*

34

After a moment : Become aware
that you are moving.

35
*It becomes bright. A third
Kaspar appears on stage from
the wings, accompanying a fourth
Kaspar, who walks on crutches,
dragging his legs, moving very
very slowly, almost imperceptibly.
The third Kaspar repeatedly
increases his pace somewhat, but
each time has to wait for the
fourth Kaspar to catch up with
him. That takes time. They walk
across stage front, Kaspar 3
nearer to the audience than
Kaspar 4. Kaspar 3 to some
extent adopts the gait of Kaspar
4, but in part retains his own
manner of walking and therefore
still has to wait for Kaspar 4 to
catch up with him. So both are
lurching, as they say, almost
'unbearably' slowly across the
stage, past Kaspar 1. When they
have finally gone, the stage
darkens instantly.*

36

After a moment : What you
can't handle, you can play with.

37
*It becomes bright. Two further
Kaspars come towards each other
across the stage from different
directions. They want to get past
each other. Both step aside in the
same direction, and bump into
each other. They step aside in the
other direction, and bump into
each other again. They repeat the
attempt in the first direction, and
almost bump into each other.
What looked awkward and
unnatural at first gradually
assumes a rhythm. The
movements become more rapid
and also more regular. The two
Kaspars no longer walk into each
other. Finally they move only the
upper part of their body, then
only their heads jerk, and finally
they stand still. The next
moment they make a wide,
elegant curve around each other
and walk off stage to the left and
right. During these attempts at
circumnavigation, Kaspar 1 has
tried to fold an unfolded road
map. He does not succeed.
Finally he begins playing with
the map, as though it were an
accordion, say. Suddenly the
map lets itself be folded thus, and
that is the moment when the
other Kaspars leave the stage
and it darkens.*

38

After a moment : To become
aware that everything falls back
into order of its own accord.

39
*It becomes bright. Another
Kaspar steps out of the wings. He
steps in front of the sofa, on
which there is a thick cushion.
He pushes with one fist into the
cushion and steps aside. The
audience sees the cushion slowly
regain its original shape. This
can also be projected on the
backdrop. With a final tiny jolt,
the cushion regains its original
form. The stage darkens at once.*

40

After a moment : Movements.

41
*Another Kaspar steps on stage.
He has a ball in one hand. He
places the ball on the floor and
steps back. The ball rolls off.
Kaspar 1 puts the ball where it
was first. The ball rolls off.
Kaspar holds his hand on the
ball for a considerable period of
time. He steps back. The ball
rolls off. The stage darkens.*

42

After a moment : Pains.

43
*It is still dark; the audience sees
two matches being lit on stage.
When it grows bright again,
Kaspar 1 is sitting in the rocking
chair, the other Kaspar on the
sofa. Each is holding a burning
match between his fingers. The
flames touch the fingers. Neither
Kaspar emits a sound. The stage
darkens.*

44

After a moment : Sounds.

45
*As it becomes bright, Kaspar 1 is
alone on stage, standing by the
large table. He takes the
broad-necked bottle and pours a
little water into the glass standing
next to the bottle. The sound of
pouring water is distinctly
audible. He stops pouring.
Quickly he pours the water from
the glass back into the bottle. He
takes the bottle and pours water
slowly into the glass. The sound
of pouring water is even more
distinct. When the glass is full,
the stage darkens.*

46

After a moment: A tone.

47
*When it becomes bright, even
more quickly than before, another
Kaspar is standing at the side of
the stage while Kaspar 1 is
standing by the table. He is
holding a thick roll of paper
which is held together by a
rubber band. Slowly but surely
he forces the rubber band off the
roll. The band snaps off, a tone
is heard. At once the stage
darkens.*

48

After a moment: A view.

49
*The audience hears a noise while
the stage is still dark. When it
becomes bright, Kaspar 1 is again
alone on the stage, sitting by the
table with the plastic fruit on it.
He is holding a partially peeled
apple in his hand. He continues
peeling, the peel growing longer
and longer, and stops peeling
shortly before the apple has been
completely peeled. He places the
apple on top of the decorative
fruit. The peel hangs way down.
The stage darkens.*

50

> *The prompters remain silent.*

51
It becomes bright. Kaspar is standing in the centre of the stage, between the table and the wardrobe. With one hand he is forcibly opening the other hand, which is a fist, finger by finger. The fist resists more and more tenaciously. Finally he wrenches open the hand. It is empty. The stage darkens.

52
It quickly becomes bright. Another Kaspar is sitting on the sofa. Kaspar sees the other Kaspar. The stage darkens.

53
It becomes bright even more quickly. Kaspar is again alone on the stage, standing in front of the wardrobe, his face to the audience. The stage darkens.

54
It becomes bright more quickly still. Kaspar looks down at himself. The stage darkens.

55
Kaspar tries to catch himself. First he runs in a wide circle across the stage, then in smaller circles, spiralling in on himself until he turns on the same spot. He reaches for himself but, because he is standing on one spot, only seizes himself with his own arms . . . whereupon he becomes still and the stage darkens.

56

It becomes bright more quickly still. Kaspar is standing in front of the wardrobe, his back to the audience. It darkens.

57

It becomes bright. Kaspar is in the process of closing the wardrobe doors. He presses on them for some time. He steps back. The doors stay shut. The stage darkens.

58

It becomes bright. It is very bright. Kaspar leans back against the wardrobe. The stage looks harmonious. A chord. A spotlight is trained on Kaspar. He assumes various poses. He continues to alter the position of his arms and legs. Say, his arms are akimbo, he shoves one leg forward, lets his arms drop, crosses his legs, puts his hands in his pockets, first in his trouser pockets, then in his jacket pockets, stands there with his legs apart, finally crosses his hands over his stomach, puts his feet close together, finally his arms are akimbo again. His legs are still close together. He begins to speak:

I am healthy and strong. I am honest and frugal. I am conscientious. I am industrious, reticent and modest. I am always friendly. I make no great demands. My ways are winning and natural. Everyone likes me. I can deal with everything. I am here for everyone. My love of order and cleanliness has never given reason for complaint. My knowledge is above average. Everything I am asked to do, I do perfectly. Anyone can provide the desired information about me. I am peace-loving and have an untarnished record. I am not one of those who start a big hue and cry over every little thing. I am calm, dutiful, and receptive. I can become enthusiastic about every worthy cause. I would like to get ahead. I would like to learn. I would like to be useful. I have a concept of length, height, and breadth. I know what matters. I treat objects with feeling. I have already become used to everything. I am better. I am well. I am ready to die. My head feels light. I can finally be left alone. I would like to put my best foot forward. I don't accuse anyone. I laugh a lot. I can make heads and

tails of everything. I have no unusual characteristics. I don't show
my upper gums when I laugh. I have no scar under the right eye and
no birthmark under the left ear. I am no public menace. I would like
to be a member. I would like to cooperate. I am proud of what has
been achieved so far. I am taken care of for the moment. I am prepared to be interrogated. A new part of my life lies ahead of me. That
is my right hand, that is my left hand. If worst comes to worst, I can
hide under the furniture. It was always my wish to be with it.

*He pulls away from the wardrobe, takes two or three steps, the wardrobe
stays shut:*

Once I felt as though I didn't even exist; now I exist almost too
much, and the objects, of which there were too many at one time,
now have become almost too few.

*In the meantime he has walked farther forward. The wardrobe stays
shut:*

Once plagued by sentences
I now can't have enough of sentences.
Once haunted by words
I now play with every single letter.

He remains standing in the same spot:

At one time I only spoke when asked,
now I speak of my own accord, but now
I can wait to speak until I am asked.

He takes one or two steps more:

Earlier on, each rational sentence was a burden to me
and I detested each rational order
but from now on
I will be rational.

He either does or does not take a step:

Earlier, I threw down one chair, then a second, and then a third:
now, with the introduction of order, my habits are changing.

He takes roughly one step:

I am quiet
now I do not want
to be someone else any more
nothing incites me
against myself any more.
Every object
has become

accessible
to me
and I
am receptive
to each object.
Now I know what I want:
I want
to be
quiet
and every object
that I find ominous
I designate as mine
so that it stops
being sinister to me.

He walks off to the side of the stage but returns after several steps, as though he still had something more to say. He says nothing. He leaves again, taking more steps than the last time, but again steps half-way back on to the stage, as though he had something left to say. He says nothing. He almost leaves, but takes one or two steps back, again as though he had something left to say. He says nothing. Then he departs rapidly. On the now uninhabited stage the wardrobe doors gradually open. When the wide-open wardrobe doors have come to a complete rest, the stage darkens at a stroke, at the same time the auditorium becomes bright. It is intermission. The auditorium doors are opened.

59

After a few moments the INTERMISSION TEXT *is piped through loudspeakers into the auditorium, into the lobbies, and even out on to the street if that is possible. At first these texts are quite low and barely audible. The texts consist of tapes of the prompters' speeches, sheer noise, actual taped speeches by party leaders, popes, public speakers of every kind, presidents and prime ministers, perhaps even statements by writers and poets speaking at official functions. The sentences should never be complete, but should be complemented and superseded by other mangled sentences. Although the audience should not be kept from entering into well-deserved conversation, its relaxed mood ought to be disturbed now and then by the intermission texts. Some members of the audience might even be able to listen with one ear while devoting themselves to their drinks. The text might be as follows: (Noises, such as the clinking of glasses.)* free of all worries of the present, we will have the last word. The surplus is lower than the criterion which has been anticipated. *(Louder clinking of glasses.)* What once was not an incalculable demand now becomes much too unexpected for many, and much too early. We need more courage if we can't be saved. A new mass flight south is more important than a murder that never occurred. It is often unjustly forgotten how healthy it is to be a Marine. We want to work to the last man. Don't think of what your country can do for you but climb up the wall. *(The sound of a large truck approaching, then disappearing.)* Criticism helps all real progress no matter the deposits in the glands. Animal herds should beware of the clear mountain air. The results exist to be burned without compunction. Without a certain number of dead each week, it neither goes upward nor downward. Hunger helps no one and doesn't teach anyone manners. *(Meanwhile, the blades of a large rotary saw have begun to clatter. This sound becomes increasingly loud.)* In recent times the voices have increased that have great difficulty playing with themselves. The sides of the scale of justice lower themselves towards each other at the end although everyone is prepared to make sacrifices. With respect to the rat plague we must reach a mutually satisfactory result. Everyone should finally open his ears and listen to the truth when the brand name is announced. What now matters most is to objectively examine the whole realm of concepts associated with each demand. No one can depend on the fact that dooms the situation. *(The saw blades penetrate wood with a screech; however, the noise soon turns into that of a gentle waterfall.)* Nothing that comes from the outside is a distorted picture simply for that and no other simple reason. The human element appears quite ineradicable. We always exist under the condition that we refuse to let irresponsible circles rob us of the view of the public nuisance which is the world. Every declaration of war is designed for each case of patience which has been exhausted. Convincing someone in the nicest possible manner does not have to end with a blow of the water level on the head. Everyone is called upon to the extent of calling the thing by its well-deserved name. The police always has a time of it because it must justify itself. None of us is entirely innocent of the time of day. *(Whistling, booing, stomping, the sound of waves.)* A sceptical stock market gets off best. At least we don't want the employees to have to pay extra even though many things speak for breaking it off. Impudence itself is no silver star. Of course the refugees have to be helped but running away with bare feet is not one of our problems. We know how to handle the glasses more and more. Uniformed persons know the difficulties when it suddenly becomes dark. The robes of the judges are breathtaking when all that is at stake is the shabby whole. We all want to move with profound seriousness which is what matters. (*A swelling football cheer which breaks off with a profound sigh, then a resurgence of it which turns into regularly increasing and decreasing cheers.*) Gripping is easier than finding oneself a well-deserved flat. We'll inflict injuries on the head and chest of anyone who is of the same opinion as we are. The right of hospitality not only cannot be superseded as a concept but one must point to it if necessary with a brain stroke. A screwdriver in the windpipe is appropriate remuneration for someone who never did anything but someone else's duty. Anyone who considers himself someone loses his nerve when angling. We'll accept anyone into the bargain who shakes the foundations. (*A sharply braking car; simultaneously, a jet of water from a firehose.*) The transformation of society into any number of possible mass demonstrations corresponds to a pacifier for a blind man. The war in the sandbox has cost many a live corpse. Anyone who thinks the way he acts only strengthens the neck of the one who thinks differently. No one deserves a fate that makes him level with the ground. Life used to be more worth while at one time but now it is no brushfire any more. (*Long-drawn-out factory siren or foghorn.*) What was said of the property owners matters even less with respect to the flesh wounds. Anyone who kills in blind fury fools himself to an extent that is questionable in the least. Anyone who protests against the delivery of goods must also protest against revisionist thinking. We value the strength of a freely reached decision more than sharks chasing swimmers. Self-assurance contributes a great deal towards continuing useful conversations. Too little has been said so far about the minorities who proudly crawl off into their corners. (*The scraping of chairs on a stone floor.*) What was once forbidden has now been outlawed. Every outward order enables a peaceful and measured exchange of ideas. We regard the either/or as the mark of a free man. We all have to make an effort to be understanding when a dead man assumes the colour of grass. A murder does not necessarily have to be equated with a nose dive. A third-degree burn clogs every petrol line. (*Sounds of horses' hoofs, together with the sound of seats being turned up, street noises, doors being slammed shut, typewriter noises.*) No one is beaten until he is ripe for retirement without good reason. The right to own estates requires no elaborate justification. A loosening-up exercise corresponds to the length of a truncheon between two legs. Whereas every suicide used to be left-handed, the regulation has now become uniform. No lull in the fighting permits time to count the sleeping flies on the ceiling of the cowshed. A single person perched on the church steeple can be equated with an incitement to riot. If one confronts a violent person by oneself, one is oneself a violent person, whereas when one confronts a violent person in the company of six or four men, thereupon the former becomes gentle of his own accord and is gentle. (*Even before this last sentence, the sounds have changed and become distorted musical noises, as if a record is being played at inordinately slow speed; a monotonous, rhythmic music should be utilized for this purpose. In between a tap is gradually turned on to full strength, then the plug in a bathtub is pulled out; in addition there may be heavy breathing noises, then the sound of whiplashes, sudden bursts of laughter as after a joke, women's laughter as if at a cocktail party. While all this is going on, the audience should be able to hear, although not quite comprehending, the spoken text. Then follows a short moment of quiet, then noise once again and the reading of texts, then a longer moment of quiet, then something like the following text by itself.*) A beautifully laid table. Everything in the best order. You're in no great hurry. You help your companion take off the coat. The colourful tablecloth delights everyone. The knife lies on the right. The napkin on the left. The plate stands in the middle. The cup stands at the right and to the back. The knife lies in front of the cup. The towel hangs to the right of the knife. Your finger rests on the towel. To the right of the towel is the first-aid kit. The plates are handed from the left. The soup is handed from the right. The drinks are handed from the right. Everything that you serve yourself is handed from the left. The stab comes from the right. You are sitting in the middle. The salt cellar stands on the left. The spoon is lying on the outside to the right of the knife. The spoon lies bottom up. The grip that chokes comes from both sides. Your hand is lying on the table. The edge of the knife is facing left. As seen from your seat, the heart of the person opposite you is on the right. The glass stands to the right of the plate. You drink in small sips. The blow is more effective when it comes from below. The bouquet of flowers is in the centre of the table. The fork lies to the left of the plate. You can't give white flowers to the dying. You sit upright on principle. The older one is on the right. The bouquet does not block your view of the person opposite you. The biscuit plate is in the middle of each setting. The coal pile is under the table. You are not resting your head on your arms. You always look for friendly words. The victim of an assassination lies in the middle of each setting. The candelabra stand in the centre of the table. A spot on a shirt is an everyday occurrence. It is not unusual for the knife to slip on the plate. Your neighbour's hand is resting on the knife. You do not swallow the wrong way. You converse to your left and to your right. (*Again the inordinately slow music has come on with a crash that is not recognizable as music at first. Houses crumble, bombs crash, but at a great distance; the text is gradually made unintelligible by the noises and finally is entirely suppressed; in between the audience begins to hear the bell as well as taped chimes; rattling, gongs, factory sirens as well as the theatre bell that calls the audience back to the auditorium.*)

60

While the lights in the auditorium are slowly dimmed in a theatrical manner, the open stage is only moderately lighted. The objects are in exactly the same position as before the intermission. The wardrobe is open. Two Kaspars are sitting on the sofa, close together. They are silent. The masks now evince an expression of contentment. After a few moments of silence, the prompters begin to recite all over the room:

61

While giving a thrashing
you are never as calm
as when beating
a rug
Intermittent smashing
of a stick
on your jug
is no balm
nor a reason

to bewail the lack of law and
order
this season
a sip of lye
in your mug
or a prick
in the guts
or a stick
in the nuts
being wriggled about
or something on that order
only pricklier
fearlessly
introduced in the ears
so
as to
get someone hopping
and pop in order
by all means
at your command
but chiefly
without being
overly
fussy
over the means –
that
is no reason
to lose any words
over the lack of order:
for
while you are popping other
to put them in order
for better or worse
you force them to sing
whereas –
once they are
completely in order
and those who were fooling
around

have been made to look
foolish –
you can sing
yourself
and after the thrashing –
when your fists and feet
are idle –
you can beat the rug
to calm yourself down.

*A third Kaspar with a small
package wrapped in wrapping
paper comes out of the wings and
sits down next to the other two
Kaspars, sits down in an orderly
fashion, the package on his knees.*

While putting other in order
you are not as quiet and orderly
as later on
when you –
having been put in order
yourself by the thrashing
that you've given others –
want to enjoy
a well-ordered
world
and can enjoy
such a world
with an untroubled
conscience.

*A fourth Kaspar comes on stage
with a similar package. Kaspar 3
makes room for him between
himself and the other two
Kaspars. Kaspar 4 sits down
quietly. All four Kaspars are
still.*

While giving
a thrashing
it would be foolish
to think of the future
but in the pauses
between punches
it's delicious
to imagine the time
of imminent order –
so that a kick
that is a touch too disorderly
won't contribute
when the thrashing
resumes
to channelling
the thoughts
of the socially sick
– when he's adjusting
later on –
in the wrong direction.

*A fifth Kaspar enters with a
similar but perhaps larger
package. Kaspar 3 gets up.
Kaspar 5 takes Kaspar 3's place.
Kaspar 3 squeezes himself into
the small space left next to
Kaspar 4. Kaspar 5 puts the
package in front of him on the
floor. All five are still.*

But should an inordinate
beating of the heart fail to
occur
while you are thrashing away
and your fists
beat the breath
from the victim's lung
like (to use the same image

again)
dust
from a rug
and you straighten out
the wretch's tongue
(to use the same image again)
like fringes on a rug
only then does the injustice
occur:
for
while you are thrashing away
you can't be as easy
as when beating a rug
while plugging up a mouth
you must be un-
easy:
so as not to become un-
easy
later on:
the failure of an inordinate
beating of the beater's hearth
to occur while he is giving a
thrashing
is BAD!
for
anyone whose hand has
suitably trembled while giving
a thrashing
has clean hands
and is just one more person
who'll have to have no qualms
later on:
thus calm reigns on earth.

The original Kaspar comes on
stage as he did at first, but
without having to look for the
slit in the curtain. His movements
are self-assured and he looks like

the other Kaspars. His mask too
should show a contented
expression. He walks with firm
steps to the front of the stage, as
though to take a bow, nicely
avoiding all objects. He stops in
front of the microphone. All six
Kaspars are still.

Those
who have been put in order –
instead of retreating
into themselves
or fleeing
society –
should now make a real effort
without being compelled to or
thrashed
but out of their own free will
to show new paths
by looking for sentences
that are valid for all:
it is not so much that they *can*
choose
but that they *must* choose
and tell the others –
without empty sayings
or blown-up phrases –
the unadorned truth
about themselves:
and the others too
should finally be able to want
to do
what they themselves
want, ought and can do.

62
Kaspar, at the microphone,
begins to speak. His voice begins

to resemble the voices of the
prompters.
Although
long in the world
I grasped
nothing
I asked
about the ob-
vious
and found
every-
thing
fi-
nite
and infi-
nite
ridi-
culous
every object
appalled me
and the whole world
galled me
neither
did I want to be
myself
nor did I want to be
somebody else
my own
hand
was unknown
to me
my own
legs
walked
of their own
accord
I was
in a deep
sleep

with open
eyes:
I was unconscious
as though
drunk
and though
I was
supposed to be of use
I was
of no use
each sight
produced dislike
in me
each sound
deceived me
about itself
each new step
caused nausea and sucking
in my chest
I couldn't keep up
I blocked my sight
myself
no light
lit up
for me
with the whole mish-
mash
of sentences
I never hit
on the idea
that it
was meant
for me
I noticed nothing
of what was happening
around me
before I began getting
on to the world.

He is quiet for a moment or
more. The other Kaspars behind
him are also rather still.

I felt
the caco-
pho-
ny
and screa-
ming
as
a roa-
ring
and gurg-
ling
in my guts
I couldn't keep one thing apart
from another
three
was not
more than two
and when I was in the sun
it rained
and when I sweated
in the sun
or was getting warm
during a run
I fended off the sweat
with an umbrella
I could keep nothing apart
neither hot
from cold
nor black
from white
neither old
from new
nor day
from night
neither people

from objects
nor prayer
from blasphemy
each room
looked flat
to me
and scarcely
was I awake
when the flat
objects
fell
all over me
as in a night-
mare:
they resisted
me
everything unknown
interrogated
me
simultaneously
everything I couldn't keep apart
confused me
and drove me
wild
so that I became lost
among the objects
and to find my way out
destroyed them.

He is quiet for a few moments.
The Kaspars behind him are
quiet too.

I got
on to the world
not
by the clock
it was the pain
when I fell

which helped me
drive
a wedge
between me
and the objects
and finally
rid me
of my babbling:
thus the pain
drove the confusion
out of me.

I learned
to fill
the void
with words
I learned
who
was
who
and to still
everything shrill
with sentences
no empty bed
confused my head
any more
everything
is at my will
never
again
will
I shudder
before an empty wardrobe
before empty
boxes
empty
rooms
I hesitate
before no walk

out
into the open
for every crack
in the wall
I have wiles
that help me keep
the situation well
under control.

He now raises his tone. The light
becomes brighter. The other
Kaspars are still silent.

Everyone must be free
everyone must be able to see
everyone must know what he
wants
no one should be bothered by
anyone's taunts
no one may miss
the drill
no one may kill
himself or anyone else
everyone must live his own life
no one may beat his wife
everyone must give his best
everyone must pass the test
no one may miss
the boat
no one may piss
on those below
everyone must look
everyone in the eye
everyone must feel loose
everyone must cook
his own goose
everyone must give
everyone what is his.

*The other Kaspars on the sofa
begin to emit peculiar noises
whose significance is unmistakable.
The audience hears suggestions of
stylized sobbing, imitation wind
sounds, giggling.*

Everyone must be his own man
everyone must know the lay of
the land
everyone must watch what
everyone says
no one may blindly trust
another man's gaze
everyone must see the other's
good side too
no one may willy nilly sail out
into the blue
everyone must let himself be
led
no one may let
lies to be spread
about anyone.

*To some extent simultaneously
with Kaspar's speaking, the
audience hears grumbling,
croaking, lamenting, falsetto
singing, owl-like hooting coming
from behind him.*

Everyone must work
on himself
Everyone must shirk
from quarrelling with others
everyone must also care for the
other
everyone must think of the
future

everyone must feel completely
secure.

The audience hears rustling,
leaves slapping against each
other, ululations, roaring,
laughter, humming, purring,
warbling, and a single sharp
scream.

Everyone must wash his hands
before eating
everyone must take off his
trousers
before a beating
no one may eat
out of anyone's hands
everyone must treat
the other
like a brother
everyone must be neat-
ly combed for the meal
says mother
no one may let the other
whimper and wail
everyone must cut his
fingernails
everyone must lend a hand
no one may spoil
the land
no one may soil
the clean doilies
everyone must clean
his nose
everyone should smell like a
rose
no one may make fun of other
blokes
with foolish jokes

no one may tickle
anyone
during the burial
no one may scribble
on toilet walls
no one may rend
the law books
everyone must lend
everyone an ear
no one is allowed to fear
everyone must tell everyone his
name.

*In the meantime, the noises and
sounds in the background have
risen to such an extent that
Kaspar in front must raise his
voice more and more. At the end
of his rhymes, the other Kaspars
are still sitting quietly on the
sofa — trilling, twittering, clearing
their throats, groaning, heckling,
etc. But these sounds have let
Kaspar's speech become so loud
that the last words resemble the
thunderous ending of a speech.*

63
*The Kaspars in back are quiet
for the moment. Kaspar in front
begins to sing, perhaps falsetto.
Slowly but surely the prompters
chime in, in canon fashion,
which, however, is not resolved.
They sing softly and delicately,
so that Kaspar is intelligible
throughout. Kaspar sings like a
true believer.*

No one may bite
the fork with his teeth
no one may cite
the names of murderers at
dinner
no one may grease
the palm of a sinner
no one may transport private
persons

in the official car
no one may start a fight
in a bar
every one must be worth
everyone's while
no one may be vile
to a woman who's giving birth
no one may call a man
by another man's
name
no one may ridicule
anyone
just because he has thick lips
no one may stick a knife
between anyone's ribs
everyone must call a cop on the
street
officer sir

The Kaspars behind him also sing along, but not words, only sounds. Nor do they really sing. They screech, yodel, buzz, trumpet, draw snot into their noses, smack their lips, grunt, burp, ululate, etc.: all of it in rhythm with the song. Now they grow gradually louder.

None of the furniture may
catch dust
no hungry man may stand in
line
no adolescent may feel lust
everybody in his golden age
must feel fine
no flag may flutter in the
wrong direction
everybody belongs into his own
section

of town
every clown is out of luck
every word that doesn't mean
well must be struck.

*The Kaspars behind become
louder still. One of them unwraps
his package, the paper rustling
loudly in the process, takes a nail
file from the package and begins
filing his nails. Another Kaspar
repeats the process, rustling the
paper even more loudly and
taking an even bigger file out of
his package to file his nails with.
Filing noises can already be
heard.*

No elbow
on the table
no fish
with the knife
no sow
in the cable-
car
no kiss
for the wife
no truffles
uncooked
every bum in jail
muffle
all dissent.

Kaspar is speaking again:

No shit
on a real stick
no genuine finger
for a lick

*The prompters sing what Kaspar
utters, and the other Kaspars
squeak, bark, make the sounds of
rain and storm, blow up bubble
gum till it bursts, etc.*

every tit
in a snit
every fresh fish
for frying
every punctual plane
to depart on time
every real person
in the clear about everything
every healthy fruit
in the can
everything nonessential
down the drain.

64
He stops speaking. There is
silence. Then Kaspar says:

What was it
that
I said
just now?
If I only knew
what it is
that I said
just now!
If I only knew
what I said
just now!
What is that
that I said
just now?
What
was I
actually
saying
just now?
What was it
that was

being said
just now?
If I only knew
what I
said
just now!
What
was that
actually
that I was
saying
just now?

Even while he is asking himself these questions, he, like the other Kaspars, begins to giggle and the like. At the same time the prompters sing his previous verses to the end. Kaspar, for instance, is snapping his finger against the microphone, producing a whine. All the Kaspars, while the prompters are singing, finally emit genuinely infectious laughter. Finally, sighing and giggling, the speaking Kaspar and the other Kaspars gradually grow quiet. The audience hears two or three of them filing their nails. Kaspar in front says:

Every sentence
is for the birds
every sentence is for
the birds
every sentence is for the birds
There is silence.
He begins to speak without versifying.
A spotlight is on him.

I was proud of the first step I took, of the second step I felt ashamed; I was just as proud of the first hand which I discovered on myself, but of the second hand I felt ashamed: I felt ashamed of everything that I repeated; yet I felt ashamed even of the first sentence I uttered, whereas I no longer felt ashamed of the second sentence and soon became accustomed to the subsequent ones. I was proud of my second sentence.

In my story I only wanted to make a noise with my first sentence, whereas with my second sentence I wanted to call attention to myself, and I wanted to *speak* with the next sentence, and I wanted to *hear* myself *speak* with the next sentence, and with my next sentence I wanted *others* to hear my speaking, and with the next sentence I wanted others to hear *what* I said, and with the next sentence I wanted others who *also* uttered a sentence not to be heard, and used only the next to last sentence to *ask questions*, and began only with the last sentence of the story to ask what the *others* had said, the others who were ignored while I said my sentence.

I saw the snow and I touched the snow. Thereupon I said the sentence: I want to be someone like somebody else was once, with which I wanted to express why the snow was biting my hands. Once I woke up in the dark and saw nothing. Thereupon I said: I want to be someone like somebody else was once, with which I wanted to express, first of all, why is it that the whole room has been moved away, and then, because I did not see myself, why have I been cut off from everything that belongs to me, whereupon, because I had heard someone, namely myself, speaking, I said once more: I want to be someone like somebody else was once? – with which I wanted to express that I would have liked to have known who else was making fun of me while I was speaking. Then once I took a look into the open, where there was a very green glow, and I said to the open: I want to be someone like somebody else was once? – and with this sentence I wanted to ask the open why it was that my feet were aching. I also noticed a curtain that was moving. Thereupon I said, but not to the curtain: I want to be someone like somebody else was once, and with that I wanted to say, but not to the curtain, I don't know to whom, why are all the table drawers out and why does my coat always get caught in the door. I also heard someone climbing stairs which creaked, and thereupon I said to the creaking that I want to be someone like somebody else was once, with which I wanted to express when will my head feel lighter again. Once I also let my plate fall to the floor, but it did not break, whereupon I exclaimed: I want to be someone like somebody else was once, with which I meant that I was afraid of nothing in the world, whereupon I said once more: I want to be someone like somebody else was once, with which I wanted to make comprehensible that something probably could make me afraid, for example a cracked icicle; and once I felt no more pain, and I shouted: I want to be someone like somebody else was once, with which I wanted to say to everyone that I finally felt no more pain, but then I felt pain once more and I whispered in everyone's ear: I want to be someone like somebody else was once, with which I wanted to inform everyone that no, on the contrary, I felt no more pain and that everything was all right with me, with which I began to lie; and finally I said to myself: I want to be someone like somebody else was once, and wanted to know with that what that sentence, which I said to myself, what it actually means.

Because the snow was white and because snow was the first white I saw, I called everything white snow. I was given a handkerchief that was white, but I believed it would bite me because the white snow bit my hand when I touched it, and I did not touch the handkerchief, and when I knew the word snow I called the white handkerchief snow: but later, when I also knew the word handkerchief, when I saw a white handkerchief, even when I uttered the word handkerchief, I still thought the word snow, and then I first began to remember. But a brown or grey handkerchief was not snow, just as the first brown or grey snow I saw was not snow, but the first grey or brown that I saw, for example animal droppings or a sweater. But a white wall was snow, and just as much as absolutely everything became snow when I looked into the sun for a long time, because I then saw only snow. Finally I even used the word snow, out of curiosity, for something that was not white, to see whether it would turn to snow because of my uttering the word snow, and even if I did not say the word snow I was thinking it and remembered at every sight if not the snow itself at least the word snow. Even while falling asleep or while walking along a country lane or while running in the dark I kept saying the word snow all the time. But finally I reached the point where I no longer believed not only words and sentences about snow, but even the snow itself when it lay there in front of me or was falling, did not believe any more and held it neither for real nor as possible, only because I no longer believed the word snow.

The landscape at that time was a brightly coloured window shutter. As of the time that I saw the shadow a chair cast on the floor, I have from that time on always designated a fallen chair on the floor as the shadow of a chair. Each movement was running because at that time I wanted to do nothing but run and run away from everything; even swimming in the water was running. Jumping was running in the wrong direction. Even falling was running. Every liquid, even when it was calm, was a possible running. When I was afraid, the objects ran very quickly. But nightfall at that time was becoming unconscious.

When I did not know where to turn next, it was explained to me that I was afraid when I did not know where to turn, and that is how I learned to be afraid; and when I saw red it was explained to me that I was angry; but when I wanted to crawl away to hide I was ashamed; and when I leapt into the air I was happy; but when I was near bursting I had a secret or was proud of something; and when I nearly expired I had pity; but when I knew neither left nor right I was in despair: and when I did not know what was up or down I was confused; but when my breath stopped I was startled; and when I became ashen-faced I was afraid of death; but when I rubbed my hands together I was satisfied; and when I stuttered it was explained to me that I was happy when I stuttered; when I stuttered I was happy.

After I had learned to say the word I, I had to be addressed as I for a time because I did not know I was meant by the word you, since I was called I; and also, when I already knew the word you I pretended for a time that I did not know who was meant, because I enjoyed not understanding anything; thus I also began to enjoy responding whenever the word you was uttered.

When I did not understand a word I doubled it and doubled it once more, so that it would no longer bother me. I said: war, war; rag, rag. I said: war, war, war; rag, rag, rag, rag. Thus I became accustomed to words.

I first saw only one person. Later, after I had seen this one person, I saw several other persons.
That certainly surprised me.

Meantime, one of the Kaspars has taken a large file out of his carton and rasped once across the carton. Thereupon he also begins to file on the Kaspar sitting next to him. The sound produced by the filing is of the kind that drives one wild. All the Kaspars wear some kind of material which, if a file, knife, or nail is applied to it, produces all manner of excruciating noises. Up to this point, only one of these noises has been produced, and briefly. The

I saw something sparkle. Because it sparkled, I wanted to have it. I wanted to have everything that sparkled. Later I also wanted to have what didn't sparkle.

I saw that someone had something. I wanted to have something like it. Later I also wanted to have something.

When I woke up I ate. Then I played and also spoke until I fell asleep again and woke up again.

Once I put my hands in my pockets and could not pull them out again.

Once every object seemed to be evidence for something, but what?

Once (*he tries to swallow*) I was unable to swallow.

Once (*he tries to sneeze*) I was unable to sneeze.

Once (*he tries to yawn*) I was unable to yawn.

Once – (*with effort he tries to speak the following sentence to the end*) pursue the others . . . I caught . . . no one vanquished . . . the objects were . . . I drove . . . no one caressed . . . the others stormed . . . the objects had . . . no one pushed . . . I shoved . . . the others

Kaspars might have on their clothing pieces of foam rubber, tin, stone, slate, etc. All these are in the carton. One might also use the noise produced by crumpling the wrapping paper. The noises now become increasingly more frequent and louder because all the Kaspars in back begin to work on the cartons and on each other with their files, knives, slate pencils, nails, fingernails, etc. One by one, they get up and form a tight, wrangling huddle. However, each noise is distinct from the others : none is produced indiscriminately ; nor do they drown out the words of the original Kaspar at the microphone; on the contrary, they make them even more distinct.

The sounds become increasingly more ample and prolonged. For instance, one will hear the sound of a door scraping along a stone floor, of a metal bar slipping along a polar bear's claws in a circus, of a sled running its runners from snow on to gravel, of chalk or a fingernail on slate, of a knife scraping a plate, of people scraping a marble floor with nails in their shoes, of a saw cutting through new wood, of a fingernail scraping across a pane of glass, of cloth tearing, etc. (Leave something to the imagination, but not too much.)

showed . . . the objects became
. . . I moved . . . the others
ripped . . . no one lowered . . .
the objects are . . . the objects
have . . . the others rub . . . no
one hits . . . I drag . . . the
objects become . . . no one
chokes . . . the others get . . . –
I was unable to speak a
sentence to the end.

Once made slip slip . . . once
madip slip slip . . . once madip
slin slin . . . monce mamin
m:m:m . . . – I made a slip of
the tongue, and they all looked
at each other.

Once I was the only one who
laughed.

Once I sat down on a fly.

Once I heard everyone scream
murder! but when I looked I
only found a peeled tomato in
the rubbish bin.

All at once I was different
from the furnishings.

Already with my first sentence I
was trapped.

*As these noises are produced, and
as the various objects in the
cartons (foam rubber, etc.) are
cut up, the Kaspars gradually
come to the front of the stage.*

I can make myself understood. I think I must have slept a long time
because I am awake now. I go to the table and use the table, but look
at that – the table continues to exist after it has been used. I can
appear because I know where my place is. I cannot fall asleep with
dry hands, but when I spit into my hands they become even drier.
By saying: the chair is harmless, it is all over with the chair's harm-
lessness. I feel good when the door, having stood open for long, is
finally closed. I know where everything belongs. I have a good eye

for the right proportion. I don't put anything into my mouth. I can
laugh to three. I am usable. I can hear wood rotting over long distances. I no longer understand anything literally. I cannot wait until
I wake up, whereas earlier I could not wait to fall asleep. I have been
made to speak. I have been sentenced to reality. – Do you hear it?
(*Silence.*) Can you hear? (*Silence.*) Psst. (*Silence.*)

The stage becomes dark.
Silence.

65
*As the stage becomes bright once more, the events on stage are again
divided into three parts: together with Kaspar's speech as follows, the
prompters come on again. Whispering, they repeat something like this:
If only. Own future. Now every second one as opposed to every fourth
one at one time. A possible object. If only. Make life easier. If only.
Development. If only. In reality. If only. In constantly growing
numbers. If only. Serves the. If only. Bears dangers. If only. It is
necessary for that. If only. Finally, they repeat over and over again,
until the end, speaking softly: If only. If only. If only. Meanwhile, the
Kaspars come forward (filing, etc.) and proceed to manhandle the
speaking Kaspar with their files, etc. They make particular fun of one
object, say a chair, laughing at it, imitating it, costuming it, dragging it
off and imitating the sound it makes as it is being dragged across the floor,
thus making it utterly ridiculous and making it and all other objects*
COMPLETELY IMPOSSIBLE. *Kaspar has gone on speaking:*

I can hear the logs comfortably crackling in the fire, with which I
want to say that I do not hear the bones crackling comfortably. The
chair stands here, the table there, with which I mean to say that I am
telling a story. I would not like to be older, but I would like for much
time to have passed, with which I mean to say that a sentence is a
monster, with which I mean to say that speaking can help temporarily,
with which I mean to say that every object becomes ticklish when I
am startled. I say: I can imagine to be everywhere now, except that
I cannot imagine really being there, with which I mean to say that the
doorknobs are empty. I can say: the air snaps shut, or: the room
creaks, or: the curtain jingles, with which I mean to say that I don't

know where I should put or leave my hand, while I when I say that I
don't know where to put my hand mean to say that all doors tempt
me under the pretence that they can be opened, which sentence I
would like to use in the sense of: my hair has gotten into the table as
into a machine and I am scalped: literally: with each new sentence I
become nauseous: figuratively: I have been turned topsy-turvy: I
am in someone's hand: I look to the other side: there prevails an
unbloody calm: I cannot rid myself of myself any more: I toss the hat
on to the meathook: every stool helps while dying: the furnishings are
waterproof: the furniture is as it ought to be: nothing is open: the
pain and its end come within sight: time must stop: thoughts become
very small: I still experienced myself: I never saw myself: I put up
no undue resistance: the shoes fit like gloves: I don't get away with
just a fright: the skin peels off: the foot sleeps itself dead: candles and
bloodsuckers: ice and mosquitoes: horses and puss: hoarfrost and
rats: eels and sicklebills:

*Meantime, the other Kaspars are producing an infernal noise with their
various tools which they have applied to the objects they have brought
with them and to Kaspar. They are giggling, behave like crowds in
crowd scenes in plays, ridicule Kaspar by speaking in the same rhythm as
he, etc. Kaspar has also produced a file and makes similar noises by
scraping with the file against the microphone while he is speaking his
sentences. But now, all at once, an almost complete silence sets in. The
Kaspars merely flap their arms about a little and gesticulate. They
wriggle a little. They snuffle. Then Kaspar says:*

Goats and monkeys	*With that, the curtain jolts a little towards the centre, where the Kaspars are wriggling. The jolt produces a shrill sound.*
Goats and monkeys	*With an even shriller sound, the curtain jerks a little farther towards the middle.*
Goats and monkeys	*With an even shriller sound, the curtain jerks still farther towards the middle.*

Goats and monkeys

With an even shriller sound, the curtain moves still more towards the centre.

Goats and monkeys

With the shrillest possible sound, the curtain makes one final jerk towards the centre, where the Kaspars are still wriggling a little. The curtain slams into them the moment Kaspar says his last word: it topples all of them. They fall over, but fall behind the curtain, which has now come together. The piece is over.

MY FOOT MY TUTOR

Das Mündel will Vormund sein

translated by Michael Roloff

'What, I say,
My foot my tutor!'

Prospero in *The Tempest*

My Foot My Tutor was first performed at the Open Space Theatre, London, on 29 September 1971, with the following cast:

THE WARD   Nickolas Grace
THE WARDEN   Garfield Morgan
Directed by Ronald Hayman

TRANSLATOR'S NOTE

The German title of *My Foot My Tutor*, *Das Mündel will Vormund sein*, means 'The ward wants to be warden!' and is the accepted German translation of Prospero's exclamation: 'My foot my tutor!'

M.R.

The curtain opens.

It is a sunny day.

In the background of the stage we see, as the stage background, the facade of a farmhouse.

The stage is not deep.

The left demarcation of the stage, from our vantage point, shows the view of a cornfield.

The right demarcation of the stage, from our vantage point, is formed by the view of a large beetfield.

Birds are circling above both fields.

In front of the farmhouse we see a peculiar, longish object and ask ourselves what it might represent.

A rubber coat, black, covers the object partially; yet it does not fit like a glove, and so we cannot recognise what the object represents onstage.

To the right of the picture of the farmhouse door, from our vantage point, in front of a window, we notice a wooden block with a hatchet in it; or rather, a large piece of wood is lying on the block, which is standing at an angle, and a hatchet is sticking in the piece of wood.

Round about the chopping block we notice many pieces of chopped wood, and also, of course, chips and splinters, strewn about the stage floor. On the chopping block, next to the large piece of wood with the hatchet sticking in it, we notice a cat: while the curtain opens the cat probably raises its head and subsequently does what it usually does, so that we recognise: the cat represents what it does.

Already, upon first glance, we have seen someone sitting next to the chopping block, on a stool: a figure.

Now, after having briefly taken in the other features of the stage, we turn back to the figure sitting on a stool in the sunshine in front of the picture of the house.

He — the figure is that of a male — is dressed in rural garb: that is, he is wearing overalls over his trousers; his shoes are heavy; on top, the person is only wearing an undershirt.

No tattoos are visible on his arms.

The person wears no covering on his head.

The sun is shining.

It is probably not necessary to mention explicitly that the person squatting on the stool in front of the picture of the house is wearing a mask.

This mask covers half of his face — the upper part, that is — and is immobile.

It represents a face which, moreover, evinces an expression of considerable glee, within limits, of course.

The figure on the stage is young — some recognize that this figure probably represents the ward.

The ward has his legs stretched out in front of him.

We see that he is wearing hobnailed boots.

The ward is holding the underside of his right knee with his left hand; the right leg, in contrast to the left, is slightly bent.

We see that the ward is leaning with his back against the back-drop representing the house wall.

In his right hand the figure is holding a rather large yellow apple. Now that the curtain has opened and is open, the figure brings the apple to his mouth.

The ward bites into the apple, as if no one were watching. The apple does not crunch especially, as if there were no one listening. The picture as a whole exudes something of the quality of what one might call profound peacefulness.

The ward eats the apple, as if no one were watching.

(If you make a point to watch, apples are often eaten with a good deal of affectation.)

The figure thus consumes the apple, not particularly slowly, not particularly quickly.

The cat does what it does. If it should decide to leave the stage, no one should stop it from doing so.

If at first we paid too much attention to the figure, we now have sufficient time to inspect the other objects and areas (see above).

Can one gather from the manner in which the ward consumes the apple that he enjoys dependent status? Actually not.

Because we have been so preoccupied with looking, we have almost overlooked that the figure has already finished eating the apple. Nothing unusual has occurred during this process, the figure has no unusual way of consuming apples, perhaps a few seeds have fallen on the floor; chickens are not in evidence.

Now it's the second apple's turn.

To accomplish this, the ward stretches out his right leg com-pletely, and with his left hand reaches under his overalls into the right pocket of his trousers.

Obviously he is not making out too well.

He couldn't reach into the pocket with his right hand though, since he would have to lean back to do so but sits too near the wall to be able to learn back as far as he would have to.

He slides forward with the stool and leans back against the picture of the wall: no, the upper and lower parts of his body are still at too much of an angle for his hand to be able to do what it wants to do.

The pause is noticeable.

Now the ward stands up and while he stands reaches into his trousers pocket and easily extracts the apple.

While still in the process of sitting down, he bites into the apple. With his seat the ward shoves the stool closer to the wall of the house again and assumes a similar, though not precisely the same, position as the initial one; the cat moves or does not move, the ward eats.

From behind the cornfield backdrop — from our vantage point, the left — a second figure emerges, the warden, judging from all visible evidence: rubber boots covered with mud up to the knee, grey working trousers, a check shirt (white & blue) with rolled-up sleeves, tattoos on his arms, an open collar, a mask covering the upper half of his face, a hat with a pheasant feather stuck in it, an insignia on the hat, a carpenter's pencil behind his ear, a pumpkin in front of his stomach.

Now that the warden has entered the stage we see that the backdrop representing the cornfield consists of many small moveable parts which are falling back into their original positions . . . the cornfield is calming down, the birds are again circling on one and the same spot.

The warden sees the ward.

The warden steps up close and takes a look at the ward.

The ward is quietly eating his apple.

The warden's watching the ward drags on.

As we see, the eating of the apple also begins to drag on gradually. The longer the warden watches the ward, the more the eating of the apple is drawn out.

When the warden has stared down the ward, the latter stops eating the apple.

The pumpkin which the warden is holding in front of his stomach is, as we see, a real pumpkin.

But we hardly notice this anymore, for after the warden has outstared the ward and the ward has simultaneously ceased eating his apple, which is now lying oddly half-eaten in the ward's hand, the stage is already becoming gradually dark. The scene is finished.

A new scene now begins in the dark, we can hear it.

What we hear is a loud, prerecorded breathing that is piped in over an amplifying system. After a period of silence the loud breathing suddenly sets in and it continues neither evenly louder nor softer but constantly wavering back and forth within its prescribed decibel range, in such a manner that we are made to think: now it will get louder and louder and become the loudest possible breathing, but at this point it suddenly becomes quite soft again, and we think: now the breathing is about to stop altogether, when it suddenly becomes loud again, and in fact far louder than what we consider natural breathing. It is 'like' the strongly amplified breathing of an old man, but not quite; on the other hand, it is 'like' the strong amplified breathing of a wild animal that has been cornered, but not quite, either; it is 'voracious', 'frightened,' 'ominous,' but not quite; at times it seems to signify someone's 'death throes' to us, but somehow it doesn't either because it appears to change location constantly. In the Italian detective film *The Chief Sends His Best Man* (with Stewart Granger and Peter van Eyck, directed by Sergio Sollima) there is a sequence in which an apartment — which someone has entered and in which he has found his dead friend — suddenly becomes dark; after a few moments of quiet the aforementioned breathing suddenly becomes audible all over the room, and for such a long time and so intensively that the intruder, in his desperation, starts shooting and jumps up from behind his chair, whereupon he is shot and the lights are turned on — a young man stands above him, a small tape recorder in his hand, which he now switches off, whereupon the 'hideous' breathing stops: that is the kind of breathing that is meant here, without the same consequences, of course — as suddenly as it started it stops again after a certain time.

We are sitting pretty much in the dark; judging from the noises coming from that direction, the stage is being rearranged.
While it is gradually becoming dark, we hear music, a succession of chords piped in very much at random, with the pauses between them varying in length. Occasionally several chords follow each other in quick succession.
The chords are taken from the instrumental 'Colors for Susan', from *I Feel Like I'm Fixin' to Die* (Fontana TFL 6087) by Country Joe and the Fish. The piece only lasts five minutes and fifty-seven seconds, so it's repeated over and over during the course of events, except for the very end of the tune which is reserved for the end of the events.
Onstage, ward and warden are in the process of rearranging the stage: what was inside before is now turned inside out.
If the stage is of the revolving kind, this process is managed by

turning the stage 180 degrees.

If the stage is not of the revolving kind, ward and warden simply turn the backdrops of the cornfield, beetfield, and house facade so that the backs of the backdrops now represent the inside walls of the house.

We look out through the back window, before which the birds are circling.

Lacking a revolving stage, ward and warden take the objects that stood in front of the house (the object under the rubber coat, etc.) to the back of the stage, and now as it becomes bright again, they bring the furnishings for the house onstage.

This is what is required for the play: a rather large table, two chairs, an electric hot plate, a coffee grinder, an assortment of bottles, glasses, cups, saucers, and plates (on the floor in back), an oil lamp, a rubber hose, a bootjack, a newspaper which lies in the crack of the door.

On a nail on the door hangs a bullwhip; on the same nail there also hangs a pair of scissors.

From our vantage point we see a large block calendar hanging on the right wall of the room.

But so that we can see all of this, the following has transpired in the meantime: the warden lit a match in the dark and turned up the oil lamp. As we already know from many other plays, the entire stage gradually becomes bright when someone lights an oil lamp: the same happens here. Now that the stage is brightly lit — let us not forget to listen to the music, which becomes neither softer nor louder — we see it in the following condition: it now represents the room of a house. But this room is still empty, except for the paper in the crack of the door, the objects on the door, and the calendar.

We see ward and warden, who come onstage from the left and right sides respectively, distribute the aforementioned objects throughout the room: each brings in a chair, then the table is brought onstage by the two of them, then comes the warden with the rubber hose which he drags across the stage before dropping it, then comes the ward with the bottles and plates, then the warden with the glasses — unhurriedly but not ceremonially either — just as though we weren't watching; circus workers would do it differently. No evincing of satisfaction, no contemplation of work well done, no moving to the music.

They both sit down, the ward almost first but he stops midway and the warden is seated, then the ward sits down too.

They both make themselves comfortable.

The music is pleasant.

The warden extends his legs under the table.

The ward also extends his legs under the table and comes to a halt when he touches the warden's feet; then, after a pause, the ward slowly withdraws his legs; the warden does not withdraw his.

The ward sits there. What to do with his legs?

Quiet, music.

The ward puts his feet on the front crosspiece of his own chair, and to accomplish this he uses his body to shove the chair back, producing the customary sound; the warden doesn't let himself be disturbed, he replies by taking off his hat and placing it on the table.

Quiet, music.

The ward slowly looks around the room, around, up, and also down, but avoids grazing the warden with his eyes, makes an about-face, so to speak, whenever he is just about to look at the warden: this is repeated so often, it loses its psychological significance.

The warden watches the ward.

The ward stands up, takes an apple from his trousers pocket underneath his overalls, and puts it beside the hat.

The warden lowers his gaze to the apple.

The ward starts gazing around the room again. What is there to see in the room?

Suddenly, as if he sensed a trap, the warden puts his head to the side.

The ward, caught by the warden's gaze, stops looking around.

Mutual staring at each other, gazing, mutual looking through each other, mutual looking away.

Each one looks at the other's ear.

The ward places both feet on the floor simultaneously; we can hear it.

The warden looks at the ward's ear.

The ward gets up carefully, softly.

The warden looks at him, at his ear.

The ward, only aware of himself, goes to the door, his steps, careful at first, becoming progressively louder as he approaches it.

The warden follows him with his eyes.

The ward bends down and pulls the newspaper out of the crack in the door.

The warden does not follow the ward with his eyes but keeps them fixed on the door: what's hanging on the door?

The ward straightens up, goes back to the table with the paper

under his arm, beginning to walk more carefully again, once by
the table walking almost soundlessly; while underway he uses his
free hand to take the paper from under his arm and holds it
neatly in his hand by the time he stands before the table.
The warden gazes at the door.
The ward neatly places the paper beside the hat and the apple.
The warden lowers his head; in the pause between the movements
we hear a louder chord.
The ward sits down without making a sound, sits the way he did
before; the next chord is suddenly softer.
The warden unfolds the paper completely.
He reads. He folds the paper together to the size of one page. He
pretends to read that page. He reads so that it is almost a pleasure
to watch him reading.
The ward, while seated, pulls, with a good deal of effort, a tiny
book out of his trousers pocket, the same trousers from which he
produced the apples, and also reads and is no less pleasure to look
at.
The warden folds the newspaper page in half and goes on reading.
The ward pulls a pencil out of his trousers pocket, a carpenter's
pencil like the warden's, only smaller; he uses it to mark the book
while reading.
The warden goes on folding the paper.
The ward no longer marks in his book but crosses something out.
The warden goes on folding as best he can.
The ward is obviously starting to draw in the little book.
The warden folds.
The ward exceeds the margins of the book while drawing and
begins to draw on the palm of his hand.
The warden: see above.
The ward draws on the back of his hand.
The warden is gradually forced to start crumpling the paper, but
we don't actually notice the transition from folding to crumpling.
The ward draws on his lower arm; what he draws doesn't
necessarily have to resemble the warden's tattoos.
The warden is obviously no longer reading or folding but is
vigorously crumpling.
Both figures are vigorously occupied, one with drawing, the other
with crumpling.
The warden completes the crumpling process and the paper is
now a tight ball.
The ward is still drawing.
The warden is quiet, the ball of paper in his fist; he looks at his

opposite who is drawing.

The ward is drawing; the longer his opposite gazes at him, the more slowly he draws. Then, instead of drawing, he only scratches himself with the pencil and finally turns it around and scratches his arm with the other end; then he pushes the pencil into his arm without moving it. Then he stops doing this and slowly places the pencil next to the hat on the table; he quickly pulls his hand away and places it, slowly, on the lower part of the arm with the drawing on it.

The warden places his fist with the crumpled paper on the table and leaves it there.

The ward starts looking around the room once more, up, down, to the side, down along his legs.

The warden unclenches the fist holding the paper ball and places his hand next to it on the table; the paper ball slowly expands.

The music, noticeably louder now, is pleasant.

A period without movement — though that is not to say that the figures become graven images — now follows, unobtrusively introducing the next sequence.

During the period without movement we just listen to the music. Now the music becomes nearly inaudible, just as the main theme may disappear almost entirely during certain sections of a film.

We see the warden slowly place his lower arms on the table.

In reply to this movement, the ward places his hands on the table, fingertips pointing at the warden.

The warden, without looking at the ward, slowly places his head on his lower arms, on his hands, that is, and in such a way that his mouth and nose are placed on the backs of his hands, with his eyes looking across them.

Thereupon the ward slowly lowers his head toward the table until his head is hanging between his arms at the height of the table. After pausing briefly in this position and at this level the ward lowers his head even further, down between his outstretched arms, which he has to bend now, until his head almost touches his knees: the ward remains in that position.

The warden draws his head toward himself until it lies not with his mouth and nose, but with his forehead on his hands.

The ward spreads his knees and sticks his head deeper down between his bent arms and spread knees.

The warden pulls his hands out from under his head and now lies with his bare face, that is, with his bare mask, on the table.

(All these movements, although they occur very slowly, are not ceremonial.)

The ward lets his arms drop from the table but leaves his head hanging between his knees at the previous level.

The warden, while keeping his face in the previous position, uses his body to push the chair as far away from the table as possible, while still keeping his face on the table, his body slipping from the chair.

The ward, if possible, clenches his knees together above his head or against it.

Both of them are completely quiet onstage, as if no one were watching.

We hear the music somewhat more distinctly.

Some time passes; it has already passed.

The objects are in their places, here and there.

The warden stands up, without our noticing the in-between movements; he stands there, he represents standing, nothing else.

What will the ward do now?

Some time passes; we wait.

Now the ward sits up, without our particularly noticing the in-between movements.

What is the warden doing? He walks about the stage and represents walking.

The ward gets up; he stands there.

The warden runs; the ward beings to walk.

The warden leaps; the warden begins to . . .

The warden climbs up on a chair and is now standing on it; the ward does not leap but stops in his tracks and stands there.

The warden climbs on the table; the ward climbs on the chair.

The warden takes the other chair and puts it on the table and climbs on the chair on the table; the ward — how could it be otherwise? — climbs on the table.

The warden attaches himself to a rope hanging down and hangs there; the ward climbs on the chair on the table.

The warden is hanging quietly, dangling a little, and the ward is quietly standing, high on the chair.

The warden lets himself drop. He lands with bent knees, then gradually straightens up to his full length.

The ward quickly climbs off the chair onto the table, from the table down onto the other chair, from this chair down onto the floor, and while doing so also takes the chair on the table down with him, putting it back in its old place and squatting down almost simultaneously.

All of this transpires so rapidly that if we wanted to count, we could hardly count farther than one.

The warden slowly squats down.
The ward sits on the floor.
The warden slowly sits down also.
As soon as the warden sits down, the ward quickly lies down on the floor.
The warden slowly, ever so slowly, lies down on his back also, and makes himself comfortable.
As soon as the warden is lying on his back, the ward quickly rolls over and lies on his stomach.
The warden, emphasizing each of his movements with the sound it produces, also rolls over on his stomach, slowly.
As best he can, the ward now bends all his extremities together. We see him diminishing everywhere and becoming smaller. But he wasn't an inflated balloon before, was he? It appears that he was. The ward becomes smaller and smaller, and flatter, the stage becomes increasingly dark. The warden stays on his stomach as we last saw him, the stage is now dark, we hear the isolated chords.

The stage becomes bright.
We see that the two figures are again seated at the table in their previous positions.
The warden gets up, goes to the bootjack, takes off his boots in a completely professional manner, without exaggerating, as if no one were watching. He kicks each boot across the stage with one kick.
The ward gets up, goes where the boots are lying and puts them next to each other beside the door.
One after the other, warden and ward go back to their places.
A brief pause.
The warden rolls his woollen socks from his feet and flings them, bunched up, across the stage, one here, the other there, without any evidence of nasty motives, just as if no one were watching.
The ward gets up, finds the socks, straightens them out, pulls them rightside out and places them as nicely as possible across the boots. Then he returns to the table and sits down.
The warden gets up, goes to the door, takes the scissors off the nail and returns with the scissors to the table.
After sitting down, he places his naked foot on the side crosspiece of the chair and cuts his toenails.
We know the sounds.
He behaves as if we were not really watching.
He cuts his toenails so slowly and for such a long time that it no longer seems funny.

When he is finally done he places the scissors on his knees.
After some time the ward gets up and walks about the stage,
picking up the clipped-off toenails and putting them in the palm
of one hand.
He, too, does this so slowly that it is no longer a laughing matter.
When the ward finally straightens up and returns to the table,
the warden takes the scissors from his knees and now begins to
clip his fingernails.
The ward turns around and goes to the calendar hanging on the
right-hand wall.
The warden cuts and the ward tears off a sheet from the calendar.
The warden cuts, and . . .
The warden cuts, and . . .
It is a slow process, without rhythm; it takes the warden a
different amount of time to cut off each nail, and the ward needs
a different amount of time to tear off each sheet from the calendar;
the noises of the snipping and tearing overlap, are not necessarily
successive, sometimes occur simultaneously; the calendar sheets
flutter to the floor. Now the calendar has been completely shorn:
all we can see of it is the rather large empty cardboard backing
left hanging on the wall.
But the warden is still cutting his fingernails, and the ward is
standing inactively by the wall, his face half to the wall.
The music, which becomes more distinct, is so pleasant that the
noise the scissors make hardly affects us.
And now that the stage is becoming dark the noise stops at once.

It becomes bright.
The two persons are sitting in their initial positions at the table,
quietly, each by himself.
The warden gets up, goes to the hot plate. He takes the kettle
from behind the row of bottles and puts one end of the rubber
hose into the kettle.
The warden exits, returns immediately.
We hear water running into the kettle.
The warden exits and returns at once.
He takes the hose out of the kettle, lets it drop. He puts the lid
on the kettle and puts the kettle on the hot plate.
The warden drags the rubber hose onstage.
As the hose is apparently very long, he has to drag for quite a long
time. Finally the warden drags the entire hose onstage.
Nothing funny happens.
He winds the hose in an orderly manner over hand and elbow,

goes to the table and places the rolled up hose with the other
objects on the table. He resumes his position.
Quietly, contemplating each other, the two figures squat onstage.
Gradually we begin to hear the water simmering in the kettle.
The noises we hear are those that are produced when water is heated.

.

The ward gets up, fetches the coffee grinder, sits down, makes himself comfortable on the chair, clasps the coffee grinder between
his knees and starts to grind. We can hear the grinding . . . The
ward is grinding, apparently unaware of anything else . . .

.

.

.

.

The kettle whistles . . . .

.

The ward gradually stops grinding . . .

.

.

Now the stopper is probably blown off the kettle, so that it
becomes quiet again.
The music sets in at the appropriate moment, when the stage once
more becomes dark.

On the bright stage we see the two persons at the table, the hot
plate having of course been turned off in the meantime.
The warden gets up and goes offstage.
But he returns quite soon, a frying pan with glowing incense in
one hand, a big piece of white chalk in the other.
We smell the incense and also see clouds of incense.
The warden goes to the door and starts writing something on the
top of the door. The moment he puts chalk to wood, the ward
turns toward him on the chair; the ward reaches into his trousers
pocket and throws something at the warden . . . it must be something very light because the warden does not stop his very slow
writing which looks almost like drawing.
The ward makes himself comfortable on his chair and throws
again, unhurriedly.
The warden writes; the ward throws.

We see that the ward's projectiles are sticking to the warden's shirt: yes they are burs.

While the warden is slowly writing, the ward occasionally throws a bur at him, yet without expressing anything with the manner in which he throws it.

We hear the music and smell the incense.

The warden's back is slowly but surely covered with a cluster of burs while he writes.

He writes slowly down along the door:

    K + M + B
     .
     .
     .
     .

The ward now takes the burs out of his fist and throws them with the other hand.

The warden, while writing, takes the bullwhip from the door. Now he steps back.

The ward happens to be throwing again.

The warden turns around as though accidentally, not quickly; at the same time, the ward throws a bur, which hits the warden's chest (or not). The warden is standing there by himself; the ward throws the remaining burs at the warden.

The warden is holding the pan with the incense in front of him. The longer the warden holds the pan, the longer the intervals between the ward's throws . . .

During this process it gradually becomes dark once again, and the music . . . (see above).

The two figures are sitting on the stage, which is bright again; they are sitting at the table, each one by himself.

They are sitting, each one by himself.
.
.
.

All at once we notice there is blood running from the ward's nose. The blood trickles out of his nose, across his mouth, over his chin, out of his nose . . .

The warden is sitting there by himself, the ward doesn't budge from the spot, doesn't budge from the spot . . .

Gradually it becomes dark again on the stage . . .

Once we can see again, both of them are sitting in their positions
at the table.
The ward gets up and stands against the back wall, with his back
to us.
The warden gets up, goes to the ward, grabs him by the shoulder,
without expressing anything (that is, not violently) and turns him
around.
The warden, after a pause, changes the position of his hands and
turns the ward around once more.
The turning gradually turns into turning around and around, now
into turning pure and simple.
The warden turns the ward with ease, almost as though he were
thinking of something else, and the ward turns easily, also as
though he were thinking of something else.
Without transition, without either of them staggering, we suddenly
see the warden standing by the bottles and plates.
The ward has been standing still for some time before we really
notice that he is standing still.
The warden has already bent down and while bending down
throws a bottle toward the ward: the ward shows how he would
like to catch but can't — the bottle falls on the floor and does
what it does.
As one can imagine, it goes on like this:
Bending down, the warden throws bottles, plates, and glasses
toward the ward, but the ward, although apparently making an
effort, lets all the objects fall on the floor, and the objects either
break or they don't. This process also lacks a regular rhythm: they
wait now and then, then the warden throws once more, then the
ward misses again . . .
Suddenly, even before the collection of bottles has been disposed
of —amidst the nicest possible throwing and breaking — the ward
catches an object, as if by accident.
We are startled.
At the same moment the stage becomes dark, abruptly.

And again it becomes bright, and both of them are sitting at the
table. The warden gets up and goes where? Apparently he doesn't
know where he should go.
No, he doesn't want to go to the calendar.
He turns round, turns round again, is turning round.
The ward gets up and walks after him; he shows how he shares
the warden's indecision and imitates the warden's gestures, his leg
movements as well as his indecisive arm movements, although the

imitation need not be a complete aping.

They almost collide when the warden suddenly changes direction — he is probably avoiding the pieces of the broken bottles and plates; more than once the ward steps on the warden's heels.

They continue moving about the stage, pretending to have a goal which, however, they never reach because they always give it up just before they are about to reach it.

Suddenly the warden is by the door, is already going out, reaches for the outside door handle to shut the door behind him — the ward seizes the door handle on the inside, wants to follow the warden, but the warden pulls tenaciously.

The ward pulls in the other direction.

The warden, by giving one hard pull, pulls the door shut behind him and in front of the ward, who has been pulled along by the violent pull.

The ward stands briefly in front of the door, his hand around the handle, then his hand merely touching the handle.

The ward lets his hand drop.

The warden is outside; it is quiet.

The ward gets down on his knees, without falling down on them however, and is already crawling through the door, quickly: we see now that the door has a cat-flap in it.

Once the ward is outside the stage slowly becomes dark.

We have already become accustomed to the music.

The pause is longer this time, for the scenery is being turned inside out.

A revolving stage only needs to revolve.

Otherwise, the scenery is turned around in the dark.

It becomes bright: it is a rainy day.

Warden and ward set up the objects on the stage: a large, longish object, covered by the black raincoat, which they have to bring onstage together, the stool, beets, melons, pumpkins.

Now that everything has been distributed on the stage the ward sits down on the stool while the warden stands next to the mysterious object.

Without an actual beginning the play has begun again: the warden takes the rubber coat off the object, so that we see that it is a beet-cutting machine.

The warden puts on the raincoat (he is still barefoot) and, to test the machine, lets the cutting knife drop down several times without, however, cutting any beets as yet.

The ward gets up and walks up to the machine.

The warden bends down for a beet, shoves it into the machine and pulls down the cutting knife with one brief, effortless movement, as he indicates with a movement: the beet falls down, its top shorn off.

The warden repeats the process in an exemplary manner: another beet falls down.

The ward watches, not completely motionless but without moving very much.

The warden repeats the process.

The ward fetches a beet but makes many superfluous movements and detours; we can hear his hobnail boots on the floor as well as the bare feet of the warden, who now goes to the side and straightens up.

The ward raises the cutting knife, shoves the beet up to its top into the machine and hacks off the top.

The warden steps up to him, stands beside him, steps back again . . .

The ward goes and fetches a few beets and puts them into place . . .

The warden steps up to him and stands there.

The cat suddenly slinks out of the house.

The ward's next attempt to cut off the top of a beet is so feckless that the beet does not fall on the floor at once.

The warden stands there watching him.

With the next attempt, the beet falls on the floor.

The cat does what it does.

The warden stands there.

The ward has problems with the beet again: he makes one attempt to sever its top, a second one, and then, without looking at the warden, who is starting to walk about the stage once more in his bare feet, a third attempt; then, after a certain time, when the warden is standing next to him again and is watching him, once more; then, later — it is already becoming darker on stage — a fifth time (the warden is starting to walk again); then — it is already quite dark (is the warden standing by the machine?) — finally once more, and now — we can't bear watching it anymore — once again, and we don't hear the sound of anything falling on the floor; thereupon it is quiet onstage, for quite some time.

After it has been quiet onstage for some time we hear, quite softly at first, a breathing that becomes increasingly louder. We recognise it. It becomes louder, that is, larger and larger — a death rattle? A very intense inhaling? Or only a bellows? Or a huge animal?

It becomes steadily louder.

Gradually it becomes too large for the house.

Is it here, is it over there?

Suddenly it is quiet.

After a long time it becomes bright again.

The house, the cornfield, the beetfield.

We see neither the cat, nor the warden, nor the ward; not even the beet-cutting machine remains onstage — except for the three backdrops, it is bare.

Now someone enters from the right: it is the ward. He is carrying a small tub in front of him, and wound about his upper body is a rubber hose.

He is no longer wearing his overalls.

The tub is placed on the floor, the hose is unrolled.

One end of the hose is placed in the tub; the ward takes the other end offstage, straightening the hose in the process.

We hear the water running into the tub for some time.

Then the ward returns, a sack of sand in one arm.

He puts the sack next to the tub. He reaches into the sack with his hand.

He straightens up and lets a handful of sand fall into the tub, without letting the sand slip between his fingers first.

He again reaches into the sack and, standing, lets a handful of sand fall into the water.

He again reaches into the sack and, standing, lets a handful of sand fall into the water, nonchalantly, irregularly, unceremoniously.

He again reaches into the sack and, standing, lets a handful of sand fall into the water.

Now we hear the isolated chords again.

The ward reaches into the sack and, when he has straightened up, lets a handful of sand fall into the water.

The ward reaches into the sack and, when he has straightened up, lets a handful of sand fall into the water.

The ward reaches into the sack and, when he has straightened up, lets a handful of sand fall into the water.

.

.

.

.

We hear both, the chords and the sand falling into the water, as the stage gradually becomes dark.

.

.

.

The curtain closes.

THE RIDE ACROSS LAKE CONSTANCE

Der Ritt über den Bodensee

translated by Michael Roloff

*'Are You Dreaming or
Are You Speaking?'*

The Ride Across Lake Constance was conceived as a continuation to *Kaspar*, i.e. as an attempt to portray the forms of human behaviour dominant in our society by closely observing

(a) the forms of daily life, as for instance being in love, work, buying and selling which seem to operate without any pattern in a 'Free Play of the Forces' and

(b) the usual presentation of these phenomena by the theatre which, although it may attack this 'Free Play of the Forces' as 'False' or 'Exploitation', itself operates just as haphazardly and is prone to 'exploitation' in the same 'Free Play of the Forces', governed by specific market requirements and market practices and the law of supply and demand as the situations of daily life it seems to portray.

First attempts to put on record these observations were realized in *Das Mündel will Vormund sein* (*My Foot my Tutor*) and *Quodlibet*. In these plays theatre forms appeared isolated from the stories so much that they become POSES which again could become identical with poses in daily life: Thus the presentation of theatre poses was also an attempt for forms of everyday behaviour to be shown as poses.

Then some time went by, and more than any other play, *The Ride Across Lake Constance* has become something quite different from its original conception, but not a single detail would be feasible without the latter.

Nothing was to be proved any more. So, in the play, proofs have the form of a farce; the suffering resulting from inability to prove or to explain takes the form of an often performed tragedy; and the joy of being free from explanation and the necessity to prove has the form of a Utopian comedy. What was clear or at least presented itself as being clear in the beginning, with each sentence and each gesture becomes more obscure in the course of the play, but I have tried to do this, sentence by sentence and gesture by gesture, as clearly and also as coarsely as possible.

The Ride Across Lake Constance is neither a tragedy, nor a comedy nor a farce. It is not educational nor is it popular entertainment. It is a projection of all these genres onto their equivalents in society and is made intelligible and obscure by the vulnerability, the pain, the callousness and the carelessness of people who are actors in the play. And the play, in its turn, also plays its part.

Peter Handke

TRANSLATOR'S NOTE

A German legend tells of a horseman who, on a winter day, sets out to ride to a village on Lake Constance. As he nears the lake, hoping to find a boat to take him across, dusk – perhaps fog – begins to settle. It is snowing, and the sharp outlines of the wide lake, the surrounding hills, and the more distant Alps gradually become obscure. The horseman, unable to see any houses or lights, fears he is lost. He eventually reaches a village, unaware that he has already crossed the lake: either the snow muffled the sound of his horse's hoofs on the ice, or the rider was so intent on not losing his sense of direction that he didn't hear it. Still thinking that he has lost his way, he asks the villagers where he might find a boat to take him across. The villagers congratulate him profusely: 'What a surprise! How did you ever make it across! The ice is no more than an inch thick!' The horseman, realizing the danger he has been in, slowly slips off his horse and drops dead.

Thus originated the proverbial expression in the southern part of Germany: that a person who has been in a situation of considerable danger and was unaware of it until afterwards has 'taken a ride across Lake Constance'.

M.R.

CHARACTERS

WOMAN WITH WHITE SCARF
EMIL JANNINGS
HEINRICH GEORGE
ELISABETH BERGNER
ERICH VON STROHEIM
HENNY PORTEN
ALICE and ELLEN KESSLER
A DOLL

To avoid character designations such as 'Actor A', 'Actor B' and 'Actress C', and so on, for reading and other purposes the characters in the play have been given the names of well-known actors.

When the play is staged, the characters should bear the names of the actors playing the roles: the actors are and play themselves at one and the same time.

The stage is large. It displays a section of an even larger room. Tne background is formed by the back wall of this room; the wall itself is covered by a brownish-green tapestry with a barely perceptible, consistent pattern. Along the back wall two parts of a staircase lead down from the right and left and meet in the centre of the wall where they form a single set of wide stairs leading forward into the room. The audience therefore sees people walking down the stairs in profile first, then from the front. In the wall beneath the right and left parts of the stairway there are two barely visible tapestry doors. A delicately curved, slender banister encircles the staircase. The floor of the room is covered with an unobtrusive carpet the same colour as the tapestry; a wine-red runner leads down the staircase steps.

Most of the furnishings in the room are covered with extremely white loose covers. In the centre of the room – not precisely the centre of course, rather a bit downstage – stands a large dark table, partially covered by a lace tablecloth; on it are an ashtray, a cigar box, a teapot, a coffeepot covered with an embroidered cosy, a longish cutlery case, also of embroidered cloth, and two candlesticks sheathed in protective covers. To the right and left and behind the table stand three fauteuils *with white loose covers; next to and behind them are an easy chair and a straight chair, loose covers over both. In front of one of the* fauteuils *stands a stool – upholstered the same and the same height as the* fauteuil *– that may serve as a footrest; a smaller footstool stands in front of the second* fauteuil*; the third* fauteuil *stands by itself. To the right of the table stands a small, uncovered bar, with several bottles with shapes indicating their respective contents. To the left of the table, a few steps away, stands a newspaper table, also uncovered, with a few bulky magazines on it, some of which are still rolled up; on top is a record player with a record on it. To the left and right behind the newspaper table and bar are two sofas, also concealed by white loose covers. To the left side of the left sofa is a brown-stained chest with several drawers; on it is a small statue covered with a white paper bag. On the right side of the right sofa leans a guitar in a bag embroidered like the tea cosy. Beneath the sections of the staircase* *on the wall hang two pictures concealed behind white sheets. Downstage to the extreme right, in line with the table, stands a Japanese screen of the kind one usually sets up in front of beds. It is small and has three panels: two are slightly pushed together, the third is open and visible to the audience. The screen has the same colour and pattern as the back wall.*

All objects are positioned so that it would be difficult to imagine them elsewhere; it is as if they could not bear to be moved ever so slightly. Everything appears as though rooted to the spot, not only the objects themselves but also the distances and empty spaces between them.

The light is that of early morning.

After the curtain has risen, two portières *to the right and left of the proscenium are revealed as* portières *to a* chambre séparée.

A WOMAN, *her hair wrapped in a white scarf, moves quickly but not hastily among the objects with a vacuum cleaner. She is in blackface. The vacuum cleaner, which was turned on the moment the curtain began to rise, makes a comparatively uniform noise.*

EMIL JANNINGS *sits at the table in the* fauteuil, *his legs on the appropriate footstool, his eyes closed. He is quite fat. His boots stand next to the stool. He is wearing red silk socks, black pants, and a light-coloured shirt, open at the collar. He seems costumed although only hints of a costume are visible: rather long frills on the sleeves of the silk shirt, a wine-red silk sash around his stomach. He is heavily made-up, his eyebrows painted. He wears several large rings on his right hand; his nails are painted black.*

He has not moved since the curtain rose, and the WOMAN *has nearly completed her work. Using one hand to push the vacuum cleaner back and forth near the newspaper table, she turns on the record player with the other. However, we hear only a few isolated sounds; the vacuum cleaner is too noisy.*

She takes the cleaner to the back wall and turns it off so that music becomes audible: 'The Garden Is Open' by Tuli Kupferberg. She pulls the cord out of the socket, rolls it up on the machine and places it behind the tapestry door.

While the record continues to play, she walks from object to object and takes off the loose covers, except those on the paintings and on the statue. Although she moves fairly slowly, her work proceeds quite rapidly – at least, one barely notices it. She pulls the cover from under EMIL JANNINGS *with a single movement and walks off to the left while the record is still playing.*

Then nothing moves onstage for a while except for the record.

The record player turns itself off and after a moment JANNINGS *slowly opens his eyes.*

JANNINGS (*with a cracked voice*). As I said – (*He clears his throat once and repeats in a firm voice.*) As I said. (*Pause.*) A bad moment.

RASPY VOICE (*behind the screen*). Why? (*He clears his throat twice, and the second time he does so he steps out from behind the screen, then repeats in a firm voice.*) Why?

It is HEINRICH GEORGE, *quite fat, his clothes also suggesting a costume, with braids trimming his jacket and lace-up shoes. He stands there.*

JANNINGS (*his head turned away slightly*). It's over already.
GEORGE (*taking a step towards* JANNINGS *and collapsing*). My foot fell asleep. (*He slowly rises again.*)

JANNINGS *reaches for the cigar box. He lifts it but cannot hold onto it so that it falls to the floor.*

So has my hand.

GEORGE *carefully walks up to* JANNINGS, *stops next to him. Both of them glance at each other for the first time, then look away again.* GEORGE *leans against the edge of the table, now sits down on it. The cigar box is lying on the floor between them. Both look at it.* JANNINGS *turns his head towards* GEORGE. GEORGE *slides off the table.* JANNINGS *points at the cigar box.* GEORGE *misunderstands the gesture and looks as if there was something to see on the box.*

JANNINGS (*going along with him; pointing as if he really wanted to point out something*). That blue sky you see on the label, my dear fellow, it really exists there.

GEORGE (*bending down for the cigar box, taking it and looking at it*). You're right! (*He puts the box back on the floor and straightens up.*)

JANNINGS. You're standing . . .

GEORGE (*interrupting him*). I can also sit down. (*He sits down in the fauteuil with the smaller footstool and makes himself comfortable.*) What did you want to say?

JANNINGS. You were standing just now: would you be kind enough to hand me the cigar box from the floor?

Pause

GEORGE. You were dreaming?

JANNINGS. When the nights were especially long, in winter.

GEORGE. You must be dreaming.

JANNINGS. Once, on a winter evening, I was sitting with someone in a restaurant. As I said, it was evening, we sat by the window and were talking about a corpse – about a suicide who leaped into the river. Outside it rained. We held the menus in our hands. 'Don't look to the right!'

GEORGE *quickly looks to the left, then to the right.*

. . . shouted the person opposite me. I looked to the right: but there was no corpse. Besides, my friend had meant I should not look on the right side of the menu because that was where the prices were marked. (*Pause.*) How do you like the story?

GEORGE. So it was only a story?

Pause

JANNINGS. When one tells it, it seems like that to oneself.

GEORGE. Like a story?

JANNINGS *nods. Pause. Then he slowly shakes his head.*

So you're wrong after all. Then it's true what you told me?

JANNINGS. I'm just wondering.

Pause

GEORGE. And how did it go on?

JANNINGS. We ordered kidneys *flambé*.

GEORGE. And you got them?

JANNINGS. Of course.

GEORGE. And asked for the bill and got it?

JANNINGS. Naturally.

GEORGE. And asked for the coats and got them?

JANNINGS. Why the coats?

GEORGE. Because it was a winter evening.

JANNINGS (*relieved*). Of course.

GEORGE. And then?

JANNINGS. We went home.

Both of them laugh with relief. Pause.

GEORGE. Only one thing I don't understand. Of what significance
     is the winter evening to the story? There was no need to
     mention it, was there?

JANNINGS *closes his eyes and thinks.*

Are you asleep?

JANNINGS (*opening his eyes*). Yes, that was it! You asked me
     whether I was dreaming and I told you of the sleep in winter
     nights when I then begin to dream towards morning, and as
     an example I wanted to tell you a dream that might occur
     during a winter evening.

GEORGE. Might occur?

JANNINGS. I invented the dream. As I said it was only an
     example. The sort of thing that goes through one's head . . .
     As I said – a story . . .

GEORGE. But the kidneys *flambé*?

JANNINGS. Have you ever had kidneys *flambé*?

GEORGE. No. Not that I know.

JANNINGS. If you don't know then you haven't had them.

GEORGE. No.

JANNINGS. You're disagreeing with me?

GEORGE. Yes. That is: no. That is: yes, I agree with you.

JANNINGS. In other words, when you mention kidneys *flambé* you talk about something you know nothing about.

GEORGE. That's what I wanted to say.

JANNINGS. And about something one doesn't know, one shouldn't talk, isn't that so?

GEORGE. Indeed.

JANNINGS *makes the appropriate gesture with his hand, turning up his palm in the process.* GEORGE *stares at it, and under the impression that* GEORGE *has found something on the palm* JANNINGS *leaves it like that. The hand now looks as if it is waiting for something – for the cigar box, say. After what has been said just now the hand has the effect of an invitation, so* GEORGE *bends down and puts the box in* JANNINGS'S *hand.*

A brief pause, as if JANNINGS *had expected something else. Then he takes the box with his other hand and puts it on his knee. He looks at his hand which is still extended.*

JANNINGS. That's not what I meant to say with that. It only seemed to me that you had noticed something on my hand. (*He opens the box top with his other hand and offers the box to* GEORGE, *who looks inside.*) Take one.

GEORGE *quickly takes a cigar.* JANNINGS *takes one too.* GEORGE *takes the box from Jannings and puts it back on the table. Each lights his own cigar. Both lean back and smoke.*

GEORGE. Haven't you noticed anything?

JANNINGS. Speak. (*Pause.*) Please go ahead and speak.

GEORGE. Didn't you notice how silly everything suddenly became when we began to talk about 'kidneys *flambé*'? No, not so much suddenly as gradually, the more often we mentioned the kidneys *flambé*. Kidneys *flambé*, kidneys *flambé*, kidneys *flambé*! And didn't it strike you why the kidneys *flambé* gradually made everything so hair-raisingly silly?

Pause

JANNINGS. Speak.

GEORGE. Because we spoke about something that wasn't visible at the same time. Because we mentioned something that wasn't there at the same time! And do you know how I happened to notice this?

Pause

JANNINGS. Speak.

GEORGE. When you made that gesture with your hand two minutes ago –

JANNINGS (*interrupting him*). Two minutes have passed since then?

GEORGE. It may also have been earlier. In any case – what was I about to say?

JANNINGS. When I made that gesture with my hand . . .

GEORGE. When you made that gesture with your hand I suddenly noticed the rings on your fingers and thought to myself: Ah, rings! Look at that, rings! Indeed: rings! And then I saw the rings again, and when what I thought and what I saw coincided so magically, I was so happy for a moment that I couldn't help but put the cigar box in your hand. And only then I noticed how ridiculous I had seemed to myself speaking all that time about kidneys *flambé*. I wasn't even myself any more, my hair stood on end when I spoke about them. And only when I saw the rings and thought: Ah, the rings! and then cast a *second* glance at the rings, did it seem to me as if I were no longer confused.

JANNINGS. And I felt you were handing me the box voluntarily.

GEORGE. Do you understand me?

JANNINGS. Personally, yes.
GEORGE. Take a look around.

They take a look around the room.

Car.

They hesitate a little, continue looking around the room.

Cattle prods.

They hesitate, continue looking around the room.

Bloodhounds.

They look around the room, hesitate.

Hunger oedemas.

Only JANNINGS *looks around the room, hesitates.*

Trigger button.
JANNINGS (*quickly looking at* GEORGE). You're right, let's talk about rings!
GEORGE. There's nothing left to say about the rings.
JANNINGS *remains silent.*

Irrelevant.
JANNINGS. Me?
GEORGE. The rings.
JANNINGS. And?
GEORGE (*irritated*). 'And' what?
JANNINGS (*irritated*). And?

Pause. The pause becomes more and more laden with animosity. Both smoke. When they notice that they are simultaneously drawing on their cigars, they stop and hold their breath. When one of them wants to blow out smoke, he notices that the other is just about to exhale and he hesitates; only then does he emit the smoke from his mouth.

(*Suddenly in a very friendly manner.*) And if they were *your* rings?

GEORGE (*suddenly looking at him in a very friendly manner*). But they are yours.

Pause. They hardly move. The pause becomes increasingly laden with animosity.

But they're *your* rings?

Suddenly JANNINGS *pulls the rings from his fingers.* GEORGE *understands, bends forward, spreading his fingers apart.* JANNINGS *places the rings on the table.* GEORGE *slips them on his fingers easily and as though routinely, almost without looking. He regards his hand.*

As though made for me! (*Pause.*) As if they had always belonged to me! (*Pause.*) They *were* made for me! (*Pause.*) And they *have* always belonged to me!

He holds the rings in the light so that they sparkle. He caresses them and touches each individually with his lips. He plays : points with the ringless hand at something, then points with the ringed hand at the same thing; places the ringless hand on his heart, then places the ringed hand on it; waves someone towards him with the ringless finger, then with the ringed one; threatens someone with the naked finger, then with the ringed one. He is intoxicated by the idea of ownership.

I can't even imagine my hand without rings any more! I can't it me – I can't myself – me myself – myself me – I can't myself me – I can't imagine myself without rings any more! Can you imagine me without rings?

JANNINGS *makes no reply.*

(GEORGE *sets out to make a speech.*) Expensive rings! Just as you, who are round, know no beginning and no end, in the same way – (*He hesitates and begins once more.*) And just as you transform the light that strikes you and are changed yourselves by the light in the same way – (*He hesitates. Pause.*) In any case – you elicit similes from me. Since I own you, you mean something to me. (*Pause.*) To wear rings on every finger – what does that mean? Wealth? Early death? To take care while climbing ladders? Job problems? Watch out, danger!?

Pause

JANNINGS. I've never dreamed of rings.
GEORGE. Because you never owned any.

Pause

JANNINGS. On the contrary, because I owned some. (*Pause.*) And they never elicited similes from me.
GEORGE. Because they weren't enough for you.

Pause

JANNINGS. On the contrary, because they were enough for me.

Pause

GEORGE. Just as . . .
JANNINGS. Again 'just – as'?
GEORGE. Bide your time! (*He begins once more.*) Just as there are born losers, born troublemakers, and born criminals . . .
JANNINGS. Who says they exist?
GEORGE. I do!
JANNINGS. That doesn't prove anything.

Pause

GEORGE. Have you ever heard people talk about a 'born loser'?
JANNINGS. Frequently.
GEORGE. And have you ever heard the expression 'born trouble-maker'?
JANNINGS. Indeed.
GEORGE. And the expression 'born criminal'?
JANNINGS. Of course.
GEORGE. But the expression 'a scurrying snake' – that you have heard quite frequently?

JANNINGS. No, never.

GEORGE. And have you ever heard of a 'fiery Eskimo'?

JANNINGS. Not that I know.

GEORGE. If you don't know it then you haven't heard of one either. But the expression 'a flying ship' – that you have heard?

JANNINGS. At most in a fairy tale.

GEORGE. But scurrying snakes *exist*?

JANNINGS. Of course not.

GEORGE. But fiery Eskimoes – they exist?

JANNINGS. I can't imagine it.

GEORGE. But flying ships exist.

JANNINGS. At most in a dream.

GEORGE. Not in reality?

JANNINGS. Not in reality.

Pause

GEORGE. But born losers?

JANNINGS. They do exist consequently.

GEORGE. And born troublemakers?

JANNINGS. They exist.

GEORGE. And therefore there are born criminals?

JANNINGS. It's only logical.

GEORGE. As I wanted to say at the time . . .

JANNINGS (*interrupting him*). 'At the time'? Has it been that long already?

GEORGE (*hesitating, astonished*). Yes, that's odd! (*He continues rapidly.*) Just as there are born losers, born troublemakers, and born criminals, there are (*he spreads his fingers*) born owners. Most people, as soon as they own something, are not themselves any more. They lose their balance and become ridiculous. Estranged from themselves they begin to squint. The bed-wetter who stands next to his bed in the morning . . . The bed signifies his possession. Or his shame? (*Brief moment of confusion, then he continues at once.*) I, on the other hand, am a born owner; only when I possess something do I become myself . . .

JANNINGS (*interrupting him*). 'Born owner?' I've never heard that expression.

Pause

GEORGE (*suddenly*). 'Life is a game' – you must have heard people say that?

JANNINGS *makes no reply.*

And a game has winners and losers, right?

JANNINGS *makes no reply.*

And those who don't get anything are the losers, and those who can have everything are the winners, right?

JANNINGS *makes no reply, only bends forwards, opens his mouth, but not to speak.*

And do you know the expression 'born winner'?

Silence. Suddenly both burst out laughing and slap each other's thighs. While doing so a woman appears above left on the staircase. She is beautiful. She is wearing a long dress in which she moves as though it were carrying her. She has appeared noiselessly and has walked down a few steps. She stops in the middle of the left staircase, puts her hand on the banister and turns her head a little: it is ELISABETH BERGNER. *Her hands are empty, no handbag.*

She observes the strange scene beneath her with eyes lowered: JANNINGS *and* GEORGE *are pulling each other's ears and patting each other's cheeks. She moves a few steps farther down and now remains standing, face forward, on the wide centre staircase.*

JANNINGS *is showing* GEORGE *the back of his hand;* GEORGE *replies by making a circle with his thumb and forefinger and then holding his hand in front of his face, and* JANNINGS *replies to this sign by holding both hands above his head, loosely clasping one wrist with thumb and forefinger of the other hand and letting the clasped hand circle about itself, whereupon both of them burst out laughing once again and start slapping each other's thighs, making exclamations such as* 'Exactly!' 'You guessed it!' *Then one of them slowly calms down while the other continues to slap his thighs.*

In the meantime two other persons have appeared on the right section of the staircase; both of them have stopped at once to observe the strange scene below. One can recognize who they are: ERICH VON STROHEIM *and* HENNY PORTEN. *He is impressive, wears – as the only hint of a costume – a red dressing gown over a grey waistcoat and trousers. She wears an evening dress with a velvet stole.*

As they appear, PORTEN *loudly claps her handbag shut and* VON STROHEIM *pulls up the zipper in the back of her dress, then fastens his collar button:* 'As I said . . .' *But it now becomes unclear how they belong together; they stand two steps apart.*

The noise of the handbag has led one of the men downstairs to quieten down gradually.

'Don't turn round!' *he says to the other.*

The other immediately turns around and sees the three persons standing on the staircase. 'No corpse,' *he says to the other.* 'You can turn round: everyone is alive.'

The other turns round, then rubs his eyes energetically.

'Don't you believe me?' *the first one asks.*
'I just wasn't prepared for such a bright light,' *the other replies.* 'I don't know that it was so late already. We've lost all track of time talking!'
'We?' *the first one asks at once.*
'I,' *answers the other.*

Pause

'Yes, me too,' *the first one says.*

PORTEN *is rocking back and forth on the stairway, playing with her stole; the others are rather quiet.*

PORTEN *slowly proceeds farther down the stairway, grazes* VON STROHEIM *with her stole, then exaggerates the way she steps around him.* VON STROHEIM *quickly overtakes her, stops with his back to her as if to block her path.* PORTEN *smoothes down the collar of his dressing gown (the back of which was turned up), blows softly on his neck and walks on. Where the two sections of the staircase join* VON STROHEIM *stops next to* BERGNER *and bends over her neck from the back. She slowly turns around, with eyes lowered, puts her arms around his neck, leans her head against his chest.* PORTEN *has come closer, touches* BERGNER'S *hip with the handbag.* BERGNER *turns her head towards* PORTEN, *frees herself from* VON STROHEIM, *with slow movements takes the handbag from* PORTEN *and dreamily hangs it over her own shoulder, and in the same manner offers her hand to* VON STROHEIM, *palm up. He suggests a kiss on the palm, then takes a step aside so that* PORTEN, *who in the meantime has stepped behind him, now 'takes her turn' and bends over the hand which* BERGNER *has turned over.* PORTEN *gives the incident a different interpretation by only looking at the hand over which she is bent. She straightens up, keeps the hand in hers, and leads it to* VON STROHEIM *as if she wanted to point out something on it to him.* VON STROHEIM *nods as if he had seen it too. This nodding, however, gradually becomes a sign that he agrees to the following :* PORTEN *leads* BERGNER'S *hand under* VON STROHEIM'S *vest and moves it around caressingly.* BERGNER *suddenly withdraws her hand and lets it drop. But it is* PORTEN *who lets out a brief scream. She makes a small curtsy in front of* BERGNER *and then suggests a bow in front of* VON STROHEIM. *Then she takes a step back, squints at one of the two — one doesn't know at whom — and proceeds to go down the few steps into the room.*

GEORGE *and* JANNINGS *have been the audience in the meantime. But when* PORTEN *begins to walk down they become alert and begin to count simultaneously:* 'One, two, three ...' PORTEN *slowly descends into the room.* 'Four, five, seven!' *She was just about to place her foot on the sixth step, now she hesitates as if she might fall, then runs back up the steps. She begins to walk down again.* 'One, two, three, four, five, six, and seven!' *But there is also an eighth step and* PORTEN, *thinking she had reached level ground, stumbles and staggers into the room, gasps for air, and quickly runs back upstairs as if she had been repulsed. She snuggles up to* VON STROHEIM.

'Courage. Get up your courage!' *they call to her from below. They whistle the way one whistles at a dog.* VON STROHEIM *puts his arm around her, supports her by the shoulder, proceeds to lead her slowly downstairs. Her eyes are closed.*

The two below have started counting again. 'One, two, three, four, five, six, seven, eight, nine!' *At* 'eight' VON STROHEIM *and* PORTEN *have safely arrived downstairs, but at* 'nine' *they walk down one more step, one that does not exist. They bounce on the floor, fall down to their knees, stagger.* PORTEN *wants to run back but* VON STROHEIM, *who is also unsteady on his feet, leads her to a sofa. He eases her down, but while he is doing so she clutches him, feels with one hand for the sofa, and then lets herself down gradually. She slowly leans back and sits there with tightly closed eyes, immobile, while* VON STROHEIM *walks step by step to the table where* JANNINGS *and* GEORGE *sit and watch. Hesitating after each movement, both hands propped up on it, he gradually sits down in the* fauteuil *without a footstool. He starts to lean back, stops, sits there quietly with open eyes. He blinks rapidly, at long intervals.*

The audience now looks up to BERGNER. *She stands there with lowered eyes.* GEORGE *and* JANNINGS *tiptoe quickly to the stairs and, each holding a finger to the other's mouth, lie down parallel to the lowest step, one on his back, the other on his stomach.* BERGNER *comes down the stairs and steps over the stomach and back on the floor, already on her way to the table. As* GEORGE *and* JANNINGS *get up and wipe the dust off each other's clothes, she has already settled in the easy chair, taken the cosy off the teapot, poured tea for herself,*

*and, without looking up, brought the cup to her lips – as if she had
done it all in a single movement.*

GEORGE *and* JANNINGS, *confused, walk back to the table.*

GEORGE. Once more, I offer you my *fauteuil.*

BERGNER *makes no reply.*

May I offer you my *fauteuil?*

BERGNER (*as if asleep*). On the street the insurmountable filth,
the frost, the snowstorms, the immense distances . . .

JANNINGS. What did she say?

GEORGE. Nothing. She is dreaming. (*To* BERGNER, *as to someone
who is talking in his sleep.*) Who are you?

BERGNER. I only walked into the parlour to turn off the light and
have been lost without a trace ever since.

GEORGE. Who?

BERGNER. Watch out! The candlestick is falling!

JANNINGS *and* GEORGE *turn around, but the candlestick stands
motionless on the table.*

BERGNER (*quickly opening her eyes; screaming*). Who are you?
What do you want? Where am I? (*During these questions she
has quietened down again and finished them only for form's sake.
She gets up and sits down in one of the free* fauteuils, *but leaps
up again at once.*) It's still warm! (*She tries the second* fauteuil
and gets up again at once.) How dare you offer me a chair that
is still warm!

JANNINGS. I?

BERGNER. No, he. (*She points at* GEORGE.)

PORTEN (*sitting quietly in the rear on the sofa, has opened her eyes.*)
What are snowstorms?

VON STROHEIM *stops blinking his eyes and follows the conversation.*

BERGNER (*to George*). Why don't you answer? (*To* JANNINGS.)
He doesn't answer.

JANNINGS *stammers.*

Think before you speak!

Pause

JANNINGS (*fluently*). Perhaps he felt you didn't expect an answer to your question.

BERGNER. Can't he answer for himself?

JANNINGS. I speak for him.

BERGNER. Are you more powerful than he is?

JANNINGS. Why? I mean, why do you ask?

BERGNER. Because you speak for him.

JANNINGS *is taken aback. He looks at* GEORGE, *who returns the glance.* JANNINGS *stammers. Pause.*

(*Quickly.*) Does he please you?

JANNINGS *nods absent-mindedly.*

Naturally, as your friend he can't help but please you.

JANNINGS. More powerful? Yes . . . yes, why not? (*To* GEORGE.) Right? I speak for you. That means you have to listen to what I say!?

GEORGE *nods playfully.*

You're not my friend! If someone has something to say here it's me!

Pause. JANNINGS *and* GEORGE *begin to play.*

JANNINGS (*dropping into the* fauteuil *and stretching out his feet*). The boots!

GEORGE *quickly steps up to him, gets down on one knee and pulls on* JANNINGS'S *boots.*

The tea!

GEORGE *quickly pours tea into a cup, hands him the cup.*

The sugar!

GEORGE *offers him the sugar bowl.*

> (*He takes a piece with the sugar tongs and elegantly lets it drop into the cup.*) A spoon!

GEORGE *hands him a spoon. Both grin, are close to giggling.*

> (JANNINGS *stirs once, snappily.*) The newspaper!

GEORGE *is already by the newspaper table and back.*

> My glasses!

GEORGE (*blurting out*). But you don't wear glasses!

JANNINGS (*snorting*). The mustard! The hairbrush! The . . . (*He hesitates.*)

GEORGE (*assisting him*). The photo album! The pincers!

JANNINGS (*with a surgeon's gesture*). The scalpel! The scissors!

GEORGE. A permanent – and fast!

JANNINGS (*reaching blindly behind him with gestures of a car mechanic*). The pliers! The monkey wrench! The soldering iron!

GEORGE. Hand over all your money, and make it snappy!

JANNINGS. The sun!

GEORGE (*hesitating*). Why the sun?

JANNINGS (*fatigued by the game*). The sun has come up.

GEORGE (*confused*). Why? I mean, why do you say that?

JANNINGS (*snapping at him*). Those are *my words*! (*As if exhausted.*) I don't know why.

GEORGE (*confused, but indifferent*). It doesn't change anything anyway, your saying so. (*He has spoken the last words to himself.*)

Meanwhile the dawn light onstage has gradually changed to a normal stage light.

VON STROHEIM (*finally*). Wrong! Entirely wrong! (*He gets up quickly.*)

BERGNER *turns towards him (previously she had turned away from the others as if disappointed).*

I'll show you how one does it!

Pause. They all prepare to watch. VON STROHEIM *slowly looks around as if he wanted to pick someone out.* GEORGE *and* JANNINGS *draw in their heads when his glance passes them. Finally* VON STROHEIM *observes* PORTEN. *Since his back is to the audience, the fact that he is looking at her can only be gleaned from her response to him. First she leans forward, sits upright. Then she rises like a sleep-walker, walks towards* VON STROHEIM, *stops in front of him. She seems to want to take off his dressing gown standing in front of him, but then she steps behind him and takes it off from behind; while doing so she does not appear to touch him. She walks to the tapestry door behind which the vacuum cleaner is stored, hangs the gown inside, takes out a wine-red smoking jacket; back again behind* VON STROHEIM, *she spreads it out and he slips into it; again they do not touch one another.*

GEORGE, *as a spectator, coughs.*

JANNINGS: Psst!

PORTEN *pulls* VON STROHEIM'S *cuffs from under his jacket sleeves. Pause.* VON STROHEIM *now describes a quarter-circle with his hand, signalling* PORTEN *to stand in front of him. She obeys immediately and in doing so makes sure never to turn her back to him. She stops in front of him. With his index finger, he beckons her to come closer. Pause.*

JANNINGS, *eagerly watching, points with a similar circular movement of his hand at the cigar box.* GEORGE, *also enthralled, has noticed the movement out of the corner of his eye and obeys blindly by handing* JANNINGS *the box from the table, still watching the two. Then he realizes what he has done and is quite startled. He looks toward* JANNINGS. *They look at one another rather startled and immediately reverse the action.* VON STROHEIM *pulls* PORTEN *closer to him by her stole. Playfully he steps a little to the side so that* PORTEN *is completely visible too. He grabs her under the chin with his index finger and lifts her face. Pause. He strokes the back of her head. Pause. He pats her fondly on the shoulder. Pause. He drums with two fingers on her cheek. Pause. He snaps his fingers against her teeth. Pause. He pulls her lower eyelid down with his finger. Pause. He gives her a pat on the behind, so that she goes half-down on her knees. Pause.* GEORGE *coughs.*

JANNINGS: Psst!

VON STROHEIM *turns* PORTEN *around – so that she stands with her back to him – and walks back a step. Pause.* GEORGE *coughs. Still sitting,* JANNINGS *gives him a kick.* GEORGE, *standing by the table, jerks forward a little; but* PORTEN, *as if she had been kicked, tumbles across the stage towards the sofa and remains lying in front of it. In fact,* VON STROHEIM *had already lifted his knee to administer a kick. Pause. Startled, they all look at each other. Pause.*

BERGNER. It's nice to watch when something is beginning to function smoothly. It's like watching a sale: move after move. Here the goods, there the money! Here the money, there the goods! Or like listening to two people talking: first the question, then the reply. Someone holds out his hand, the other shakes it. How are you, I'm fine! How do you like him, I think he's okay! Someone gets up, you're already leaving? Someone sighs, and you pat him. Oh, that's beautiful!

VON STROHEIM *slowly lowers his leg, turns around slightly dazed.* PORTEN *pulls herself up on the sofa and sits down, her face half turned away.*

GEORGE *sits down bewildered in the* fauteuil. JANNINGS *looks at the boot with which he kicked him. He pinches* GEORGE'S *leg and upper arm a few times.* GEORGE, *too, fiercely pinches his own upper arm once.* BERGNER *sighs. She walks up to* VON STROHEIM *then stops short. He comes towards her then stops. She takes his hand, puts it on her breast. She caresses herself with his hand until he begins to caress her.* PORTEN *suddenly gets up and runs towards the table.* GEORGE, *who from* PORTEN'S *viewpoint is sitting behind the table, stands up unintentionally.* BERGNER *and* VON STROHEIM *stop caressing each other and watch.*

GEORGE. What would you like? (*The words slipped out.*)
PORTEN (*like a customer*). Do you carry tear gas guns?
GEORGE. Tear gas guns? You mean 'tear gas guns'?
PORTEN. Aren't you a salesman?

GEORGE *makes no reply.*

> You were sitting behind the table and got up when I came in; you're a salesman, aren't you?

GEORGE *looks at* JANNINGS, *who signals to him to agree with her.*

GEORGE. Salesman? You mean I am a 'salesman'? Well, why shouldn't I be a salesman? I asked you, didn't I, 'What would you like?' What would you like? A weapon perhaps, for going home after dark?
PORTEN. A tear gas gun!
GEORGE (*to* JANNINGS, *who sits in his* fauteuil, *as if he were the boss*). Do we carry tear gas guns?

JANNINGS *pulls a small riding whip out of his boot and hands it to* GEORGE, *who puts it on the table.* PORTEN *looks at it without touching it.*

JANNINGS (*sitting with his face turned away from her*). This riding whip will do the trick too.
GEORGE. A riding whip like this one will do the trick too.
PORTEN. I want *this one.*
JANNINGS. Is she our first customer today?
GEORGE (*translating*). A customer like you should be treated like the first customer of the day. It's yours!
PORTEN (*taking the whip*). Is it a good one?
GEORGE. First-rate.
PORTEN. Can I believe you?

GEORGE. What reason would I have to trick you?

She hands the whip back to him, and he slashes through the air with it, audibly. Then he slaps the whip on the table.

Just imagine the sound in the dark! (*He hands her the whip.*)

PORTEN *repeats what he did, producing the same sounds. The whip still in her hand she pulls her dress up as far as her hip and pulls a large note of stage money out of her garter belt. She puts the note on the table and also places the whip next to it.*

GEORGE, *astonished, hands the whip back to her, then takes a few coins out of his trousers pocket and puts them on the table. While he is looking for banknotes in his other pockets,* PORTEN *takes the coins; but when he continues to search, she puts the coins back on the table.*

JANNINGS *gets up and flashes a few notes, which he counts into her hand one by one. He closes her fingers one by one over the notes; she closes the last finger (the index finger) herself, very slowly. It seems that she is beckoning him to come to her. At the same time they look into each other's eyes. All hold their breath.*

PORTEN *pushes the notes into her bodice; then slowly withdraws her hand, careful to indicate that the hand is now empty; touches her upper lip with her tongue; and gently flipping the whip back and forth, looks for a long time at the two salesmen until* GEORGE *shifts his weight from one leg to the other and shouts much too loud at* VON STROHEIM: 'Do you belong together?' VON STROHEIM *and* PORTEN *give each other a fleeting glance, then look away. A second glance: they look at each other as though for the first time.*

VON STROHEIM. Can't one tell by looking at us? (*He steps towards* PORTEN *and grabs her around the waist.*)

PORTEN *stops flipping the whip.*

GEORGE. Now, I guess.

PORTEN (*to* GEORGE *and* JANNINGS). And how is it with you two? Do you belong together?

GEORGE *and* JANNINGS *look at each other, look away. The second glance; they look at each other as though for the first time.*

GEORGE AND JANNINGS (*simultaneously*). Yes, he belongs to me.
GEORGE. Why?
JANNINGS. Because it has always been like that.
GEORGE. Who says that?
JANNINGS. People in general.
GEORGE. And why do you tell me that only now?
JANNINGS. There was no need to tell you until now.
GEORGE. And now it has become necessary?
JANNINGS (*looking at his old cigar*). Yes. (*He points with the cigar at the box of matches lying on the footstool.*)

GEORGE *bends down then hesitates and straightens up again.*

There, you see how necessary it was.

GEORGE, *confused, thereupon hands him the matches and* JANNINGS, *content, lights his cigar. He drops the match.*

You've lost something there.

GEORGE *glances briefly at the match, looks away. The second glance: he picks up the match and puts it in the ashtray.*

VON STROHEIM (*applauding by way of suggestion, but one can hear no clapping*). Much better already! Much better! Of course, if I were you . . .
PORTEN. Who's stopping you?
VON STROHEIM. Yes, who's stopping me? (*He takes a deep breath and assumes a pose.*)

JANNINGS *takes the coins from the table and flings them into* VON STROHEIM'S *face.* VON STROHEIM *shakes himself and comes to his senses.*

VON STROHEIM (*to* JANNINGS *and* GEORGE, *as if teaching them something*). You're still here?

JANNINGS (*repeating, but twice as loud*). You're still here?

VON STROHEIM. That's it! Exactly! That's how I would have done it!

Pause

    (*Signalling* JANNINGS *to go on speaking; prompting him.*) What do you want here?

JANNINGS. What do you want here?

VON STROHEIM. We just want to take a look around.

JANNINGS. This isn't an amusement park!

VON STROHEIM. Why don't you let *him* speak for himself?

JANNINGS *nods to* GEORGE *and sits down on the* fauteuil, *his back to the others.*

GEORGE. This is private property.

JANNINGS *nods.*

    You're not in a restaurant. You have nothing to say here. Please talk to each other only in whispers. If you must intrude here, at least take off your hats. Didn't you see the felt slippers by the entrance? Look at me: I'm talking to you. You're not at home here, where you can put your feet on the table. Where are we that anybody can come in? Look where you walk, mantraps and self-detonating charges have been set. Danger, rat poison. Don't touch anything. Vicious hounds. Long hard winter. Floods in spring, mud in the closets, no more cranes wake with their shrill screams in the meadows, no more May bugs buzz through the lime trees. (*Pause.*) It's terribly painful to be alive and alone at one and the same time.

Pause

VON STROHEIM. He'll never learn it.

Pause

GEORGE. It wasn't raining yet, but farther away one could hear it already raining . . .

VON STROHEIM turns away with PORTEN and walks around with her as if he wanted to inspect the furnishings. He tries to take out a magazine but when he straightens up with it, it turns out that the magazine is chained to the table, like a telephone book, and he quickly puts it back. Then PORTEN tries to pick up the little statue which is covered with a paper bag, but it turns out that the statue is either screwed or glued to the chest of drawers. She pulls the paper bag from the statue: it is a multicoloured painted dog, sitting in an upright position. She touches it and it squeaks: it is made of rubber. VON STROHEIM joins her and pulls on one of the chest drawers. It will not open although he makes repeated attempts. Finally he tries a different drawer, which opens very easily.

VON STROHEIM. You see!

They leave the drawer open and continue their inspection tour. He takes off and drops the cover from the first picture: a seascape, not a rough sea, not a calm sea, no ships, only ocean and sky.

Almost simultaneously PORTEN removes the cover from the second picture: a mirror with no particular characteristics. She settles down on the second, so far unused, sofa while VON STROHEIM returns from the bar with a bottle and two glasses. He sits down next to her and twists the bottle top but cannot open it. He casually blows into the glasses and a cloud of dust swirls into his face. He casually puts the glasses and bottle aside. He looks at his hands, turns one palm up and down.

PORTEN (*suddenly seizing his hand*). Watch out! (*Pause. She sees his hand.*) Oh, I see, it's only your hand. I thought, an animal.
VON STROHEIM. Why don't you look at me?
PORTEN. I don't dare look at you closely because I'm afraid I might catch you at something! (*She looks at him.*)

Pause. BERGNER has in the meantime gone to the mirror and calmly viewed herself in it.

C

GEORGE, *still standing, carefully wipes the cutlery on the table with a large red cloth he pulled out of his pocket and then places it – now and then he tries to set it up – on a second red cloth as if he were putting the cutlery on display. He and* JANNINGS *are spectators.*

PORTEN *has put* VON STROHEIM'S *hand on his knee and caresses her own hand with her other one.*

VON STROHEIM (*moving his lips soundlessly, though every so often a word becomes audible*). Snowploughs ... hedges ... a dog portrait? (*At one point he presses down the intertwined fingers of both hands so that the joints crack.*)

BERGNER *is combing her hair but with increasingly insecure movements. She does not know in which direction to comb while viewing herself in the mirror. With a small pair of scissors she wants to cut a strand of hair, holding it away from her head, but keeps missing until she finally lets go of the strand. She wants to put on make-up, pencils in eyebrows and eyelines, puts rouge on her cheeks, powders her nose, puts on lipstick. But as she does this her movements become shaky and contradictory. She confuses the direction in which she wishes to draw the lines. She is mixed up. She starts to put the cosmetics back into her handbag but they fall down. She walks away. She turns around, walks in the opposite direction, looking back over her shoulder at the same time, turns around again. She is completely confused, her face is badly made-up. She walks in a direction where no one is and says:* 'Help me!' *but with gestures, hopping around. She bumps into things, bends down for things that already lie behind her.*

PORTEN (*calling to her*). Open your eyes! Say something! Pull yourself together!

But BERGNER *turns her head not towards her, but in another direction.*

(PORTEN *gets up and walks up to her from behind.*) Don't be frightened.

BERGNER (*startled, looking up towards the stairs; trying to point to the seascape but unable*). It winked at me! It's winking at me!

PORTEN *calms her down by caressing her and leading her around the room. Together they bend down for the coins and other things on the floor. At first* PORTEN *guides* BERGNER'S *hand; then* BERGNER *reaches for the things herself and also points at them correctly again. While doing this they talk to each other, and the longer they talk, the more sure of themselves and graceful they become.*

PORTEN. Once when it rained I walked with an open umbrella across a wide, heavily travelled street. When I had finally reached the other side, I caught myself closing the umbrella.

BERGNER. And once when I – please, help me. (*She is still unsure of herself.*)

PORTEN (*taking her and wiping her face with the stole*). Once when I bent down over a bouquet of carnations while there was a great deal of noise around me, I couldn't smell anything at first.

BERGNER. Once when I put a tablecloth over – (*She can't think of the word and becomes afraid again.*) Please help me.

PORTEN (*now speaking very distinctly to set an example*). Once I walked down a stairway and had such a desire to let myself fall that I began to run out of fear as soon as I had reached the bottom.

BERGNER (*breathing a sigh of relief*). Once when I wanted to put a tablecloth over a table, I was with my thoughts (*she delicately points to the picture*) at the seashore and caught myself shaking the tablecloth as if wanting to signal with it.

They embrace, then dance around while they put the coins and cosmetics into the handbag. They talk and move more and more lightheartedly.

PORTEN. Why 'caught myself'? Why not: 'I saw myself,' 'I noticed'?

BERGNER. I saw myself! I noticed myself! I heard myself!

They stand facing one another.

PORTEN. Someone keeps looking over his shoulder while he's
    walking – does he have a bad conscience?
BERGNER. No, he's simply looking over his shoulder from time to
    time.
PORTEN. Someone is sitting there with lowered head – is he sad?
BERGNER (*assuming a modelling pose for her reply*). No, he's simply
    sitting there with lowered head!
PORTEN. Someone is flinching. Conscience-stricken?
BERGNER (*answering in another modelling pose*). No, he's simply
    flinching.
PORTEN. Two people sit there, don't look at each other and are
    silent – are they angry with one another?
BERGNER (*delivering her sentence in a new pose*). No, they simply
    sit there, don't look at each other and are silent!
PORTEN. Someone is banging on the table – to get his way?
BERGNER (*in a different pose*). Couldn't he simply be banging on
    the table?

*They run towards each other with a little yelp of joy, embrace and
separate again at once, looking at one another tensely.*

(*Points to* GEORGE.) He's polishing the cutlery and putting it
on display on a red cloth – does he want to sell it?

PORTEN, *standing there with arms hanging down, just shakes her
head briefly.*

GEORGE, *feeling as if released, begins to polish the utensils lightheartedly.*

(*Pointing to* JANNINGS.) He turns his back on us, sits in the
most comfortable *fauteuil* – does that mean he's more powerful than all of us?

PORTEN *looks into her eyes and just shakes her head briefly.*

JANNINGS, *relieved, stretches in his* fauteuil, *obviously delighted to have lost his significance.*

> (*Pointing with her head to* VON STROHEIM.) He's sitting alone in the corner on a big sofa – does he want to tell us that we should sit down next to him?

PORTEN *now merely smiles indulgently, as one does about something that has turned out to be a dream.* VON STROHEIM *also forgets himself, smiles amiably and is obviously relaxing.*

And the mirror over there?

JANNINGS (*getting up and strolling towards the women*). It's quite simply a mirror.

GEORGE (*joining in*). Perhaps there's fly shit on it!

BERGNER. And why can't the drawer be pulled out of the chest?

JANNINGS (*hesitating just slightly*). It's stuck!

BERGNER. And why is it stuck?

VON STROHEIM (*jumping off the sofa*). Let it be stuck!

GEORGE. Yes, let it be stuck!

GEORGE AND VON STROHEIM (*skipping and dancing towards each other, lifting their legs like dancing bears*). Let it be stuck!

JANNINGS (*joining them*). Let it be stuck! Let it be stuck!

GEORGE, VON STROHEIM AND JANNINGS (*dancing around one another*). Let it be stuck, the drawer! The drawer, oh, let it be stuck! Let it, the drawer, let it, oh, let it be stuck! (*They sing in unison.*) Oh, let the drawer be stuck, oh, oh, let the drawer be stuck!

They stand still and sing the same words to the melody of 'Whisky, Please Let Me Alone' in a canon with assigned voices, with a break in the middle, after an 'Oh,' whereupon they all look at one another in silence, raise their index fingers, and one of them continues singing an octave lower: '. . . Let the drawer be stuck!' whereupon the other two voices also join in one by one, also an octave lower, and they finish singing the song in harmony. They all look at one another gravely and tenderly.

We're free? We're free? (*Pell-mell.*) We only dreamed all
that! Did we only dream all that? What? I have already
forgotten! And I'm just noticing how I'm forgetting! I'm
standing quite still and am observing how I gradually forget.
I'm trying to remember, but as I'm trying to remember, I
notice that it sinks down lower and lower – it is as if I had
swallowed something, and with each attempt to regurgitate
it, it slips down lower and lower. It is sinking and you loom
more and more prominently! Where have you been, I was
looking for you?! Who are you? Do I know you?

*They embrace, bend their heads towards each other, hide their heads
among each other, rub them together, caress each other with heads and
hands. They let go of each other and busy themselves lightheartedly
with the objects, touch them, press them to their bodies, lean playfully
against them, prop them up, cradle them in their arms, bring two
objects into contact as if in an embrace, pinch, pat, and caress them,
wipe dust off them, remove hairs from them . . . While doing so they
sigh, hum, giggle, laugh, trill . . . Only once do they become briefly
uncertain and quiet: one of the women stands leaning against the
banister, her face turned away and her shoulders twitching. After an
anxious moment one of the men walks up to her and timidly turns her
around: she is laughing quietly, and gradually they all become merry
again.*

*At one point one of the men walks from one end of the stage towards the
others, who are simultaneously walking towards him. It appears they
will collide, but at the very moment one pictures them colliding he
feints with his body and steps elegantly aside. He does that across the
entire stage. The other men imitate him, walk towards the women and
skirt them elegantly before walking on in the same direction; likewise
the three men avoid objects. They are delighted with each other, and
the women laugh.*

*One of them turns a cartwheel; the other leaps merrily over an
obstacle when he could have just as simply stepped; the third makes*

an elegant gesture with his lower arm by lifting it and quickly bending his elbow, letting, as if by magic, his sleeve slip to his elbow. He repeats this several times and finally, with the same movement, playfully gives himself a light. Finally, as if a matter of course, one after the other sits down by the table, the women in the fauteuils *with the footstools,* VON STROHEIM *in the* fauteuil *without footstool,* JANNINGS *in the easy chair,* GEORGE *in the straight chair. As in an after-image they still hint at their previous playful acts, still repeat what they said to one another :* 'I forgot myself completely! "I?" We! We forgot ourselves!'

Finally they calm down. Only BERGNER *is still playing with her handbag and doesn't know where she should leave it.*

VON STROHEIM. Why don't you leave it on your lap? Having something on your lap is most pleasant.

GEORGE (*it having occurred to him simultaneously*). . . . Something on your lap is most pleasant.

They laugh.

In your lap you have the most pleasant feeling for something.

PORTEN (*it occurred to her too, but a little later*). In your lap you have the most pleasant feeling for something.

They all laugh.

BERGNER *cautiously puts the handbag on her lap, and with little wiggling movements puts herself into a comfortable position in the* fauteuil. *She emits a small sound. All of them try what it is like to have things on one's lap, are satisfied and put the things back in their places.*

(PORTEN *shows her naked arm to* VON STROHEIM.) You see, I've got goose pimples.

VON STROHEIM. Are you . . . Do you feel – (*He stops in time.*) So you have goose pimples, do you? (*He laughs.*)

All laugh as if it were an unpleasant memory.

PORTEN. Yes, I simply have goose pimples.

Pause. JANNINGS *pulls something out of his upholstered seat. He holds it up and shows it to* GEORGE. *At the same time, as if unintentionally, he elongates one eye with the index finger of his other hand.* GEORGE *ignores this, bends towards what* JANNINGS *has in his hand.*

VON STROHEIM (*also turning his head towards* JANNINGS; *in a playful mood*). You have something there. What is it? Nothing special I assume. There's no need to talk about it, is there?

BERGNER *and* PORTEN *turn their heads slightly too but look away again immediately.*

JANNINGS. A pin.

They all look at it as though surprised.

VON STROHEIM. A pin? You don't mean 'the pin'?
JANNINGS. The very one.
PORTEN. And it really exists? It isn't merely a figure of speech?
JANNINGS. Please, convince yourself.

He hands the pin to GEORGE, *who hands it to* VON STROHEIM *very matter-of-factly, who hands it to* PORTEN.

PORTEN. It has all turned out to be true. Not even the ruby-red pinhead is missing. It has all come true.
VON STROHEIM. Did you dream of it?
PORTEN. Someone mentioned it in the dream. (*She hands the pin to* BERGNER.) When I saw the pin just now. I remembered it again. And I had thought it was just another word.
GEORGE. Once someone told me about a corpse with a pinhead-sized wound on its neck. (*Pause. To* JANNINGS.) Did *you* tell me about that?
JANNINGS. I can't remember. But when you started telling the story, it seemed familiar to me too.
GEORGE. No it was a movie. (*Pause.*) It was thundering and at the same time fog banks on the village street . . .

BERGNER. Should I drop it?

They all become quiet and do not move. She drops the pin.

GEORGE (*negating the effect by speaking again too soon*). Children
with lumps of plaster on their eyes – (*He breaks off, but it is
already too late.*)

They only smile, leave the pin where it fell.

VON STROHEIM. I already told you the story about the lake?
PORTEN. No.

He looks at BERGNER: *she shakes her head tenderly.*

JANNINGS (*simultaneously*). No.
VON STROHEIM. Then I probably only thought I did.
PORTEN. Has it anything to do with the pin?
VON STROHEIM. I was sitting by a lake shore in the morning
and the lake was sparkling. Suddenly I noticed: the lake is
sparkling. It is really sparkling.

Pause.

PORTEN. Something similar happened to me once when someone told me that his pockets were empty. 'My pockets are
empty!' I didn't believe him and he turned his pockets
inside out. They really were empty. Incredible!

GEORGE *takes a cigar out of the cigar box, then offers the box to*
JANNINGS, *who takes out a cigar.* GEORGE *strikes a match and
hands it to* JANNINGS *who lights his cigar and blows out the match.*
GEORGE *lights himself another match.*

VON STROHEIM *takes the red cloth from the table, jumps up with it,
walks around with it, shakes it as if he wanted to display it to them.
They bend forward, inspect.* VON STROHEIM *looks around trium-
phantly. They nod, shake their heads surprised, laugh with delight,
slap their thighs with laughter. Exclamations such as:* 'A red cloth,
indeed!' 'No doubt about it!' '*Lupus in fabula,*' 'Talk of the devil!'
'Atlantis has reappeared!'

VON STROHEIM *stands in front of the others, like a magician. He turns all his pockets inside out very fast – the pockets are very wide and light-coloured – and strikes a pose.* PORTEN *claps her hands vigorously.* VON STROHEIM, *as magician, takes off his smoking jacket in a jiffy, turns it inside out and quickly puts it back on.*

JANNINGS (*enthusiastically*). So it is true!

VON STROHEIM *produces a small imitation of a rolling pin out of his pocket, which is now the magician's pocket.*

(*Exclaiming so that the cigar drops out of his mouth.*) Not merely in jest then!

GEORGE *hands him the cigar.*

JANNINGS (*wiping the ashes off his knees; stopping suddenly, noticing what he's doing; continuing to clean in a merry ritual*). Ashes on my suit! When I tell about that no one will believe me.

They all laugh. VON STROHEIM *conjures up the magician's magic cloth, a flag with colours not signifying any particular country. He blows on the flag briskly, making it flutter.*

JANNINGS. Indeed, it flutters! The flag flutters!

VON STROHEIM *stashes the things in his pockets, becomes an actor: he walks to the bar, takes out a bottle, fondles it, then leans back, supporting himself with one hand on the table.*

(*Calmly translating this for* GEORGE.) He is fondling the bottle and supporting himself with his hand on the table.

VON STROHEIM *moves to the side of the table, dangles the bottle by the neck, and begins to squint.*

(*To* GEORGE.) He is holding the bottle by the neck and squinting.

VON STROHEIM *puts the bottle back and moves through the room*

*with hunched shoulders, making an unnecessarily wide curve around
each object but at the same time scrutinizing each.*

He is hunching his shoulders, looking at the objects, yet
making a curve around them.

VON STROHEIM (*returns to the table; as a teacher*). And now for
the practical application: someone fondles an object or leans
against it?

GEORGE. The proprietor.

VON STROHEIM. Someone moves with hunched shoulders among
objects, makes a curve around them?

GEORGE. The guest.

VON STROHEIM. Someone who is squinting holds an object in his
hand?

GEORGE. The thief.

JANNINGS. Someone fondles an object because it belongs to
him. Because someone fondles the object, does it belong to
him?

VON STROHEIM. Unless you prove the opposite.

JANNINGS. Someone with an object in his hand begins to squint.
Because he has stolen it?

VON STROHEIM. Unless he proves his innocence.

JANNINGS. Someone suddenly puckers up his mouth and nose.
(*He demonstrates how.*) Because he's afraid and a coward?

VON STROHEIM. Unless his actions prove the opposite.

JANNINGS. But if there's nothing to do?

VON STROHEIM. What else would he be afraid of?

JANNINGS. I don't understand that.

VON STROHEIM. What you're sitting in is an easy chair, isn't
it?

JANNINGS. Yes.

VON STROHEIM. Or is it perhaps a life preserver?

JANNINGS *laughs at this extraordinary suggestion.*

Just as ridiculous as it seems to you when I claim that you
are sitting on a life preserver would it therefore be to claim

that someone's mouth and nose pucker up (*he imitates the expression*) because he feels like doing something.

Pause

JANNINGS. But an easy chair is an easy chair, and an expression (*he makes one*) is an expression. How can the two be compared?

VON STROHEIM. I'll demonstrate it to you.

Pause. They all wait. Pause.

(*Suddenly.*) What do you have in your mouth?

JANNINGS *quickly takes the cigar out of his mouth and puts it out.*

(*Smiling.*) Why is your collar button open?

JANNINGS *nimbly closes his collar button.*

You are so serious.

JANNINGS *laughs resoundingly. Pause. Quiet. Pause.*

JANNINGS (*softly*). You have something on your nose.

VON STROHEIM (*about to wipe it off, hesitating; softly*). You've understood?

Pause

JANNINGS (*suddenly loud*). You're just standing there, please hand me the bottle.

VON STROHEIM *plays along, hands him the bottle.*

No, not that one, the other one! (*He points.*) No, not that one, one can't ask for anything any more. Yes that's the one! (*But he hands the bottle back to him at once.*) Put it back in its place!

VON STROHEIM (*like a teacher who is playing a student*). Why?

JANNINGS. Because you took it from its place.

VON STROHEIM *nods, puts the bottle back.*

No, not there. Back in its place, I said. Over there, to the right.

VON STROHEIM. Why precisely there?

JANNINGS. Because that's where it stood before.

VON STROHEIM *nods.*

Give me another bottle.

VON STROHEIM. Why?

JANNINGS. Because you gave me a bottle once before.

VON STROHEIM. That's perfect! (*He hands him the bottle.*)

JANNINGS: You're standing?

VON STROHEIM *moves to sit down on a sofa.*

Back in your place!

VON STROHEIM *sits down in his place. Playfully,* JANNINGS *assigns the following roles: he hits the bottleneck with a teaspoon;* GEORGE *gets up.*

(*Without looking at him.*) Cartwheels!

GEORGE *stands there.*

VON STROHEIM (*prompting him*). Why?

GEORGE. Why?

JANNINGS. Because you did a cartwheel before!

Pause. GEORGE *turns a cartwheel.* JANNINGS *hands him the magazine.* GEORGE *does not yet understand this language; he doesn't know what to do with the magazine, glances into it.*

Pass it on.

GEORGE. Why?

JANNINGS. Didn't you also pass the pin before?

Pause. GEORGE *hands the magazine to* VON STROHEIM *who gives it back to* GEORGE *as if the pages were mixed up.* GEORGE *understands: he arranges the pages and hands the magazine back to* VON STROHEIM, *who puts it on the table.*

JANNINGS *pulls the second red cloth from under the cutlery on the table and lets it drop. He points to it with the spoon. Pause.*

Well?

GEORGE. Why?

JANNINGS. Didn't you just do a cartwheel?

GEORGE. But how can you compare the two?

JANNINGS. For whom did you do the cartwheel?

GEORGE. For you – (*He hesitates.*)

JANNINGS. 'Of course,' you wanted to say, right?

GEORGE. For you, of course.

JANNINGS. If you can do a cartwheel for me, you can also pick
up a cloth for me.

Pause

GEORGE (*starting to bend down for the piece of cloth, hesitating*). But
what if I don't want to?

JANNINGS. It's too late for that now. All the time you did as I
asked and never said anything. You were content until now
or you would have said something. So why should you be
dissatisfied now? You didn't contradict me at any time. Why
should you be allowed to contradict me now? No, what you
utter now isn't valid any more. Do as I say!

Pause. GEORGE *picks up the cloth, moves to hand it to* JANNINGS
(*who doesn't even bother to extend his hand*), *hesitates, lets it drop
again as if his hand had fallen asleep. Pause.*

JANNINGS (*in a sensible tone of voice*). Look at the others. (*He
turns his head to* VON STROHEIM, *then to* PORTEN.)

VON STROHEIM *at once goes up to* BERGNER *with the guitar* (*which
he takes out of its bag while walking*), *sits down behind her and
picturesquely strikes two soft chords.* PORTEN *sits down on*
JANNINGS'S *knees and makes herself comfortable.*

If *they* do as they are told – why don't you too?

Pause

GEORGE. But why do they do it?

JANNINGS. First obey! Then we can talk about it.

Pause. GEORGE *hands him the cloth, which* JANNINGS *places
picturesquely around* PORTEN'S *shoulders, tying it under her chin.*

(*To* PORTEN.) Well?

She kisses him without moving her head.

Now ask!

GEORGE. Why do they do that? Why do they listen to you?

VON STROHEIM *strikes another picturesque chord.*

JANNINGS. Because it is natural to them. They did it once without my saying anything while they were half asleep, or
because it just happened like that. Then I said it and they did
it again. Then they asked me: 'May I do that for you?' and I
said: 'You shall!' And from then on they did it without my
having to say anything. It had become the custom. I could
point my *foot* at something and they would jump and get it.
Nothing but laws of nature. People began to socialize with
one another and it became the rule.

BERGNER (*on cue, as though talking in her sleep*). How are you; I'm
fine, thanks. (*She sighs.*)

JANNINGS. An order resulted; and for people to continue to
socialize with one another, this order was made explicit: it
was formulated. And once it had been formulated, people
had to stick to it because, after all, they had formulated it.
That's natural, isn't it? Say something! No, don't say anything, *I* am speaking now. Don't touch that, it's mine. (*He
pushes a candlestick away.*) Don't dare stare at it, it's my
property! What was I talking about? Help me! No, don't say
anything. About the laws of nature. (*He takes an ashtray into
his hand, then lets it drop.*) Just as this ashtray obeys the law of
gravity, so you obey me. Well?

He points with his foot, GEORGE *puts the ashtray back on the table.*

You see? Do you believe me now? No, don't answer. I'll
answer for you. I can imagine your answer: Yes, that business
with the ashtray and force of gravity is true enough. Do you
know what the difference is between you and me?

GEORGE *laughs as though before a joke.*

No, no joke: I *can* imagine you sometimes, you *must* imagine me always. Why aren't you laughing? By the way, this reminds me of a real joke: What's the name of the man who invented the chair? Well? Nothing? I'll help you. What's the name of the man who invented the zeppelin? (*Pause. He laughs invitingly.*) You're not laughing. Okay! But I'll make a note of it. Where was I? Hadn't I asked you to remind me what else I wanted to talk about? Didn't I see you nod? Then I only imagined that I saw you nod. Once I thought of a conversation I had with someone, and I remembered distinctly how he'd smiled when he answered me, and then it occurred to me that I had been talking to him on the telephone! The laws of nature! The trains! The ocean! He stood where you're standing now!

GEORGE, *startled, steps aside;* JANNINGS *bursts out laughing, drops the ashtray again.*

I'd like to pick it up for you, but I have to stick to what I said. (*To* PORTEN.) Right?

She nods.

I can't say something and then do the opposite. Inconceivable! That would be a topsy-turvy world. Do you understand that?

PORTEN *tries to reach backwards for the ashtray.*

Stop, that's his job!

GEORGE *puts the ashtray on the table;* VON STROHEIM *touches the guitar almost accidentally – a gentle chord.*

So you understand. Just as the trains must obey a schedule so that there is no disorder, you must obey me. That business with the trains and their schedule is probably true, you say? I dare you to tell me that! Keep quiet! Answer!

GEORGE *tries to speak.*

Forget it! Like a maggot that crawls across one's palm – no, that belongs somewhere else. The ocean! What are you thinking of just now? You can say it? Then you're not thinking of anything. I once lived for some time by the ocean, and since I lived there, in what categories would you imagine I began to think? In the categories of low and high tide! And that's how it is generally (*as though to the audience*): the manner in which one thinks is determined by laws of nature! (*Again to* GEORGE.) For example, since I've started taking walks through the woods, at the sight of the weak and the strong, I always think in terms of the law of nature. And since I learned how to read menus – (*he pushes* PORTEN *off his knees and she runs quickly to the sofa, cuddles up on it; he looks towards her*) – I think about women, whether I want to or not, in categories of hors d'oeuvre and main dish.

She looks at him, but one feels the look rather than actually seeing it.

She doesn't want it differently – ask her yourself. She'll show you. (*He snaps his fingers at her and she responds.*)

PORTEN (*as though by rote*). Do I talk too much for you? Are my knees too bony? Am I too heavy? Is my nose too big? Am I too intelligent for you? Do you find me too loud? Are my breasts too small? Do you think I'm too fat? Am I too fast for you? Am I too skinny for you? Was I good?

JANNINGS. You see, she herself uses the categories in which one thinks of her. (*To* PORTEN.) Hey!

She comes back and sits down on his knees.

When I was called all I said at first was 'Yes!' After all, it was possible that they only wanted to know whether I was still there. Where were we?

GEORGE *puts his hand to the back of his head, lowers his hand again.*

Stop! Repeat that gesture!

GEORGE *repeats the gesture.*

D

It reminds me of something. More slowly!

GEORGE *repeats the gesture.*

The hat! Do you know the song 'Me Hat, It Has Three Corners'? It's a folksong. (*He recites it seriously.*)

> Me hat, it has three corners
> Three corners has me hat
> And if it hadn't three corners
> It wouldn't be me hat.

Ever since I've known that song I've been incapable of imagining such a hat. A three-cornered hat: an impossible idea! A hat: an impossible, a forbidden idea! Once I ordered (or did I?) that a cake be cut. 'Where?' I was asked. Ever since then I've been unable to imagine a cake. You try drawing a circle in your mind but you don't know where to begin. Finally there's a noise in the brain as if a boiling egg were popping. Quiet! Shut up! I can imagine what you want to say! The circle! I become dizzy when I'm supposed to imagine it! And when I become dizzy, I become furious. For example, someone asks me what time it is. Can you imagine a person who doesn't have a watch? I certainly can't. Dizziness and anger! Or: a person looks 'desperate', starts all sorts of jobs but stops them all again at once. Can you imagine anyone still being seriously desperate? Dizziness! Dizziness and anger! Or someone ashamed? Dizziness and anger, dizziness and anger! Then the contrary: someone is ashamed for someone else? I for you? At once – you cannot imagine me ashamed for you? (*He pushes the cigar box off the table so that all the cigars fall out, puts* PORTEN *in her* fauteuil, *stands in front of* GEORGE *and claps his hands, pretending to slap him, and sits down again.*) Like chocolate and soap – yes, like chocolate that lies next to a piece of soap. I, at any event, have never felt ashamed – except for that time when I compared two feelings I had for someone to chocolate and soap. And then once more. (*Pause.*) And then the story with the maggot on the palm of the hand. (*Pause.*) And then once when I was asked: 'Who is that?' and I answered: 'That one? Yes, she's very touching, isn't she?' (*Pause.*) Yes, and then one more time. (*He laughs shamefully, remembering.*) And then once when I said: 'Those present naturally excluded!' And another time when I heard someone say 'She's ugly!' and replied: 'But she has pretty eyes.' (*Pause.*) And then just one more time when I put a book of matches on the counter and the salesman asked me: 'Is that *you*?' (*Pause; puzzled.*) Actually, I've been ashamed quite frequently. (*Pause; to* VON STROHEIM.) Should I make *him* feel ashamed?

VON STROHEIM (*striking the body of the guitar and spreading his fingers*). Just so he doesn't put you to shame.

JANNINGS (*turning to* GEORGE). Look over here!

Successively, he takes several objects from the table or out of his pocket and shows them to GEORGE. GEORGE *looks helplessly at each of them. Finally* JANNINGS *shows him some paper money, waves it, and* GEORGE *quickly tries to grab it.*

(*Laughing.*) This language he understands! This language he understands! (*He laughs again.*)

Pause. They both lower their heads.

(JANNINGS *scratches himself vehemently once. Suddenly pointing angrily at the cigars.*) What's that?

GEORGE. Cigars.

JANNINGS. And what's that supposed to mean? Pick them up!

GEORGE *bends down.*

(*Giggling.*) Can you imagine doing anything but what I tell you to?

GEORGE *tries to imagine it. Finally he also starts giggling, but stops again and tries to think once more.*

Imagine you're sitting in my place.

GEORGE *looks up at him. He begins to giggle.* JANNINGS *giggles too, but differently; he looks around himself.* PORTEN *is also giggling.* VON STROHEIM *is smiling.* BERGNER *appears absent-minded.* GEORGE *collects the cigars and carefully puts them back in the box.*

(*Watching him; starting to tell a story.*) Once – (*To* PORTEN.) Why are you grinning?

PORTEN. I'm not grinning. I'm smiling.

JANNINGS. Stop fidgeting!

PORTEN. I'm not fidgeting, I'm making myself comfortable.

JANNINGS. Shut your trap!

PORTEN. I don't have a trap.

JANNINGS (*already turning back to his story*). I had a bad day. You know what that is like.

GEORGE *nods.*

I burned my tongue on the coffee; as I was tying my shoe-laces I suddenly had two pieces in my hands, you know what that's like.

GEORGE *nods.*

Just as suddenly – Why 'just as suddenly'? What's the difference! In any case, as I was writing down what I planned to do, the tip of the pencil broke off. I found another pencil (no, not what you're thinking: the pencil did write); however, all at once I noticed that overnight I'd begun to write one letter differently from the way I used to, with a curlicue where I'd never before made a curlicue in my entire life! You know what that's like.

GEORGE *nods, but only after* JANNINGS *has given him a look.*

To top it all, I suddenly saw before me a woman stamping on eggshells. I tore her away by the hair, you know what that's like. But it turned out that she was purposely breaking up the shells for the birds. Dazed, I walked on and noticed another madman. He was running back and forth on a piece of land, and a crowd had already formed around him. Then it turned out that he wasn't mad at all, but the owner of the land was trying to keep people from trespassing. Even more dazed, I walked on and my thoughts were busy with a goose that I was in the process of carving up, very fastidiously – you know what I'm like, very fastidious – when someone grabbed me by the arm from behind. Despite or just *because* of my dazed state – (*he smirks*) whenever I say *despite* I must also say *because* of – I swivelled around and gave this some-one a slap in the face. My hand slipped, you know what that is like: I thought someone with greasy fingers had grabbed me. Suddenly – yes, another *suddenly*, that day passed in leaps and bounds – I stood before a dog squatting with quivering behind at the kerb – *quivering*: I've never used that word before! – to take a crap, you know what that's like. I, no lazybones myself – (*to* GEORGE, *who hesitates*) don't let me stop you from your work – gave him a kick . . .

PORTEN. Don't go on, please! I don't want to have to dream about it!

GEORGE. Once my mind was on a child and a hot iron, and when I suddenly saw someone reaching for the door handle, I shouted at him: *Don't touch!*

JANNINGS. You can talk and stack cigars *evenly* at one and the same time?

GEORGE *continues to work in silence.*

. . . and went home. Luckily the sun set very rapidly as it always does in the tropics – that's how it's decribed in all the stories, right? – and as I slowly opened the door, there was a soft rustling behind it. (*Slowly* and *softly* usually go together!) I immediately fired through the panel – and I had spread the papers on the floor myself to frighten burglars when they opened the door. A bad day! Later, I dozed off in my rocking chair. Suddenly I awoke and saw the dog running past. A quick slap with the riding whip – you know what that's like?

GEORGE *nods.*

> But it was my own feet: waking up, I'd taken my black socks
> for the dog. (*Pause.*) You have nothing to say?

GEORGE. I feel no need to say anything.

JANNINGS. It's enough that I feel the need to hear something
from you.

GEORGE. But what if I feel the need to remain silent?

JANNINGS. Then you must say to yourself that in regard to your
needs, what matters for me is I have the need that you do
what you must do in any case. (*Pause.*) Say something!

Pause.

GEORGE. But what did you want to prove with the story? You
didn't tell the story just to tell a story?

JANNINGS. I told it so you would know what it is like when a
whole day passes and one feels at odds.

GEORGE. At odds with what?

JANNINGS. With one's work.

GEORGE. You were working at the time?

JANNINGS. I was working but I felt at odds with my work.

GEORGE. And what is it like if one feels at odds with one's work
while one is working?

JANNINGS. I told you: a rapid sunset, a rustling behind the door,
strange dogs in the room.

GEORGE. What is it like if one does not feel at odds with one's
work while one is working?

JANNINGS. It becomes play.

GEORGE. And how do you manage not to feel at odds while you
work?

JANNINGS. One must imagine that it's play.

GEORGE. And who determines the rules of play?

JANNINGS. The one who plays it: the one who works.

GEORGE. Is it like that or does one have to imagine it?

JANNINGS. If you're not at odds, it's like that.

GEORGE. But if I feel at odds, then I first have to imagine it?

JANNINGS. If you feel at odds, you cannot imagine it. Instead: a rapid sunset, a rustling behind the door . . .

GEORGE. But I feel at odds.

JANNINGS. I'll show you. (*He gets up and puts a cigar in the box with playful little movements, a finger dance. Then he sits down.*) For me work is play.

GEORGE. Well, it isn't *your* work. But it is your *thing*. And it's up to you to tell me how *my* work on *your* thing can be called play. I, who feel at odds – you're so right – cannot imagine it.

Pause

JANNINGS. You must regard work like a bet: whoever is faster, more elegant, more thorough – then there are winners and losers.

GEORGE. But who should I bet with if I'm by myself?

JANNINGS. With yourself.

GEORGE. Whether I'm faster than myself?

JANNINGS. No irony! You can't allow yourself to be ironical until you've finished your work . . . Don't you have two hands?

GEORGE. Obviously.

JANNINGS. Which hand is more nimble?

GEORGE. The right one, I suppose.

JANNINGS. Then make a bet with yourself and give it a try.

Pause. GEORGE *starts putting cigars back in the box first with his left hand, then the right. He becomes increasingly faster, gets into a frenzy. He finishes and puts the box on the table.*

Which hand won?

GEORGE (*remaining silent; then suddenly*). Let's bet on something else!

JANNINGS. Fine, let's make a bet!

GEORGE (*pointing to* PORTEN). Put her over your knee and slap her.

JANNINGS. And what's the bet?

GEORGE. First put her over your knee.

JANNINGS *puts* PORTEN *over his knee.*

You hit her with the riding whip as fast as you can for one
minute. While doing so you keep your mouth shut. If you
open it you lose.

JANNINGS. The bet stands.

*Pause. He starts beating her vigorously, but after only a few slaps his
lips part. Startled, he lets go of her and sits down, pinches his lips
tight. He wipes his forehead.*

GEORGE *also sits down. Pause.*

VON STROHEIM *touches the guitar as if by chance. A very gentle
sound. Pause. He laughs.*

JANNINGS *opens his mouth as if to roar and moves as if to hit the
table. He instantly shuts his mouth again and lets his fist sink, opening
his fingers.*

I believe – (*He breaks off; he starts to reach for something but
stops in mid-air and lets his hand drop.*)

GEORGE (*to* PORTEN). You'd best imagine it all once more right
now; then you won't need to dream of it later on –

PORTEN (*smiling*). Of water and of madness, of . . .

VON STROHEIM (*at the other end, wanting to say something at the
same time*). I was so very . . .

They both break off. Pause.

PORTEN (*turning to* GEORGE). Of water and of madness, of ships
of fools on great rivers where . . .

VON STROHEIM (*again at the same time, to* BERGNER). I was so
very afraid, I was so very afraid for . . .

Pause

JANNINGS (*pointing to* VON STROHEIM *while looking at* PORTEN).
It's his turn.

Pause

VON STROHEIM (*as in a game, to* BERGNER). I was so very afraid
for you that I suddenly burst out laughing. You were sitting
there and didn't move. Only your jugular vein throbbed.

BERGNER. I haven't been listening.

VON STROHEIM *bends over her so that she has to see his face upside
down. She opens her eyes, gives a small cry of horror; he turns his
head so that she sees his face normally again. She calms down
instantly and looks at the guitar.*

Is that for me?

VON STROHEIM *hesitates, hands it to her.*

And what do I have to do for that? (*She turns the guitar
around as if it were a present, then hands it back to him.*)

VON STROHEIM *puts it on the table. He strokes* BERGNER'S *neck
with his finger. Pause.*

(*She slaps his hand.*) Don't touch me!

JANNINGS (*prompting*). Why?

VON STROHEIM. Why don't you want to be touched? You used
to let people touch you.

BERGNER. Don't look at me!

VON STROHEIM. You looked at me tenderly before.

BERGNER. Does that mean that I should 'look at you tenderly'
now as well?

VON STROHEIM *posts himself in front of her.*

(*She looks away.*) Every time you men begin to speak, it feels
as if a beggar were accosting one.

VON STROHEIM. All of us?

BERGNER. Yes, you too.

VON STROHEIM. Give me your hand.

BERGNER. Why?

He takes her hand.

Are you a palm reader?

He strokes her hair.

> I know that my hair is a mess.

VON STROHEIM. You are beautiful.

BERGNER. Have you seen my handbag anywhere?

VON STROHEIM (*putting a necklace around her neck*). What do I get for that?

BERGNER. Why do you want to spoil my fun with the necklace?

VON STROHEIM. What must I do to make you stop despising me? Is it the way I move that you dislike? Is it my hairline? Is it the way I hold my head that makes you look away? Do the hairs on my hands disgust you? Do you find it exaggerated the way I move my arms up and down when I walk? Do I talk too much?

PORTEN, *watching from some distance away, laughs. Pause.*

> (*As on the telephone.*) Are you still there?

BERGNER *looks at him.*

> Where were you? Why don't you say something? Do say something! Come back! You were so beautiful, it was painful to look at you; so beautiful that I was suddenly very much afraid for you. You were so painfully beautiful that you left me behind – me, who was suddenly so alive – left me behind – terribly *alone*. You said nothing, and I talked to you as if to someone who had just died. Why don't you say something? Do say something! Can you imagine it?

Pause

BERGNER. Not any more. For a moment – (*Pause.*) No. It's over.

VON STROHEIM. Don't stop talking. I am afraid to interrupt when you stop talking. At the moment my tenderness for you is so vehement that I want to hit you.

Pause. He hits her. She stands up. He stares at her. She lets him stare at her.

Abandoning her long rigidity, she moves slowly and walks up and down in front of him. She interrupts her smooth movements now and then to turn abruptly, puts her hand on her hip, stretches herself loosely, lets her arms drop, grazes, while moving like this, a number of objects, supports herself everywhere, once swings towards VON STROHEIM, stops in front of him, takes off her necklace. She stands there as if she had just come through a door and is leaning against it. She strokes him with the necklace and lets it drop into his pocket.

BERGNER (*looking at him*). Don't move!

He moves to touch her, she stands still, smiling; he hesitates briefly, now touches her neck and tries to pull her towards him; but he is a moment too late, her neck resists him, she shakes off his hand and steps back.

    Why don't you look at me as if you didn't care?

VON STROHEIM. For that I would have to imagine that you were mine.

BERGNER. Then imagine it.

VON STROHEIM. Where should I begin?

BERGNER (*pointing to the guitar*). Does that belong to you? (*She shoves it away contemptuously.*)

VON STROHEIM. The longer I look at you, the ghostlier you seem to me.

BERGNER. And with every one of the feelings you describe to me you take a possible feeling away from me.

VON STROHEIM. I'm not describing my feelings for you.

BERGNER. But you are *intimating* them to me. And every time you intimate your love for me, my feelings for you grow duller and I shrivel up. Your feelings move me, but I can't respond to them, that's all. At first I loved you, you were so serious. It struck me that usually it can be said only of a child that he is 'serious'. Besides (*she laughs*), you had such beautiful eating habits. You really ate beautifully! And once when I said, 'I got wet to the skin!' you said, 'To *your* skin!' When I speak of it I almost love you again. (*She embraces him suddenly, but immediately steps back again even farther away.*) But I only have to mention that and I become insensitive right away. You talked all the time and I forgot you more and more. Then I was startled and you were still there ... A complete stranger, you talked to me with shameless intimacy, as to someone at the end of a film. Do you understand? I am taboo for you! Suddenly I was taboo for you. Two seconds! Two seconds of pain, that's what having loved you will mean to me later on. (*Pause.*) I'm not disappointed, I'm not sad, I'm only tired of you. (*She moves almost imperceptibly under her dress.*) I have wronged you so much.

VON STROHEIM. Wronged – in what way?

BERGNER. The wrong of loving you.

PORTEN *suddenly claps her hands vehemently,* GEORGE *gives a dirty laugh,* VON STROHEIM *and* BERGNER *slowly move away from the spot and begin to walk around aimlessly in different directions. Pause.*

JANNINGS (*beginning to tell a story*). Not very long ago I saw a stewardess, but an ugly one ...

VON STROHEIM (*interrupting him*). Let's talk about something else.

JANNINGS (*beginning another story*). Not long ago I saw a woman standing in the street – not a streetwalker, I must add ...

GEORGE (*interrupting him*). Something else!

JANNINGS. It is less than a week ago that I saw behind a bank counter someone with a rather long nose. But when I talked to him it turned out that despite ...

PORTEN AND BERGNER (*interrupting him*). Let's change the subject.

JANNINGS. All right. Not five minutes have passed since a man approached me in the park – no, not a faggot ...

He is interrupted by a girl who comes onstage from the right, a suit-case in her hand : ALICE KESSLER. *She is wearing an afternoon dress and looks as if she had come to this performance by mistake.*

ALICE (*putting down the suitcase; beginning to speak very matter-of-factly*). Is it you? Am I in the right place? I heard you talking from a distance and came in. The sounds I heard were so inviting, voices and laughter – what is more beautiful than that? What are you showing each other there? I'd like to see something too. What are you whispering there? I'd like to hear something too. (*She tosses her hat to* VON STROHEIM.)

VON STROHEIM *is so disconcerted that he turns aside instead of catching it.*

How are you?

Pause. All of them seem petrified.

How are you?

BERGNER (*suddenly loosening up and moving; practising her reply*). Fine? Fine. Fine! We are fine. Indeed! We're fine! (*Pause. She tries to talk normally again.*) And how – and how are you?

ALICE (*answering quite naturally*). I'm fine too. Though my hand is still trembling from carrying that heavy suitcase, and I'm still a little weak in the knees because I'm not used to walking on high heels; but I can cope with all that because I'm so happy to see you. What are you doing here?

BERGNER (*glad to be able to answer so simply*). We're talking.

ALICE. And now you don't know how to go on?

BERGNER. Perhaps. (*She falters.*) Yes. Yes!

ALICE. Good day!

BERGNER. Good day!

ALICE (*to the others*). Good day!

They raise their heads, perplexed. As if awakening, still half-asleep, not knowing yet what they are saying, they say 'Hello!' one after the other. Then they comprehend what they have said and become lively.

The stage light gradually turns into early morning light again.

What time is it?

GEORGE *nudges* JANNINGS *in the hip.*

JANNINGS (*as if back to sleep already*). Don't you have a watch?
(*He gives a start.*) 'How late is it?' Of course: how late is it?
Well, how late is it now? You could have said so right away!
(*He opens his pocket watch in front of* ALICE.)

ALICE. Thanks!

He shuts the watch again.

JANNINGS (*after a pause*). Don't mention it. (*He spreads his arms
wide as if he had just found a solution and plays with the
answer.*) Don't mention it? (*To* GEORGE.) Ask me what time
it is.

GEORGE (*merrily*). What time is it?

JANNINGS *shows him the pocket watch.*

Thanks!

JANNINGS (*closing the watch*). Don't mention it.

GEORGE (*merrily*). Thanks!

JANNINGS (*cheerfully*). But I insist: don't mention it!

ALICE *holds out her hand to* JANNINGS. *He shakes it instantly. She
also holds out her hand to* GEORGE *and he shakes it instantly. She
holds out her hand to* PORTEN *and* PORTEN *shakes it gratefully.*
VON STROHEIM *understands too and takes her hand.*

*Now she takes off her gloves and everyone watches very inquisitively.
She hands them to* VON STROHEIM *and he takes them. He now picks
up the hat and tosses it playfully to* GEORGE. GEORGE *catches the
hat and puts it on the table.* VON STROHEIM *adds the gloves to it.
Everything is working well.* BERGNER *sits down, apparently relieved.*

ALICE (*to* VON STROHEIM). What do you have there in your
hand?

VON STROHEIM (*opening his fist*). A necklace. Yes, a necklace!

ALICE. It's beautiful.

VOICE (*from the wings*). It's *not* beautiful.

ELLEN KESSLER *now appears from the left, also with a suitcase, dressed exactly like* ALICE. *She tosses* VON STROHEIM *her hat, then takes off her gloves and hands them to him.*

VON STROHEIM (*putting the things on the table; to* ELLEN). So you would like to have it?

ALICE. Yes.

He turns to ALICE *and puts the necklace around her neck. She moves voluptuously.*

ELLEN *begins to walk around. She walks about with the same movements as* ALICE *did before. Shakes hands with everyone and says:* 'Good day!' *They answer her – at least the first two do – after an initial pause, then laugh at each other as over a joke. Behind her back* GEORGE *takes a cigar out of the box and shows it to* JANNINGS, *then he takes out a second one; they laugh silently; finally* GEORGE *shows* JANNINGS *a third cigar;* JANNINGS *becomes serious and looks to the left and right, but no one else appears.*

VON STROHEIM (*to Alice*). Why is it that whenever I look at you, I know I've seen you before, although when I actually say it . . .

ELLEN *taps* VON STROHEIM *on the shoulder; he turns to her since she has tapped him on the shoulder, and continues speaking to her as if it were quite normal.*

. . . it strikes me as the usual cliché?

ELLEN *holds out her hand to him and he bends over it. She shies back, and* ALICE, *remaining motionless while* ELLEN *performs the appropriate gestures, says:* 'He bit me!'

(*To* ALICE.) In my thoughts I was about to pinch myself in the arm.

ALICE (*motionless*). Already forgotten.

VON STROHEIM. Already forgotten?

ALICE. You always ask. Were you alone too long?

VON STROHEIM. Why?

ELLEN. Or did you work too hard?

VON STROHEIM. Why?

ALICE. Or do you pose counterquestions only to win time for your reply? Because you're figuring out a lie? Because in the meantime you've become so distraught that you can't answer any more without lying? 'I came in quietly and you all sat there looking distraught, but you looked at me as though *you* had been quiet until then, and *I*, by entering so suddenly, should actually be the one to look distraught.'

VON STROHEIM. What are you talking about?

ELLEN. About you. I only wanted to show you how you talk.

She leans against his back, shoves one leg between his. He looks down at himself. She puts her arms around his neck. ALICE *waves to him with a finger.* ELLEN *doubles the gesture by holding her hand to his face from the back and also bending a finger. He tries to take a step forward, but leans back at the same time, remains standing there.*

VON STROHEIM. I'll talk as I please.

ELLEN *puts her hand over his eyes.*

ALICE. Then say something.

VON STROHEIM *opens his mouth and shuts it. He moves his hands as if he were looking for something that keeps eluding him. He stammers, but whenever his hand seems to seize something he produces whole syllables :* 'be, what, un, re'; *then he reaches for it and it escapes him again, and he goes on stammering.* ELLEN *takes her hands away from his eyes and he calms down instantly.*

VON STROHEIM. I can't, it's like reaching for a piece of soap under water.

ALICE. What?

VON STROHEIM. Already forgotten. When you covered my eyes I had it perfectly clear in front of me, but now I have forgotten it. (*He falters.*) 'Already forgotten?' That was it! You said, 'Already forgotten!' And I remembered something, but what? It escaped me again and again, and I had a feeling like searching for a piece of soap under water – (*He makes a perfunctory gesture, suddenly sniffs his fingers, repeats the gesture.*)

Pause

ELLEN. Perhaps you'll think of it . . .

ALICE. . . . if you watch me?

ELLEN (*with a fluttering voice; ambiguously*). Perhaps, if you watch me, you'll also remember where you should put me – (*she laughs*) – where you carried me to – (*she laughs*) – before, do you remember? – (*she laughs*) – and you'll also remember what you should do with me now. (*She laughs.*)

Because ELLEN *stands behind him one does not see her talking;* ALICE *moves her lips and makes the appropriate gestures.*

They let him stand there and skip and dance across the stage side by side. Taking fervent pleasure in their work, their movements nearly parallel, they busy themselves with the objects and people: while one takes off JANNINGS'S *boots, the other is loosening* GEORGE'S *shoelaces; finished at the same time they begin to brush* PORTEN'S *and* BERGNER'S *hair; again they finish at the same time and skip over to the open drawer of the chest; they return with four fancy cushions and, running helter-skelter but with similar movements, stuff them behind the backs of the four people. There has hardly been time to perceive these actions when they are back at the table with four glasses and two bottles, which they place in front of the characters.*

But now their movements suddenly slow down and begin to contradict one another. The work of one is revoked by the other: one takes away the glasses and bottles which the other has set up; one dishevels the hair which the other has just brushed; then one takes the cushions away from the persons to whom the other has just given them. At the same time the other removes the bottles and the glasses which the one . . . Then one ties the shoelaces which the other has untied, while in the meantime the other takes away the cushions from . . . Where-

upon one of them dishevels the hair which . . . While the other puts
JANNINGS'S *boots back on . . . But they stop at the same time and
start to run quickly offstage in opposite directions; they return and
change directions, finally run into the wings. As soon as they have
disappeared, they cannot be heard running anywhere.*

Everyone onstage is holding his breath. Suddenly, JANNINGS *and*
GEORGE *leap up out of their state of complete immobilization, and
rush to the suitcases which have been left onstage. They fling them
into the wings after* ELLEN *and* ALICE, *but no crashing sound can
be heard. They listen. Then they stop listening. While they are
returning to their places,* PORTEN *suddenly leaps up too and throws
the remaining things – hats and gloves – into the wings after the girls,
tossing the hats as if they were gloves, letting the gloves sail through
the air as if they were hats. One hears them crashing like suitcases.
They all settle in their places.*

PORTEN. Goo – (*As in good.*)

The others instantly turn to BERGNER.

I'm speaking.

They turn awkwardly towards PORTEN. BERGNER *seems to have
fallen asleep.*

Good day!
GEORGE (*a little too late*). Good day!
PORTEN (*a little too late*). How are you?
GEORGE (*a little too late*). Fine. (*A little too late.*) And how are you?
PORTEN (*a little too late*). Fine – Please hand me the paper.

A brief pause. GEORGE *hands her the newspaper from the table. She
holds it in her hand. Pause. Then she looks at it.*

GEORGE. Is there anything in it?

Pause

PORTEN (*as though she had answered immediately*). I'm looking.
(*Pause. She puts the paper away.*)

GEORGE. Give me the paper.

Pause. Then she gives him the paper, but as if she were giving it to him at once. GEORGE *opens it but looks into it only after an interval. Pause. Then he exclaims as if he had seen the picture at first glance.* 'Ice floes!'

Pause

PORTEN (*lively*). Seriously? (*Pause.*) How much do you weigh?

Pause

GEORGE. Two hundred and eighteen pounds.

Pause

PORTEN. Oh God!

Pause

JANNINGS (*shaking his head; hesitating and looking at* GEORGE). Why are you shaking your head? Do you wish to contradict me?

GEORGE. I am not shaking my head, nor would I, even if I were shaking my head, wish to contradict you!

PORTEN (*to* JANNINGS). You yourself were shaking your head.

JANNINGS. That was me?

VON STROHEIM. That was you.

JANNINGS (*looking to* GEORGE). Who is speaking?

VON STROHEIM. I am.

JANNINGS (*to* VON STROHEIM). That was you?

GEORGE. Are you dreaming?

JANNINGS.

> Am I in earth, in heaven or in hell?
> Sleeping or waking, mad or well-advised?
> Known unto these, and to myself disguised?
> Am I transformed, master, am not I?

(*Pause. To* GEORGE.) Do you have a match?

GEORGE. Yes.

Pause. JANNINGS *points with his finger at the table but the others look at his finger. At last he looks at his finger too and lets his hand drop. Pause.* VON STROHEIM *starts to pull out the red cloth.*

JANNINGS (*seeing it, screaming*). No!

VON STROHEIM *puts it away again instantly. Pause.* PORTEN *begins to laugh, becomes quiet again immediately.* GEORGE *looks at her questioningly : she only shakes her head. Pause.*

    Let us pray to God.

PORTEN (*instantly*). My chocolate.

BERGNER (*in her sleep*). There's a rat in the kitchen.

Pause

VON STROHEIM (*reaching into the cigar box*). May I take one?

They look at him; he pulls back his hand.

    (*He asks once more.*) May I take a cigar? (*He is already extending his hand.*)

They look at him and he pulls back his hand.

    (*With arms pressed to his sides he asks once more.*) May I take one?

No one looks at him and he takes a cigar. PORTEN *gives him an ashtray.*

GEORGE (*to* PORTEN). Thanks.

PORTEN. Why are you thanking me?

GEORGE. Because that would have been my job.

Long pause. GEORGE *lifts up the teapot and puts it down again.*

JANNINGS (*upbraiding him*). What do you mean by that?

GEORGE *pulls in his head. Pause. He takes out a piece of chocolate. removes the silver foil, and eats it. He consumes it.*

GEORGE (*to* PORTEN). Or do you want a piece of it?

She doesn't reply.

> (*Staring into the paper.*) Just now I read the word *snowstorm*, and now I can't find it any more!

All stare into the paper. Pause.

VON STROHEIM (*to* PORTEN). Is your number 23–32–322?

PORTEN. No, my number is 233–23–22. (*Brief pause.*) In my neighbourhood there is a shopping centre with stores, restaurants, and . . .

VON STROHEIM. A cinema?

PORTEN. Why? (*Pause.*) I once attended a sale . . .

GEORGE. And everyone screamed, ran around and turned over the furniture?

PORTEN. No. You're – Yes! They turned over the furniture, screamed and ran around! (*She looks at him happily, becomes serious again instantly. Suddenly, delighted, to* VON STROHEIM.) 23–32–322? Yes, that is my number. (*Pause. She looks at* GEORGE *for a long time.*)

GEORGE. Why do you look at me like that?

PORTEN. I'm afraid I might not be able to recognize you again. (*She was serious beginning her reply but ends it as a joke. She cuddles her head against his shoulder.*)

Pause. GEORGE *lowers his head.*

> Hey!

GEORGE (*shouting at her*). What kind of feelings do you have? (*He comes to his senses and asks her again kindly.*) I meant to ask, what kind of feelings do you have?

PORTEN. Too many of them.

JANNINGS. In those days, before a thunderstorm, the grass would smell of dog piss.

PORTEN. Who's saying that?

JANNINGS. I?

PORTEN. I see. (*She continues at once.*) As a child, if I wanted something, I always had to say what it was called first.

GEORGE (*wanting to say something*). And I –

VON STROHEIM (*irritated*). Yes, people showed me something and then walked away with it (*contemplatively*) and I had to follow and get it for myself.

GEORGE (*wanting to say something*). And I –

VON STROHEIM. Or people simply opened the drawer in which the thing was and went away.

GEORGE (*to* VON STROHEIM). And so that I could learn to get my way –

VON STROHEIM *looks away*, GEORGE *turns to* JANNINGS.

– I was shoved towards the objects that had been taken from me.

JANNINGS *looks away and* GEORGE *turns to* PORTEN.

I was supposed to get them back myself.

PORTEN (*remembering*). Yes! How I fidgeted then!

VON STROHEIM (*looking away, speaking to* JANNINGS, *who has been clearing his throat*). You were about to say something?

JANNINGS. No.

Pause.

GEORGE. How strange!

With this exclamation he means to call attention to himself, but no one turns to him. Instead PORTEN *winks at* JANNINGS, *who thereupon puts a finger to his lips and shakes his head.* VON STROHEIM *then bends forward and elongates an eye with one finger. This time attention is paid to the signal; as a reply,* JANNINGS *pulls his mouth apart with two fingers; thereupon* VON STROHEIM *turns up the lapel of his jacket by grasping it conspicuously with thumb and little finger, and* JANNINGS *nods twice.* PORTEN, VON STROHEIM *and* JANNINGS *laugh.*

Strange!

PORTEN (*as if irritated*). What's strange?

GEORGE (*relieved*). Suddenly I remembered a hill I had climbed with someone and the cloud shadows that appeared and vanished.

PORTEN. And what's strange about that?

GEORGE. That I should remember it for no reason.

PORTEN (*cleaning her eye as if he had spat at her during his discourse; very hostilely*). Put that paper of yours away.

GEORGE. It's my paper.

PORTEN (*snapping the paper away*). And move your cup away from there. (*She snaps her fingers against the cup so that it turns over.*)

GEORGE. It isn't my cup.

PORTEN. And spare me your recollections. (*She instantly continues talking to* VON STROHEIM *kindly.*) Do you know the expression 'To mention a noose in the house of a man who's been hanged'?

JANNINGS *laughs,* VON STROHEIM *smiles.*

GEORGE. Why are you so hostile?

PORTEN. And why are you so pale?

GEORGE. I'm not pale!

PORTEN. And I'm not hostile! (*She continues at once.*) Do you know the expression 'Put your hands on your head'?

GEORGE (*looking at* JANNINGS, *then replying*). Certainly.

PORTEN. Why do you look at *him* before answering?

GEORGE. It's a habit.

PORTEN. Put your hands on your head!

He hesitates.

Did you hear what I said?

GEORGE (*again looking at* JANNINGS *first*). I'm still thinking about it.

PORTEN. But the expression exists, doesn't it?

He slowly places his hands on his head.

VON STROHEIM (*playing along*). Put your hands on the table.

GEORGE (*testing whether the sentence exists*). 'Put your hands

on the table.' (*Relieved.*) Yes. (*He puts his hands on the
table.*)

PORTEN. Make your hands into fists and caress me!

GEORGE *tries to do so.*

No!

VON STROHEIM. Hand me the cup.

GEORGE *hands him the cup without thinking.*

PORTEN. I'll show you something! (*She smiles at* VON STROHEIM
as her initiate and starts searching through her clothes.)

GEORGE *stretches out his hand while she is still looking. Now and
then she looks at his hand and continues to search. Suddenly she hits
his hand and shoves it away.*

(*Maliciously.*) That's what I wanted to show you!

*He writhes and draws in his head. All at once she covers her eyes with
both hands and shudders.*

GEORGE (*startled*). What's the matter?

PORTEN (*takes her hands from her eyes*). Oh, it's nothing.

GEORGE *wants to reach for the cup which* VON STROHEIM *has put
down in the meantime, but* VON STROHEIM *moves it a little and*
GEORGE *withdraws his hand. They repeat this manoeuvre several
times, both displaying a lot of patience.*

(*Interrupting the game; to* GEORGE, *very hostilely.*) Who are
you?

GEORGE *gets up quickly and assumes a pose behind the table as if his
picture were about to be taken.*

Now I remember. You're the salesman. You gave me the . . .
(*She puts the riding whip on the table.*) How much is it? (*A
slip of the tongue.*)

GEORGE. Riding whip.

PORTEN. Yes, I wanted to ask that too. You sold me the riding whip.

GEORGE *sits down;* PORTEN *again puts her hands over her eyes and shudders. She pushes the riding whip away.*

JANNINGS. Don't you like it any more?

PORTEN. No, I just pushed it away.

JANNINGS (*in a disguised voice*). The *riding whip* on the table – that means someone who's very close to you will be swallowed up by a swamp and you will stand there slowly clapping your hands above your head. (*He laughs in a strange voice.*)

PORTEN *gets up quickly, pushing the guitar off the table in the process.*

(*In a disguised voice.*) A *guitar* falls off the table – that means hats staggering into glacial fissures during the next mountain-climbing expedition. (*He laughs in a strange voice.*)

VON STROHEIM (*to* PORTEN, *who is standing there motionless*). You want to leave?

PORTEN (*sitting down*). No, I just stood up. (*She suddenly crosses her arms over her chest and hunches her shoulders.*)

GEORGE. Are you cold?

PORTEN (*dropping her arms*). No. (*To* VON STROHEIM.) And who are you?

VON STROHEIM *picks up the guitar and holds it as he did previously.*

(*Tenderly.*) Oh, it's you. (*She instantly becomes serious again.*)

VON STROHEIM. Did you remember something?

Helplessly, PORTEN *tries to give him another affectionate look, stops, reaches for a cigar.*

GEORGE. Are you restless?

PORTEN (*putting the cigar back in the box; quietly*). No, I only wanted to take a cigar. (*Suddenly she screams.*) I only wanted to take a cigar!

GEORGE *shies back, pulls his jacket over his head as if trying to protect himself from the rain, and stays hunched up like that.*

(*Screaming.*) I only wanted to take a cigar! I ONLY
WANTED TO TAKE A CIGAR!

*They all hunch up more and more. Now one hears a noise emanating
from backstage, a high-pitched, pathetic howling, which coincides
with a slight darkening onstage.* PORTEN *immediately stops
screaming and also hunches up.*

The WOMAN WITH THE SCARF *steps out of the wings and walks
swiftly to the second tapestry door without looking at anyone. As
soon as she opens the door, the shrill noise behind it immediately
subsides. Instead one hears the rustling of a newspaper which is lying
just inside the door. The* WOMAN *goes inside and returns with a big*
DOLL *which represents a child. The child is quiet now; it has the
hiccups. It is wearing a gold-embroidered white nightgown and looks
very lifelike. Its mouth is enormous and open. As the* WOMAN
*reaches centre stage with the child, it starts to bawl terribly, without
any preliminaries somehow.* GEORGE, *jacket over his head, quickly
leaps towards the chest and closes the drawer. The bawling stops at
once.*

The WOMAN *now carries the child from one to the other very quickly;
in passing, during brief stops, the child reaches for the women's
breasts and between the men's legs. It also very rapidly wipes off all
the things which had been lying on the table, then pulls away the lace
tablecloth and drops it. When the* WOMAN *stands with the child
beside* BERGNER, *who seems to be still asleep, it begins to bawl again –
so suddenly, it is as if it had never stopped. The* WOMAN *holds it in
such a way that the child sees* BERGNER *from the front. It stops
bawling at once and is carried away.*

The WOMAN *returns alone, closes the tapestry door and goes off.
After she has gone, the others sit there motionless. One of them tries
to reach for something, but stops almost as soon as the movement has
begun. Someone else tries a gesture that atrophies instantly. A third
wants to reply with a gesture, interrupts it, twitching. They squat
there, start to do something simultaneously; one of them futilely tries*

to pull his hand out of his pocket; one, two of them even open their mouths – a few sounds, then all of them grow stiff again and cuddle up, make themselves very small as if freezing to death.

Only BERGNER *sits there motionless the whole time, eyes closed. All of a sudden, as though playing 'waking up', she moves slightly. By and by the others look towards her.* VON STROHEIM *gets up and bends down to her. She moves a little again. The others are motionless.*

She opens her eyes and recognizes VON STROHEIM; *she begins to smile.*

The stage becomes dark.

THEY ARE DYING OUT

Die Unvernünftigen sterben aus

translated by Michael Roloff
in collaboration with Karl Weber

'It suddenly occurs to me that I am playing something that doesn't even exist, and that is the difference. That is the despair of it.'

CHARACTERS

HERMANN QUITT
HANS, *his confidant*
FRANZ KILB, *minority shareholder*
HARALD VON WULLNOW ⎫
BERTHOLD KOERBER-KENT⎬   *businessmen and friends of* QUITT
KARL-HEINZ LUTZ ⎭
PAULA TAX
QUITT'S WIFE

TRANSLATOR'S NOTE

This translation was made from the playscript made available by Verlag der Autoren. It incorporates the author's alterations for the first Suhrkamp Taschenbuch edition of 1973 and the author's subsequent alterations of 15 February 1974.   M.R.

ACT ONE

A large room. The afternoon sun is shining in from one side. The distant silhouette of a city, as though it were seen through a huge window, is visible in the background. (The background might also be formed by a backdrop, similar to a cinema screen, with the silhouette of the city vaguely outlined against it.) QUITT, *wearing a track-suit, is belabouring a punch bag with his fists, feet and knees.* HANS, *his confidant, wearing a dress-suit, stands next to him with a tray and a bottle of mineral water, watching.* QUITT *takes a sip from the bottle, pours some on his head, and sits down on a stool.*

QUITT. I feel sad today.

HANS. So?

QUITT. I saw my wife in a dressing-gown and her lacquered toes and suddenly I felt lonely. It was such a matter-of-fact loneliness that I have no trouble speaking about it now. It relieved me, I crumbled, melted away in it. The loneliness was objective, a quality of a world, not something of myself. Everything stood with its back to me, in gentle harmony with itself. While I was taking a shit I heard the sounds I was making as if they came from a stranger in the next cubicle. When I took the bus to the office . . .

HANS. So as to maintain contact with the people and to study their needs with the aim of producing new products?

QUITT. . . . the sad curve which the bus described at one point at a wide traffic circle cut like a yearning dream deep into my heart.

HANS. The world's sorrow.
Cut Mr Quitt's feelings
To the marrow.
Hold on to your senses, Mr Quitt. Someone as wealthy as you can't afford these moods. A businessman who talks like that, even if he really feels like that, is only giving a campaign speech. Your feelings are a luxury and are useless. They might be useful

to those who could live according to them. Mr Quitt: for example, why don't you make *me* a gift of the sorrows from your leisure time to reflect about my work. Or . . .

QUITT. Or?

HANS. Or become an artist. You're already supporting violin recitals; you even condescended to collect money in public for the acquisition of a painting by the National Gallery. The wealth of feeling that is yours as of such and such a date this month is not only useful but is even essential for an artist. Why don't you paint the curve, the curve of yearning which your bus described on canvas. Why don't you sell your experience as a painting?

QUITT (*stands up*). Hans, you're playing your daily role as if you knew it by rote. More realistically, please! More lovingly! Grander!

HANS. And the way Mr Quitt has just stepped out of his role was pure make-believe, too?

QUITT. Let's not start splitting hairs. I admit: the shop assistant in the aforementioned bus eating chips that smelled of rancid oil ruined my feelings – well, I would have loved to have slapped her face. On the other hand: shortly afterwards I met a black man on the street; he was completely absorbed in the photos he'd just picked up from the chemist's, grinning to himself, swept away in remembrance, so that I suddenly remembered along with him, I felt solidarity with him. You're laughing. But there are moments when one's consciousness, too, takes a great leap forward.

HANS. But brutal reality
In no time destroys that sense of solidarity.
However, I am laughing because you told me many times how you like to remember the time when you lived for days on end in Paris on nothing but bagfuls of chips.

QUITT. I had guests when I was telling that story. And in company, I sometimes also mention 'the wood anemones and the hazelnut bushes from the springtime of my youth'.

HANS. Does the addition of these artistic elements facilitate negotiations?

QUITT. Yes: by serving as an allegory for what is being left unsaid. The wood anemones beneath the hazelnut bushes then signify something altogether different. Only those who speak know that. The poetic element is for us a manifestation of the historic element, even if it is only a convention. Without poetry we would be ashamed of our deals, would feel like primordial man. By the way, who exactly is coming today?

HANS. Harald von Wullnow
Karl-Heinz Lutz
Berthold Koerber-Kent
Paula Tax
all of them businessmen and friends of Quitt.

QUITT. I still have to change. If my wife comes, tell her to take care of the guests – then we can be sure that she'll go 'bargain hunting' instead of flushing the lavatory the whole time. Incidentally, I feel genuinely sad. Almost a comfortable feeling . . . (*Off.*)

HANS. How easily Mr Quitt talks about himself! You have to envy him his sadness. He becomes talkative then, like someone who's just being filmed. In any event, time passes more quickly with a sad Quitt, because when he feels good he is distant, unapproachable, rubs his hands together briskly, hops up and down once, that's his Rumpelstiltzkin act. (*He sits down on the stool.*) And what about me? What was I allowed to feel this morning? Isn't it true that you can tell more stories about yourself when you've just woken up than at any other time? Thus: the sun rose and shone into my open mouth. I hadn't had any dreams. I even find it repulsive the way people purse their mouth when they say 'dream'. When I brushed my teeth my gums bled. I would have liked to do it. But there was nothing doing. I: made a list of the meat to be ordered. Who am I, where did I come from, where am I going? Me . . . Yes, me, me! Always me. Why not someone else? (*He reflects and shakes his head.*) I have to try it when I'm with people. (*He gets up.*)

KILB, *the minority shareholder, appears in the background.*

I can't remember anything personal about myself. The last time anyone talked about me was when I had to learn the catechism. 'Your humble servant' of 'Your Grace'. Once I had a thought but I forgot it at once. I'm trying to remember it even now. So I never learned to think. But I have no personal needs. Still, I can indulge in a few gestures. (*He raises his fist but pulls it down again at once with the other hand. Now he notices* KILB.) Who are you, where did you come from, et cetera, et cetera.

KILB. My name is Franz Kilb. (HANS *laughs.*) Don't you like the name?

HANS. It's something else. I was talking to myself just now – fluently almost. We don't have anything against names here. And *what* are you?

KILB. A minority shareholder.

HANS. *The* minority shareholder perhaps?

KILB. Yes, *the* minority shareholder, Franz Kilb, the terror of the boards of directors, the clown of all the annual general meetings, the tick in the navel of the economy, with a nuisance value of 100 – it's me, popping up again. (HANS *steps forward and puts one fist in front of* KILB's *face while showing him out with the other hand.*) Are you serious?

HANS (*steps back and drops his arms*). I'd like to be. But I'm only serious when Mr Quitt is serious. Nonetheless: it is my honour – scram! (KILB *sits down on the stool.*) So now you're going to tell us the story of your life, is that it?

KILB. I own one share of every major corporation in the country. I travel from one annual general meeting to the other and spend the nights in my sleeping bag. I go by bike – here, look at the trouser-clips. I'm a bachelor in my best years, my reflexes function perfectly. (*He strikes his kneecap and his foot hits* HANS.) This is my Boy Scout knife: during the Third Reich I passed my lifeguard test, I can pull you out of the water with my teeth. There are people who hold me in high esteem, but I don't put my name on any political endorsement. I once appeared on *What's My Line*, I said I was self-employed, no one guessed what I did. At the AGMs I sit with my rucksack and keep my hand up all the time. AGMs where the board ignores someone who asks for the floor are null and void. How quiet it is here. Can you hear how quietly I am speaking? My last mistress called me demonic, the press – (*He quickly proffers a few newspaper clippings.*) – calls me a gadfly. I am quicker than you think. (*He has tripped up* HANS *who has fallen on his knees.*) I live from my dividends and am a free person, in every respect. My motto is: 'Anyone who's for me gets nothing from me; anyone against me will get to know me.' That's a warning for you.

QUITT *returns.* KILB *gets up at once, makes a bow and steps into the background.*

QUITT. The ubiquitous Mr Kilb. (*To* HANS.) Stop dusting your tails. As I was looking in the mirror while changing it struck me as ridiculous that I was growing hair. These insensitive, indifferent threads. I was sitting on the bed, my head in my hands. After some time, I thought: If I keep holding my head like that all my thoughts will cease. Besides, I was really touched by my plight when I and my sadness regarded the blanket that I had pulled back in the morning. I will prove to you that my feelings are useful.

HANS. Watch out, if you say it once more you'll suddenly really mean it. But seriously, I've never heard of a mad businessman. Only the other-directed find themselves ominous. But you're incapable of being at odds with the world. And if you are, you make a profit on it.

QUITT. You're becoming schematic, Hans.

HANS. Because I'm a compulsive speaker.

KILB. Ask him about his parents. His father was an actor. His mother made dolls which she couldn't sell. Both of them failed to return from a trip around the world. They're supposed to have jumped into a volcano. He's their only child.

QUITT (*to* HANS). I'm not ill. Let's talk about something more harmless.

Pause.

KILB. For example, the immortality of the soul?

Pause.

QUITT. The reason I'm not ill is because I as Hermann Quitt can be just the way I feel. And I'd like to be the way I feel. I've got the blues, Hans. (*Pause.*) In any event, sometimes I go somewhere and I think I've come in through the wrong door. Another second and they'll ask me who I am. Or I suddenly stand on an incline in my empty office, see the pencil roll down from the table top and the papers slip down. Even when I come in here I often become suspicious that I've intruded. Frequently when I look at a familiar object I think: where's the trick? People I've known for ages I suddenly call by their last name. That's not just an old dream. But I wanted to talk about something else. (*Pause.* KILB *raises his arm.* QUITT *has suddenly butted his head against the punch bag.*) What's still possible? What's there left for me to do? Recently I drove through a suburban street where I used to walk every day. Suddenly I saw an old poster hoarding. In those days I used to read everything on it. Now the hoarding was nearly empty, only one poster left, an ad for a powdered milk that's long off the market. (*He raises his arms.*) While I drove slowly past, the posters for all the bygone chocolates, tooth pastes and elections passed before my mind's eye, and in this gentle moment of recollection I was overcome by a profound sense of history.

KILB *and* HANS (*simultaneously*). And then you fraternised with your driver?

Pause. Honking off-stage.

QUITT. That's Lutz. He also honks that way at night when he comes home. It's a signal for his wife to turn on the microwave oven, Made in Japan. Go and help him with his coat. (HANS *leaves.*)

KILB (*steps forward*). How does that story about your parents go?

QUITT. It's not idiotic enough. I once dreamt I was losing my hair. Whereupon someone told me that I was afraid of becoming impotent. But perhaps it only meant that I was afraid of losing my hair.

KILB. But why are you afraid of losing your hair? For instance, what does that mean? Besides, I caught sight of you recently. You were sitting on a bench by the river, rather absentmindedly engrossed in nature.

QUITT. Absentminded?

KILB. You hadn't even wiped the pigeon droppings off the bench. Besides, experience tells me that the contemplation of nature is the first sign of a waning sense of reality. And your eyelids scarcely blinked, like a child's.

QUITT. Oh, go on, go on. It's beautiful to hear a story about oneself.

KILB. I went to have lunch. Fish and chips. After all, I exist too.

QUITT. Kilb, I've admired you for a long time. I like your ruthlessness. That time when you brought an effigy of me into the AGM and hung it on the lectern! And had yourself carried bodily out of the hall! I also envy you. Next to you I feel constricted, caught inside my skin, and notice how limited I am. I can tell you this now that it's just the two of us.

KILB *draws him toward himself by both ears and smacks a kiss on his lips.* QUITT *gives him a kick.*

KILB. So as to re-establish the previous state of affairs. (*He retreats.*)

Simultaneously HANS *leads* LUTZ, VON WULLNOW *and* KOERBER-KENT *into the room.* KOERBER-KENT, *a businessman-priest, represents a Catholic-owned company; he is dressed in civilian clothes, but wears the collar of his profession.*

LUTZ (*to his colleagues*). As I said, we weren't the first ones. We just observed them in the beginning, let them over-extend themselves, then we got the green light from our overseas affiliates, tackled them and down they went. He of course tried to bluff us, but we were on to him long ago. We let him twist in the wind a while longer and then we bagged him. (*They laugh, each in his own way.*)

VON WULLNOW (*to* QUITT). Quite something, that bike out there leaning against your fence. My father once gave me one almost like it, together with my first pair of long trousers. They don't do work like that any more nowadays. Instead of selling you a bike they dress it up like a machine, with tachometer and horn. And a machine of course is allowed to wear out more quickly than a simple bike. It is also characteristic of machines that they become obsolete. A bike wouldn't. Do you ride to the office on it?

QUITT *points to* KILB.

VON WULLNOW. I wondered straight away why it was so dirty.

LUTZ. I'll take his arms. Who'll take the legs?

QUITT. And if we trip, the poisoned apple falls out of his mouth. And the new Adam leaps to his feet.

KOERBER-KENT. He doesn't bother me. I find him entertaining. He reminds me of some dark urge inside myself. Besides, he doesn't really mean it. He can't help it that's all. Ever since we had a chat, just the two of us, I believe in him.

LUTZ. It's easy to believe in someone if it's just the two of you. I believe in anyone if it's just the two of us. But I get nothing out of it. That's why I try not to be alone with anyone. It falsifies the facts.

VON WULLNOW. He has no sense of honour, that creature. He reminds me of an old nag we used to have at home. He pissed every time he stepped from his stall out on the pavement. It made such a wonderful splashing sound. He moved through the world with his joint dangling. And look how bow-legged he is. And his middle-parting – which isn't really in the middle. His threadbare flies, the pointy shoes, that's no way to live!

KOERBER-KENT. Von Wullnow, you're wasting your time. There's no insulting him. Your despising him so elaborately only increases his self-esteem. Let's sit down and begin. I have to prepare a sermon today.

LUTZ. What are you going to preach on?

KOERBER-KENT. About the fact that death makes all men equal. Us as well.

VON WULLNOW (*indicating* KILB). He's like that. But now – should he hear everything?

LUTZ. But we're not going to say anything that no one besides us should hear, are we?

Pause. The businessmen laugh. KILB *is playing with his tongue in his mouth.* HANS *leaves. The businessmen sit down on a suite of matching chairs and sofa.*

VON WULLNOW. Are you standing comfortably, Kilb? We're only human, after all.

The businessmen laugh again. QUITT'S WIFE *appears. She looks at all of them, then walks diagonally through the room and disappears.*

(*To* KOERBER-KENT.) Do you as a priest also employ female help in your enterprises?

KOERBER-KENT. How do you mean?

VON WULLNOW. I was just thinking about the fact that *you* aren't married, neither happily, nor at all.

KOERBER-KENT. No, we can't marry.

VON WULLNOW. I didn't mean it that way.

QUITT. I don't understand your allusions.

VON WULLNOW. But you understand that they are allusions?

LUTZ (*distracting them*). Of course, women are cheaper. But you have to be careful. Every month a few of them pull a fast one on us.

KOERBER-KENT. By pilfering the products?

LUTZ. No, by becoming pregnant. Scarcely have they started work when they turn up with child – not out of passion, mind you, but out of cold calculation; and we have to pay the maternity benefits.

VON WULLNOW. One shouldn't always be talking about the good old days, but things *were* different in the past. And you didn't need to talk about the good old days either in those days. Everyone was one big happy family in my grandfather's shop. They didn't work for my father but for the shop and that also meant for themselves – at least that's the feeling you got, and that's what mattered. Anyway, our system is the only one in which it is possible to work for oneself. It's incredible how strong my sense of solidarity was with my workers. It cut through all class differences and thresholds of natural feeling when they made their work easier for themselves by singing songs or urging each other on during particularly difficult jobs, with original chants which, incidentally, should be collected before they are forgotten altogether. Today they get the work over and done with, mutely and indifferently, that's all. Their thoughts are somewhere else, nothing creative any more, no imagination. I must say I admire our imports from the sunnier parts of the world. They're alive during their work, are happy to be together. Work is still part of their life for them. Moreover, in the good old days the workers used to take pride in their products; when they went for their Sunday walks they proudly pointed out to their children anything in the vicinity made by their own hands. Meanwhile, most children haven't the faintest idea what their parents do at work.

KILB. Why, do you want them to point out the bolt in the car which your father personally screwed in, or the packet of margarine mother wrapped herself?

VON WULLNOW. I don't have my cane with me. I refuse to touch you with my bare hands.

KOERBER-KENT. I recently had my library redecorated. Of course, I helped with the work, and then I noticed the lack of enthusiasm with which the decorators were working, despite the fact that I was paying better than minimum wages. Why is it, I asked them, that you can't develop any passion for your work even though you are paid for it? The good souls didn't have any answer to that one.

VON WULLNOW. Typical.

KILB *is meanwhile clipping his fingernails.*

KOERBER-KENT. They only think of the money. They've got nothing in their minds except pounds, shillings and smut, as I used to put it. Instead of enrolling in evening courses or absorbing our cultural heritage, they spend their wages on refrigerators, crystal mirrors and cuckoo clocks. Since they no longer have any respect for the public good – not to use a religious word in this circle – they have become possessed by the Beelzebub of personal happiness, as I sometimes say jokingly. And yet there's no way for them to be personally happy without considering the public good. You're scarcely born and already you're pushing into the revolving door of the here and now and can't push your way back out, I always say. Paper wraps stone, consumption cracks character.

VON WULLNOW. A story. No sermon without a little story, right? I know my rhetoric. Which, incidentally, is another art that has gone to the dogs among us . . . I was walking through the supermarket.

QUITT. You in a supermarket?

VON WULLNOW. Mine, of course. But I was trying to tell a story.

QUITT. Von Wullnow, the supermarket baron, that's news.

VON WULLNOW. I had to invest, taxes forced us to. I don't have to explain that to you. And besides, a big chain is just the right market for some of our products. That way we have our own outlets and don't need to discount to the retailers.

QUITT. 'Harald Count Von Wullnow Supermarkets.'

VON WULLNOW. We called them Miller-Markets. Anyway, when I went to inspect one of them I couldn't help noticing a woman

who made herself conspicuous by standing around a long time
with an empty shopping trolley. I watched her and wondered to
myself, because, aside from the furtive glances she was casting
about, she seemed almost lady-like. Suddenly she came up to me
and said softly: Do you think they still have the Special Offer on
the giant-size detergent that was in the paper last week? Too bad,
I thought afterwards. She was just my shirt size, I liked her
layout. But to lose one's dignity over a consumer article like that!
I felt quite ashamed for her.

KILB *has meanwhile placed his hands underneath his armpits and is
producing farting noises.*

LUTZ. All I have to say against consumers is that they aren't
informed. Why don't they read the business sections in their
papers which publish the results of product testing? Why don't
they join the consumer action groups? No wonder they can't tell
the products apart. Have you ever watched the faces of housewives, during a sale? A mass of mindless, dehumanised, panic-
stricken grimaces that don't even perceive each other any more,
staring hypnotically at objects. No logic, no brains, nothing but
the seething stinking subconscious. A happening at the zoo,
gentlemen. No consciousness, no life, no feeling for quality. I
know what I'm talking about.

KILB (*interrupting*). Fire!

QUITT (*ignoring him*). And what are you talking about?

LUTZ. You know very well. We have just stopped production. Our
quality article had no chance against your mass-produced one.
Your brand is a household name; even our packaging, a three-
dimensional picture on a hexagonal cover, was too revolutionary.
Consumers are conservative, their curiosity about what is progressive is fly-by-night. That was our first fire – I mean, fiasco.
(*Looks at* KILB.)

QUITT. When your product came on the market I immediately put
ours on the steal-me list.

KOERBER-KENT. Please explain.

QUITT. The steal-me list is a full-page ad which we publish once a week in the major newspapers. It lists the ten products of ours that are shoplifted with the greatest frequency. Simultaneously we send this list as posters to the trade. There they construct a kind of altar display of the listed objects and the poster with the legend SHOPLIFTERS' HIT PARADE is hung above it. This boosts sales. I immediately put my article at the top of the list and left it there, until Lutz gave up. I must say I've grown fond of it in the meantime and look at it in its plain square package with genuine affection. Still, I'm going to stop production on it.

LUTZ. What do you mean?

QUITT. It was a losing proposition for a long time. I just didn't want you to think you knew better.

VON WULLNOW. Marvellous, Quitt. That's the old school spirit, but I can see even now how important it is that we reach an agreement in time.

QUITT. Otherwise why would you be here?

VON WULLNOW. Businessmen are people who get things moving, as Schumpeter says. Let's oil the machinery of the world.

KILB. Someone's coming.

VON WULLNOW (*ignoring him*). This is an important day. It is the first time that we have wanted to give up our separatism. We've been lonely long enough. We planned in loneliness, in sad isolation we watched the market, helplessly each of us set his price by himself, hoping for the best. Despising everything that was alien, each of us on his little island watched the other's advertising campaigns. We did not recognise our mutual needs, were even proud of our individualism. That has to change; we can't go on like this.

PAULA TAX *enters hurriedly.*

QUITT. I was just thinking of you, Paula.

PAULA. And?

QUITT. Nothing bad.

VON WULLNOW. Have a seat. (*To the others.*) I always found it embarrassing to say to a woman: sit down. (*To* PAULA.) All of us were thinking of you. Even the Vicar-General, I think?

KOERBER-KENT (*jokingly*). Now I know why I felt the whole time as if a door had been left open somewhere.

KILB. Your signet ring is tarnished, Monsignore.

KOERBER-KENT. Continue, my friend. (KILB *remains silent.*) He's never got more than one sentence in him. The habit of quick interjections has ruined him.

PAULA *has sat down. She is still wearing riding clothes.* QUITT'S WIFE *comes in again. She pretends she is looking for something.* PAULA *loosens her scarf and shakes her hair.* QUITT'S WIFE *stamps her feet. As she walks on, the heel of her shoe gets caught in a crack in the floor. She hops backward, slips back into the shoe and tries to walk out with measured steps.* KILB *barks after her and she disappears with a scream.*

QUITT. Perhaps the reason for the nausea is that only a minute previously you could have held an entirely different opinion of the matter, and in that case the story would have taken an entirely different turn.

PAULA. You look at me as if I should ask what that means.

QUITT. Please remind me later that I still have something to explain to you.

PAULA. When?

QUITT. Later.

LUTZ. I don't want to harass you. There's a lot at stake today. Had it not been for my autogenic training I wouldn't have been able to get to sleep last night. I usually think of the ocean when that happens but even that sparkled for a long time like freshly pureed spinach in my new frozen food packaging, and the moon above had been crossed out with a felt pen and a smaller one circled in beside it.

VON WULLNOW. All right, let's get down to business. I assume, if not our conversation then what we mean by it is for our ears only.

In any event, you have my word of honour. (*He takes a look around.*) The Vicar-General swears on this, doesn't he? Lutz promises. Yes? And Quitt? Nods. Mrs Tax's thoughts are still nudging her horse with her thighs. And our guest of honour? (*He nods briefly at* KILB.)

QUITT. Hans.

HANS *appears at once, frisks* KILB, *shakes his head – no microphone – and withdraws again.* KILB *thereupon takes his stool and sits down with the others, assumes the pose of a kibitzer.*

VON WULLNOW. We're no sharks. But we've learned that free enterprise is a dog-eat-dog business. Public opinion regards us as monsters, belching cigar smoke. And in the often so poetically quoted moments of those overly long cross-country trips, we see ourselves like that: we've become what once we didn't want to become at any price. Don't shake your head Vicar-General. You know that's not the way I mean it. No, we aren't just the baddies in a game: we really are bad. Even as a gourmet – although for a long time I hoped for the opposite – my face has slowly but surely become less and less soulful. Just take a look at your colleagues business-lunching in the five-star restaurants, Lutz: their jowls reflect a life-long sell-out. A life-long circus, not just twice a year like the housewives. Still, it is premature undialectical impressionism, as Mrs Tax would surely say, to slander ourselves. After all, we didn't become monsters because we relished it. My primal experience is the thought that there's no such thing as a human being who becomes inhuman of his own accord. That's what I tell myself whenever I have to put myself together again after having done something I actually abhor in my heart of hearts.

QUITT. What you're trying to say is that it's futile to try to enlarge the market any further by means of the price war.

LUTZ (*glancing at* KILB). Not like that. Everyone should be able to translate it into his own terms.

QUITT. Competition is a game. Fighting is childish. Together we can undercut the small fry until they long to live from dividends.

Not force but the gentle law of displacement. When I was a child I would sometimes quietly sit down on something that someone else wanted, and absentmindedly whistle a song to myself.

KOERBER-KENT. You're not at confession here, Quitt.

QUITT. What matters is this. First of all: there are too many products, the market has become opaque. Who is producing too much? One of us? Perish the thought. Who then? They, of course. We're going to make the market transparent again. Second: now there are no longer too many products but too many units of the same products. The refrigeration plants are bursting with butter, I read at breakfast today. Is our supply too large? No. Demand is too low, and that's the catch we live off. Third: is demand too low because prices are too high? Of course. And prices are too high because wages are too high, correct? So we are going to have to pay lower wages. But how? By having the work done more cheaply somewhere else. For instance, 'Mauritius represents an excellent labour market. The plantations have accustomed the population to hard work for generations. The nimble Asiatic fingers have become skilled and are of proven value.' Therefore we will be able to claim that our merchandise is a bigger bargain. That's the biggest drawing card. Besides, imagine that all goods will bear the legend: 'Made in Mauritius.' I remember the yearning such labels used to instill in me as a child. Why shouldn't they exert the same effect on our beloved consumers? In any event, demand will rise and we will match up our prices again. Fourth: from time to time we take a walk through the forest by ourselves so as to feel like human beings. Fifth: – (*To* VON WULLNOW.) All this time I've felt the irresistible urge to wipe the moisture off your lips. (*He wipes* VON WULLNOW's *mouth with a handkerchief. To* KILB.) Repeat what I've just said.

Pause. KILB *moves his lips, falters, tries again, shakes his head. He hops on his stool towards* QUITT.

KILB. Anyway, it sounded logical. As logical as this here. (*He tugs at both his ears 'so that' his tongue sticks out of his mouth, grabs his chin 'so that'* the tongue slips back inside. *The businessmen meanwhile have exchanged significant glances.*

LUTZ. So we're celebrating already?

QUITT. I'm not finished yet.

KOERBER-KENT. What were you playing at just now? It was only a game, wasn't it? Because in reality you are . . .

QUITT (*interrupting him*). Yes, but only in reality. (*To* VON WULL-NOW.) And you are speechless?

VON WULLNOW. I'm just getting used to you again. Perhaps you're just one of those people who likes squeezing other people's pimples.

QUITT (*strikes his forehead histrionically*). True, I was carried away by something. But now I'm normal again.

VON WULLNOW. It passed so quickly I've already forgotten it. I was brushed by a bat. Did something happen? Besides, you haven't finished yet.

QUITT. What is important is that from now on none of us does anything without the other. When I buy raw materials without informing you of my source, that's treason. When Lutz brings a new product on the market to corner a share of the turf, that is treason. If the Vicar-General plays his female labour a lower rate than we do, because they are pious farm girls, and so depresses the prices, that's treason. If you, Paula, let your workers share in the profits and have to raise your prices all by yourself, that's treason. (*To* VON WULLNOW.) That's the way you want it, isn't it?

VON WULLNOW. Mrs Tax would probably pose the counter question: but what if I let them share because I find it reasonable – say, to increase production?

QUITT (*to* PAULA, *as if she had answered for herself*). It isn't treason as long as you don't raise your prices without first consulting us.

And as long as you and I have the same habits you can't betray me. And now the champagne, Hans.

A cork pops off-stage, HANS *appears at once, carrying a tray with champagne glasses and a bottle which is still smoking. The ceremony of pouring the champagne.* QUITT *points ironically to the quality of the champagne and glasses, for example: 'Dom Perignon 1935, Biedermeier glasses, handmade, notice the irregularities in the glass.' The group rises to its feet, clinks glasses, drinks quietly, looking into each other's eyes.* KILB *has not stood up. While the others are drinking he briefly laughs a few times without the others paying him any heed. He pulls out his knife, turns it back and forth and lets it fall blade downwards on the floor. They look at him without interest. He puts the knife away and plays a little on his harmonica.* HANS *has already left with the tray.* KILB *gets up and spits in front of everybody's feet, one after the other. In front of* PAULA *he uses his hand to pull out his chin simultaneously sticking out his behind. The rest continue to regard him benignly. Suddenly he picks up* LUTZ *and the priest, who don't object, one after the other, and puts them down somewhere else. He criss-crosses the stage. In passing, he kicks them lightly on the backs of their knees so that their legs give a little, except for the last one. He offers* PAULA *his thigh, Harpo Marx fashion, which she holds and then lets drop again; he makes an exception of* QUITT, *only casting sidelong glances at him. Now he has also begun to speak.*

KILB. And I? Is it my job to take care of the entertainment? Am I the dumb animal whose ears are allowed to hear everything? Or the poodle in front of whom you lie down naked in bed? I can drag you across your beautiful lawns with my teeth. I'll smear pus over your beautiful whole sentences. I'll wrap your spray-deodorised private parts in heat-sealed cellophane. You singe the fluff off slaughtered chickens with a candle. 'Chickenskin' they say in Switzerland instead of 'goose pimples'. Cheers! Cheers! I always speak this calmly, dear lady. Here, you've dropped your supersoft toilet tissue. (*He pulls out a strip of toilet paper and places it over her arm; she smiles, unimpressed.*) If you ever catch fire it will be me who wraps you in blankets until you choke to death. And when you all freeze to death I'll sit beside you cracking my knuckles. Demonic, don't you agree? (*More and more embar-*

rassed.) Let yourselves be conjured up out of your personal thorn hedges, you, the bewitched of the business world, a free man stands before you, a model, a figure from a picture book. (*He slaps his hands together, slaps his thighs and the soles of his shoes like a folk dancer, only more slowly and awkwardly.*) Let's swing a little! Action! Lights! A little circus atmosphere! Not just words against which the brain is defenceless anyway! Conserve your vocal chords! More body language! (*He picks up a champagne glass and lets it drop somewhat helplessly, makes a vain reflex movement to catch it which he tries to overplay.*) And don't stand around like stiffs! Anyway, far too statuesque! Move. You will be recognised by your movements. Let's celebrate.

He dances PAULA *a few steps further across the stage, then stops in front of her. He starts unbuttoning her blouse . . . He encourages himself by beating his fists together and blowing into the hollow of his hands. In between he sticks his hands into his armpits as if they were freezing. No one stops him. Sidelong glances at* QUITT. QUITT *watches him attentively as well as remotely, almost impatiently.* KILB *tugs the blouse out of her jodhpurs somewhat indecisively.* PAULA *merely smiles. He steps back as if he were giving up, performs another pathetic slapping gesture without really slapping his hands together. Suddenly* QUITT *leaps forward, seizes* KILB'S *hand and tries to use it to tear off* PAULA'S *blouse himself.* KILB *resists.* QUITT'S WIFE *enters, watches with interest.* QUITT *lets go of* KILB *and tears off the blouse himself.* PAULA *crosses her arms in front of her breasts without undue hurry.* QUITT'S WIFE *leaves.* QUITT *places another champagne glass into* KILB'S *hand, simultaneously takes the other glasses into his fist and smashes them, one after the other, on the floor, repeating* KILB'S *words – Cheers! Cheers! – while doing so and nudges him in the side until he, too, drops his glass, somewhat indecisively. He walks from one person to the other and spits into each face; lifts up a splinter of glass and attacks* KILB *with it, throws the splinter away and puts* KILB *into a headlock; leads him back and forth like this and butts his head against the others.*

KILB (*in the headlock, trying to free himself*). You misunderstood me, Quitt. There's no method to your madness. It is unaesthetic, vulgar, formless. But worst of all, it is unmusical, has neither melody nor rhythm. That wasn't how we planned it. Don't you understand a joke? Can't you distinguish between ritual and reality any more? Know your limits, Quitt.

QUITT (*while pushing him into a chair and dragging him off-stage on it*). Until now you have lived off the fact that I have my limits, you phoney. Now show me my limits, you model of the independent life.

Far upstage he tips him out of sight and comes back. PAULA *walks off with measured steps.* HANS *reappears with a dustpan and brush. The others are tidying themselves up. Everyone begins to smile.* QUITT *does not smile.* HANS *sweeps the splinters together.* PAULA *returns dressed and also smiles with closed lips.*

VON WULLNOW. I believe he's finally learned his lesson.

KOERBER-KENT. He'll never learn anything. He's got no memory. The jack-in-the-box only uses the floor to propel himself. He doesn't forget because he doesn't remember anything. The horsefly settles on the very spot from which it's just been shooed away. He doesn't think backwards and forwards like us who have a sense of history – as Mrs Tax might say – he only has a good nose. I would call him a mere animal, an involuntary fidgeting animal. The sparrows in the field, by not living but by being lived, are the divine principle. I can see him now on his bicycle animalistically rushing down the tree-lined avenues.

QUITT. Don't always look at me when you speak; I can't listen to you that way.

VON WULLNOW. It's a pity that there are no more tree-lined avenues. How sweet, for instance, the dawning recollection of the manor house at the vanishing point of two rows of chestnut trees, the windows still mirroring darkly, only the dormers of the servants' quarters already lit up, a hedgehog rustles in the dry leaves at our feet, the special stagnant air of that time of day when the sick retreat into themselves and die willingly, and a chestnut suddenly bursts open on the gun on our shoulder while we have turned around for one last look at our parents' house before we stalk cross-country to our hunting ground. Yes, a delicate being, our minority shareholder, the delicacy of a thief when it comes to opening a drawer, the delicacy of the murderer when it comes to handling a knife.

LUTZ. Von Wullnow, your language is so elevated it makes me hesitate to tell my joke now.

VON WULLNOW. I order you to. You've been looking all this time as if you had something to get off your chest.

LUTZ. Two people love each other. They make love so rapidly the way you sometimes devour a slice of bread with honey on it. When they are finished . . . (*Glances at* PAULA.) Oh, pardon me.

VON WULLNOW. Mrs Tax isn't listening anyway. And besides, she's above that sort of thing. She'd probably consider our dirty jokes as proof of our commercialised sexuality, wouldn't you? Go on.

LUTZ. . . . the man gets up at once. Oh, says the woman, you've scarcely finished and you're aleady leaving? And that's supposed to be love? Look, the man replies, I counted to ten, didn't I?

There's either brief laughter or there isn't. VON WULLNOW *is already in the process of leaving with* LUTZ *and* KOERBER-KENT – *only* HANS, *who is still sweeping up broken glass, giggles, kneeling on the floor. The gentlemen turn around towards him, he gets up and proceeds out in front of them, giggling.*

VON WULLNOW. Quitt, we trust you as you trust us. Forget your super annuated sensitivity. Sensitive is a word I only associate with condoms.

QUITT (*to* PAULA). Aren't you leaving?

PAULA. I was to remind you that you still wanted to explain something to me.

QUITT. I merely wished you would stay, now you can go. (*Pause.* PAULA *sits down again. Pause.*) I noticed how I happened to think of you disgustingly by chance. One minute before and all I could

have attached to you was your name. Suddenly there was
something conspicuous about you. I wanted to get up and grab
you between the legs.

PAULA. Are you speaking about me or about a thing?

QUITT (*laughs briefly. Pause*). I almost said: about you, you thing.
Something seems to want to slip out of me today, something of
which I'm afraid but which still tantalises me. You know the
stories about laughing funerals. Once I sat opposite a woman I
didn't know. We looked at each other's eyes until I felt hot.
Suddenly she stuck out her tongue at me, not just mockingly, a
little between her lips, but all the way to the root, with the whole
face a gruesome grimace – as though she wanted to stick herself
out at me. Ever since then I've felt like doing something like that
myself. Usually I manage to do it only in my head, for just a
moment. It starts with my wanting to undo someone's shoelaces
who's walking by or pull a hair out of his nose, and ends with the
urge to undo my flies in public.

PAULA. Shouldn't we rather talk about our arrangement?

QUITT. But I'm finally beginning to enjoy talking. I am speaking
now. Before, my lips just moved. I had to strain my muscles to
articulate properly. My whole chin ached, the cheeks became
numb. Now I know what I am saying.

PAULA. Are you Catholic?

QUITT. Why! You're actually listening to me!

PAULA. Because you're talking about yourself like a representative
of universal truth. What you experience personally you want to
experience for all of us. The blood you sweat in private you bring
as a sacrifice to us and our stubbornness. Your ego wants to be
more than itself, your sentimentality makes appeal to my
inability to feel, your urge to confess only seeks to demonstrate to
me that I'm still unawakened. You behave as though your time
had finally come. Actually, your time as Quitt who suffers his life
in exemplary bourgeois fashion has long since passed. Your

suffering is over with. The fact that you insist so much on yourself makes you suspect. You lack a sense of history, you're much too western for me.

QUITT. But, even if it is for the last time, I'd like to be at the centre of things, just by myself. Otherwise I would feel written off once and for all, like a machine, wouldn't be able to utter a single word meant for someone else. Once when I stepped out of the house the children yelled after me: 'I know who you are! I know who you are!' Spitefully, as though the fact that I could be identified was something bad. Besides, it seemed inappropriate to me just now to tell something like a story after having been considered so abstractly by you.

Pause.

PAULA. Sit down. (QUITT *does so. Pause. They look at each other.* PAULA *looks away.*) Yes, my outfit bothers me too now. And I can't think of anything I might want to say to you. But I would like to say something to you. (*Pause.*) It's pleasant to sit here while the light is fading. I wasn't thinking of anything just now. That was nice too. (*Pause.*) Do you like evaporated milk? I suddenly feel like having evaporated milk. (*Pause. She speaks as if she wants to avoid speaking of something else.*) My workers should never see me like this. Normally, I buy my clothes off the peg, I even feel good in them. By the way, it occurred to me before that we should also plan our advertising together from now on. I would like to start from the basis that we don't generate any artificial needs but only awaken the natural ones of which people aren't conscious yet. Most people don't even know their needs. Advertising, inasmuch as it describes a product, is only another word for raising the level of awareness. What we should object to is advertising which is inappropriate to its product because it creates misconceptions among the consumers about the nature of the product. That would be the very deception or simulation of something that isn't there which we are always accused of. But our products exist and their very existence makes them rational – otherwise we, as rational beings, would not have had them produced in a rational manner from rational raw materials by rational people. And if our advertisements don't lie but only provide an exact description of our rational products, then the advertising will be just as rational. Take a look at the socialist states. They have no irrational products – and still they advertise, because the rational needs advertising most of all. That's what transmits the idea of what is rational. For me advertising is the only materialistic poetry. As an anthropomorphic system it endears us once more to the objects from which we have been alienated by ideology. It animates the world of goods and humanises them, so that we can feel at home with them. I can't tell you how deeply moved I am when I read on an old gable end in giant letters 'Your shoes need Erdal' or I see a picture of a washing powder packet with the sun behind it. It sends me ten feet off the ground. Today, twenty years later the same shoe-cream bears the rubbishy label 'Tested in the Himalayas', and I'm back down with a bump. When I'm merely feeling unproductive I look at ads in magazines, it makes my mood seem ridiculous; so advertising is also a form of consolation, but of a concrete, rational kind as distinct from bourgeois obscurantist poetry. And think with how much more dignity and how much more progressively the copywriters can work than the poets! While the poets in their isolation conjure up something vague, the copywriters, working as an efficient team, describe the definite. Indeed, they are the only truly creative ones – they think something they had no idea about beforehand. Incidentally, we noticed recently what was wrong with the slogan for one of our products. It contained the phrase 'a level dessertspoon' and the product didn't sell. Finally it occurred to one member of the team to substitute the word 'heaped' for 'level'. Instead of 'level dessertspoon' we used 'a heaped teaspoon' and suddenly sales increased by almost 100%.

HANS *enters during the last sentence and turns on the light.*

QUITT (*to* HANS). We don't need any light.

HANS *turns off the light and leaves.*

PAULA. I can hear my wristwatch ticking.

QUITT. You should be able to afford a noiseless watch. But it probably isn't just any old watch but a memento. So please try to remember. (*Pause.*) Or don't try to remember – as you please.

PAULA. If you tell a child that is singing to itself: 'Very nice, go on singing!' it will stop singing. But if you say: 'Stop!' it will go on singing.

QUITT. There are women who . . .

PAULA. Stop it, nothing can come of that.

QUITT. There are women you can't touch because if you did you would be desecrating a memento. A necklace then has a story which makes every caress of the neck a mere afterthought. Everything about the woman is so complete that every experience you share with her only reminds her of something in her past. Whatever you tell her, she immediately interrupts you with this introverted nodding of the head. She is untouchable, inside and out. She is so full of memories. The most mysterious, delicately stuttering impulse immediately evoked a doppleganger who has already made the impulse crystal-clear to the woman. You begin to understand sex killers: only the slitting open of the belly provides him with the attention every individual deserves. You can't run your hands thrugh a whore's hair – or else her hairdo will get messed up.

PAULA. It's just as you say it is. But why is it like that? Who is responsible for that? And who makes sure that it stays that way? And who profits by it? Instead of naming the causes you make fun of their appearances. And precisely that happens to be one of the causes. To describe pure appearances is a man's kind of joke. Van Wullnow would say that I would say: undialectical impressionism.

QUITT. And you: because you've got so many causes on your mind you forget to bother with the appearances. Instead of things you see nothing but causes. And when you eliminate the causes so as to change the appearances, they have already changed so that you have to eliminate entirely different causes. And if you look at me now, please become aware of me for once and not my causes.

PAULA. You have a beautiful tie-pin. Your shirt is so new that one can still see the pinholes. Your grinding jaws manifest willpower. Your delicate hands might be those of a pianist. One of your earlobes has dried shaving-cream on it. And while you behave animalistically the creases on your trousers give you away.

QUITT *gets up and pulls* PAULA *towards him. She wraps her arms exaggeratedly around him and also puts one leg around his hip, throws back her head and sighs derisively. He lets go of her at once and walks away. She walks backwards. They pursue each other alternately for a short time. Then they walk around by themselves and finally stop.*

QUITT. Please stop being conceptual. I once gave someone a present, some chocolate for his child. The chocolate was wrapped in small squares, each one with a picture of a different fairy-tale motif. 'Oh,' the father said disappointedly, 'it's not a puzzle!' And then he said: 'That's it, deprivation of the imagination by the chocolate manufacturers.' When he said that, I suddenly stood very distantly beside him and felt radically alone. I looked down on the floor in utter loneliness. So, please stop.

PAULA. But you were the one who started it.

QUITT. Do you see that nail sticking out of the wall there?

PAULA. Yes.

QUITT. It's long, isn't it?

PAULA. Very long.

QUITT. And how thick is your head?

Pause.

PAULA. Perhaps I should turn on the light after all.

Pause.

QUITT. Today the door-bell rang. Because I was curious who it was I went to open the door myself. It was only the eggman whom the so-called estate sends around from house to house once a week.

He always comes at the same time. I'd forgotten. 'Can't you be someone else for once?' I wanted to scream.

Pause.

PAULA. And what if *I* were someone else?

QUITT *takes one step towards her. She does not step back.*

QUITT. And recently I saw a silent film. No music had been dubbed in, so it was almost completely quiet in the cinema. Only now and then when something funny happened a few scattered children laughed and stopped again at once. Suddenly I had a sense of death. The feeling was so strong that I yanked my legs far apart and spread my fingers. What social conditioning can you use to explain that? Does this syndrome already bear someone's name? If so, whose?

PAULA. I can't explain it to you in terms of social conditioning. It is unconditionally yours and can't be emulated. As a social factor it's not worth mentioning. The masses have other worries.

QUITT. But which will pass.

PAULA. Yes, because the conditions will pass too.

QUITT. And then the masses will perhaps have my worries, which do not pass.

QUITT'S WIFE *appears with a magazine in her hand.*

WIFE. Austrian dramatist, dead, seven letters?

QUITT. Nestroy.

WIFE. No.

QUITT. Across or down?

WIFE. Across.

QUITT. Raimund.

WIFE. Of course. (*Off.*)

Pause.

PAULA. The watch . . . it isn't a memento. (*Pause.*) Is that still too conceptual?

QUITT. Now I won't tell you what I'm thinking.

PAULA. And what are you thinking?

QUITT. It's kind of you to ask. But why don't you ask me of your own volition? I yearn to be questioned by you. Do I have to bang my head against the floor to make you ask about me? (*He throws himself on the floor and actually bangs his head a few times against it, then stands up at once and steps up to* PAULA.) I would like to snap at the world now and swallow it, that's how inaccessible everything seems to me. And I too am inaccessible, I twist away from everything. Every story I could possibly experience slowly but surely transforms itself back into lifeless nature where I no longer play a role. I can stand before it as I do before you and I am back in prehistory without human beings. I imagine the ocean, the fire-spewing volcanoes, the primordial mountains on the horizon but the conception has nothing to do with me. I don't even appear dimly within it as a premonition. When I regard you now I see you only as you are, and as you are entirely without me, but not as you were or could be with me; that is inhuman.

PAULA. Excuse me, but I can't concentrate any longer. (*She takes a step, so that their bodies touch.*) So what were you thinking?

Pause.

QUITT. You know anyway.

PAULA. Perhaps. But I'd like to hear you say it.

QUITT. Now I feel strong enough not to tell you any more.

PAULA (*steps back*). We are alone.

QUITT. I am alone and you are alone, not we. I would not want to transpose the 'we' of our plans to you and me at this moment.

PAULA. Isn't this moment, too, part of our plan?

QUITT. Don't you get out of your box even for a second?

PAULA. Your impatience is what keeps me boxed in.

QUITT *flings her on the floor. She lies there, supporting herself on one elbow. Then she gets up.*

QUITT. How gracefully you get back on your feet!

PAULA. I'd like to leave now.

QUITT. Hans!

HANS *appears with a long fur coat over his arm and first walks in the wrong direction.*

QUITT. Over here. Where did you think you were?

HANS (*helping* PAULA *into her coat*). Always with you, Mr Quitt. The lights were on in the room I just left.

PAULA. Hans, you're good at helping people into their coats.

HANS. Mr Quitt has the same one.

PAULA (*to* QUITT). I would like to tell you something about myself, Quitt, just like this, without being asked to. And note that for the first time, I'm speaking about myself. After your wife left I slowly exhaled. And while exhaling . . . please don't laugh.

QUITT. I'm not laughing.

PAULA. While exhaling . . . please don't laugh.

QUITT. Another second and I will.

PAULA (*loudly*). As I exhaled love set in. (*She leaves.*)

QUITT (*to* HANS). Don't say anything.

HANS. I'm not saying anything.

QUITT'S WIFE *enters, turns on some mild indirect lighting and sits down. She gives* HANS *a signal to leave.*

QUITT. Nobody's done any dusting yet.

HANS *proceeds to dust.*

   (*To his* WIFE). And what did you do all day?

WIFE. You saw what I did: I went in and out and back and forth.

QUITT. And what was it like in town?

WIFE. People respected me.

HANS *leaves*.

QUITT. Was there anything new?

WIFE. I stole this blouse.

QUITT. The main thing is not to get caught. Anything else?

WIFE. I stopped here and there and then walked on. Why don't you sit down too?

QUITT. You don't look well.

Pause.

WIFE. Yes, but at least it's already evening. (*She gets up and walks out quickly.*)

QUITT *sits down even before she has gone. He remains alone for a while. The silhouette of the city is completely illuminated in the meantime.* HANS *returns with a book.* QUITT *looks up.*

HANS. It's me, still.

QUITT. Tell me, Hans, what's your life actually like?

HANS *sits down*.

HANS. I knew what you would say the moment you opened your mouth. But I couldn't interrupt you at that point. So let's forget it.

Pause.

QUITT. Stop looking me in the eyes.

HANS. I do that whenever I'm at a loss how to please you.

QUITT. Tell me about yourself.

HANS. What do you mean?

QUITT. Don't you understand; I am curious to know your story. How do *you* behave when you would like to speak but can only scream? Don't you sometimes get so tired that you can only imagine everything flat on the ground? Doesn't it also happen to you sometimes that when you think of your relationship to others you only see heavy wet rags lying around everywhere? Now tell me about yourself.

HANS. You mention me.
Yourself you mean.

Pause.

QUITT. Why does my teeny little scrap of consciousness go squawking about the big wide world so affectedly? And can't help itself? (*Shouts.*) And doesn't want it any differently? I am important. I am important. I am important. Incidentally, why don't you look me in the eyes now?

HANS. Because there's nothing new to see there.

Pause.

QUITT. Please read to me.

HANS (*sits down and reads*). ' "I shall have to let you go after all," his uncle said one day at the end of the midday meal, just as a magnificent thunderstorm was breaking, sending the rustling rain like diamond missiles down into the lake, so that it twitched and seethed and heaved. Victor made no reply whatever but listened for what else would come. "Everything is futile in the end," his uncle started up again in a slow drawn-out voice, "it's futile, youth and old age don't belong together. The years that could have been used have passed now, they are lowering down on the other side of the mountains and no power on earth can drag them back to the near side where cold shadows are aleady falling." Victor could not have been more awed. The venerable old man happened to be sitting in such a way that the lightning flashes illuminated his face, and sometimes, in the dusky room, it seemed as though fire flowed through the man's grey hair and light trickled across his weatherbeaten face. "Oh Victor, do you know life? Do you know that thing that people call old age?" "How could I, Uncle, as I am still so young?" "True, you don't know it, and there's no way you could. Life is boundless as long as you are still young. You always think you still have a long stretch ahead of you, that you've travelled only a short way. That's why you put so much off to the next day, why you put this and that aside, to tackle it later on. But then when you want to tackle it, it is too late and you notice that you are old. That is why life is a limitless field if you look at it from the beginning, and is scarcely two paces long when you regard it from the end. It is a sparkling thing, something so beautiful that you feel like plunging into it, and you feel that it would have to last forever . . . and old age is a moth darting in the dusk, fluttering ominously about our ears. That is why you would like to stretch out your hands so as not to have to leave, because you have missed so much. When an aged man stands on a mountain of achievements, what good is it to him? I have done much, all sorts of things and have nothing from it. Everything turns to dust the moment you haven't built an existence that outlasts your coffin. The man who has sons, nephews and grandsons around him in his old age will often become a thousand years old. Then the same many-sided life persists even when he is gone, life continues just the same; yes, you don't even notice that one small segment of this life veered off to the side and never came back any more. With my death everything will disappear that I myself have been . . ." After these words the old man stopped speaking. He folded his napkin together, as was his custom, rolled it into a cylinder and pushed it into the silver ring which he kept for the purpose. Then he assembled the various bottles into a certain order, put the cheese and sweetmeats on their plates and plunged the glass bells over them. Yet of all these objects he took none away from the table as was his usual habit, but left them standing there and sat before them. Meanwhile the thunderstorm had passed; with softer flashes and a muted thundering it moved down the far slope of the craggy eastern mountain range, and the sun fought its way out again, gradually filling the room with a lovely fire. At daybreak the next morning Victor took his walking-stick in his hand and slung one strap of his satchel over his arm. The spitz, who understood everything, bounded with joy. Breakfast was consumed amid much small talk. "I'll take you as far as the gate," the uncle said when Victor had stood up, had hitched his satchel on his shoulder and was about to take his leave. The old man had gone into the adjacent room and must have triggered a spring or set off some kind of mechanical contraption; for at that moment Victor heard the rattling of the gate and saw, through the window, how the gate was opening slowly by itself. "Well," said his uncle as he stepped out, "everything is ready." Victor reached for his walking-stick and placed his cap on his head. The uncle walked down the steps with him and across the open space in the garden as far as the gate. Neither said a word during their walk. At the gate the uncle stopped. Victor looked at him for a while. Tears shimmered in his bright eyes, testifying to a profound emotion . . . then he suddenly bent down and vehemently kissed the wrinkled hand. The old man emitted a dull uncanny sound like a sob . . . and pushed the youth out through the gate. In two hours the latter had reached Attmaning, and as he strode out from the dark trees towards the town he happened to hear its bells tolling, and never had a sound sounded so sweet to him as this tolling which fell so endearingly upon his ears, a sound he had not heard for so long. The Wirtsgasse was filled with the beautiful brown animals of the mountains which the cattle dealers were driving down towards the lowlands, and the inn's guest-room was full of people since it was market day. It seemed to Victor as if he had been dreaming for a long time and had only now returned to the world. Now that he was back out in the fields of the people, on their highways, part of their merry doings, now that the expanse of gentle rolling hills stretched out wide and endless before him, and the mountains which he had left hovered behind as a blue wreath: now his heart came apart in this great circumambient view and outraced him far, far beyond the distant scarcely visible line of the horizon . . .'

QUITT. How nice that this armchair has a headrest. (*Pause.*) How much time has passed since then! In those days, in the nineteenth century, even if you didn't have some feeling for the world, there at least existed a memory of a universal feeling, and a yearning. That is why you could replay the feeling and replay it for the others as in this story. And because you could replay the feeling

as seriously and patiently and conscientiously as a restorer –
Adalbert Stifter after all was a restorer – that feeling was really
produced, perhaps. In any event, people believed that what was
being played there existed, or at least that it was possible. All I
actually do is quote; everything that is meant to be serious
immediately becomes a joke with me, genuine signs of life of my
own slip out of me purely by accident, and they only exist at the
moment when they slip out. Afterwards then they are – well –
where you once used to see the whole, I see nothing but
particulars now. Hey, you with your ingrown earlobes! It
suddenly slips out of me, and, instead of speaking to someone I
notice, I step on his heels so that his shoe comes off. I would so
like to be full of pathos! Von Wullnow bathing in the nude with a
couple of women at sunrise bawled nothing but old college songs
in the water – that's what's left of him. What slips out of me is
only the raw sewage of previous centuries. I lead a businessman's
life as camouflage. I go to the telephone as soon as it rings. I talk
faster if the door behind me is held open. We fix our prices and
faithfully stick to our agreements. Suddenly it occurs to me that I
am playing something that doesn't even exist, and that's the
difference. That's the despair of it! Do you know what I'm going
to do? I won't stick to our arrangement. I'm going to ruin their
prices and them with it. I'm going to employ my old-fashioned
sense of self as a means of production. I haven't had anything of
myself as yet, Hans. And they are going to cool their hot little
heads with their clammy hands, and their heads will grow cold as
well. It will be a tragedy. A tragedy of business life, and I will be
the survivor. And the investment in the business will be me, just
me alone. I will slip out of myself and the raw sewage will sweep
them away. There will be lightning and thunder, and the idea
will become flesh.

There is thunder.

HANS. I can't find a rhyme this time.

QUITT. Good night.

HANS *leaves.* QUITT *drums his fist on his chest and emits Tarzan-like
screams. Pause. His* WIFE *comes in and stops in front of him.*

WIFE. I have something else to say to you.

QUITT. Don't speak to me. I want to get out of myself now. I am now myself and as such I am on speaking terms only with myself.

WIFE. But I would like to say something to you. Please.

Pause.

QUITT (*suddenly very tender*). Then tell me. (*He takes her around the waist, she moves in his embrace.*) Tell me.

WIFE. I . . . where it . . . because . . . hm . . . (*She clears her throat.*) . . . and you . . . isn't it . . . (*She laughs indecisively.*) . . . this and that . . . and autumn . . . like a stone . . . that roaring . . . the Ammonites . . . and the mud on the soles of the shoes . . .

She puts her hand before her face and the stage becomes dark.

ACT TWO

The silhouette of the city. The punch bag has been replaced by a huge balloon which, almost imperceptibly, is shrinking. A large, slowly melting block of ice with a spotlight shining on it has replaced the matching sofa and armchairs, a glass trough with dough rising in it somewhere else, also with a spot on it. A piano. A large boulder in the background with phrases slowly and constantly appearing and fading on it: 'Our greatest sin . . . The impatience of concepts' and 'The worst is over . . . The last hope'. Next to them are children's drawings. The usual stage lighting constant throughout. HANS *is lying on an old deck-chair, dressed as before, and is asleep. He is mumbling in his sleep and laughing. Time passes.* QUITT *walks in from behind the wall, rubbing his hands. He executes a little dance step while walking. He whistles to himself.*

QUITT. It's been ages since I've whistled! (*He hums. The humming makes him want to talk.*) Hey Hans! (HANS *leaps up out of his sleep and immediately goes to relieve* QUITT *of the coat which he isn't wearing.*) You can't stop acting the servant even in your sleep, can you? When I was singing to myself like that I suddenly couldn't stand being alone any more. (*He regards* HANS.) And now you're already annoying me again. Were you dreaming of me? Oh, forget it, I don't even want to know. (*He whistles again.* HANS *whistles along.*) Stop whistling. It's no fun if you're whistling too.

HANS. I dreamed. Really, I was dreaming. The dream was about a pocket calendar with rough and smooth sides. The rough sides were the work-days, the smooth ones the days I have off. I slithered for days on end over calendar pages.

QUITT. Dream on, little dreamer, dream – just as long as you don't interpret your dreams.

HANS. But what if the dream interprets itself – as it did just now?

QUITT. You are talking about yourself – why is that?

HANS. You've infected me.

QUITT. And how?

HANS. By employing your personality . . . and having success with yourself too. Suddenly I saw there was something I lacked. And when I thought about it I realised that I lacked everything. For the first time I didn't just sort of exist for myself, but existed as someone who is comparable, say, with you. I couldn't bear the comparing any more, began to dream, evaluated myself. Incidentally, you just interrupted me and it was important. (*He sits down and closes his eyes. He shakes his head.*) Too bad. It's over. I felt really connected when I was dreaming. (*To* QUITT.) I don't want to have to go on shaking my head much longer.

QUITT. It occurs to me I should have got you up earlier. Then you wouldn't be getting ideas like this. You want to leave me, then?

HANS. On the contrary, I want to stay forever. I still have much to learn from you.

QUITT. Would you like to be like me?

HANS. I have to be. Recently I've been forcing myself to copy your handwriting. I no longer write with a slant but vertically. That is like standing up after a life time of bowing down. But it hurts, too. I also no longer put my hand like this – (*Thumbs forward, fingers backward on his hips.*) – on my hips; but like you do. (*Fingers forward, thumbs backward.*) That gives me more self-confidence. Or standing up – (*He stands up.*) – I stand on one leg and play with the other like you. A new sense of leisure. Only when I buy something, say at the butcher's, I place my legs quite close together and parallel and don't move from the spot. That makes an upper class impression, and I always get the best cut and the freshest calf's liver. (*He yawns.*) Have you noticed that I no longer yawn as unceremoniously as I used to but with a pursed mouth, like you?

QUITT. The long and short of it: you are still here for me?

HANS. Because I am compelled to be as free as you are. You have everything, live only for yourself, don't have to make any comparisons any more. Your life is poetic, Mr Quitt, and poetry as we know, produces a sense of power that oppresses no one – but rather dances the dance of freedom for us, the oppressed. At one time I felt caught in the act even when someone watched me licking stamps. Now I don't bat an eyelash when someone calls me a lackey; carry the dustbin out onto the pavement in my tails with complete peace of mind; walk self-confidently arm in arm with the ugliest woman; do work, willy-nilly, which isn't mine to do – that is my freedom, which I have learned from you. At one time I used to be envious of what you could afford to do. I felt treated like a butt and not a butler – notice my new freedom, I'm already playing with words! – cursed you under my breath as a bloodsucker, did not see the human being in you but only the corporation mogul. That's how unfree I was. Now, as soon as I imagine you, I see the self-assured curve that your watch chain describes over your belly and already I am moved.

QUITT. This sounds familiar. (HANS *laughs*.) So you're just making fun of me. I should have known that someone with your history would never change. But you're not the one who matters. It's the others that count.

HANS. Do you actually despise yourself, Mr Quitt? . . . Now that you've mucked everyone up?

QUITT. Myself? No. But I might despise someone *like* me. (*Long pause*.) Why don't you react? Just now when you weren't answering, what I said began to crawl back into me at a certain moment and wanted to make itself unsaid, and me too, by shrivelling me deep inside. (*Pause*.) You're making fun of my language. I would much prefer to express myself inarticulately like the simple people in that play recently, do you remember? Then you would finally pity me. This way I suffer from my articulateness being part of my suffering. The only ones that you and your kind pity are those who can't speak about their suffering.

HANS. How do you want to be pitied? Even if you became speechless with suffering your money would speak for you, and the money is a fact, and you, you're nothing but a consciousness.

QUITT (*derisively*). Pity only occurred to me because the characters in the play moved me so . . . not that they were speechless, but that despite their seemingly dehumanised demeanour they really wanted to be as kind to each other as we spectators who all live in more human surroundings are already to each other. They too wanted tenderness, a life together, et cetera – they just can't express it, and that is why they rape and murder each other. Those who live in inhuman conditions represent the last humans on stage. I like that paradox. Because, I like to see human beings on the stage. Not monsters, human beings, gnarled with suffering, unschematic, drenched with pain and joy. The animalistic attracts me, the defenceless, the abused and insulted. Simple people, do you understand? Real people whom I can feel and taste, living people. Do you know what I mean? People! Simply . . . people! Do you know what I mean? Not paper tigers but . . . (*He thinks for quite a while.*) . . . people. You understand: people. I hope you know what I mean.

HANS. I can't take your jokes so soon after waking up. But let's suppose you're being serious. There must be another possibility which makes your alternative – here paper tigers, there human beings – look ridiculous.

QUITT. Which?

HANS. I don't know.

QUITT. Why not?

HANS. That I don't know is the very thing that lends me hope. Besides, as one of those whom you have in mind, I can say it: every time the curtain rises I become discouraged at the prospect that things will be human again up there any moment now. Let's further assume that you mean what you say: perhaps the people on stage moved you – not because they were people but because everything was shown as it is. For example, if you recognise a portrait as true to life, you frequently develop a peculiar sympathy for the person in the portrait without necessarily having any feeling for the real person. Couldn't the same thing have happened to you when you saw the play? That you

empathised with the inarticulate people represented on the stage
and think therefore that you have done so with the real ones? And
why do you want to see real characters on stage at all? They
belong in the past and are alien to you.

QUITT. Because I like to think back to the days when I was poor too,
and couldn't express myself, and primarily because the painted
dummies from my own social stratum are sitting in the audience
anyway. On stage I want to see the other class, as crude and as
unadorned as possible. After all, I go to the theatre to relax.

HANS (*laughs*). Now *you're* being derisive.

QUITT. I meant that seriously. (*He laughs. Both of them laugh.*)

QUITT'S WIFE *comes in*.

HANS. Here comes one of your real people.

WIFE. Are you laughing at me?

QUITT. Who else?

WIFE. And what were you saying about me?

HANS. Nothing. We were only laughing about you.

QUITT'S WIFE *laughs too; she slaps* QUITT *on the shoulder, nudges him
in the ribs.*

QUITT. We're all happy for once, right?

HANS. Since business is so good, Mr Quitt . . . why don't you cross
my palm with silver?

QUITT. You're welcome.

He goes to put the coin into HANS's *outstretched hand but* HANS *pulls
back the hand and stretches out the other. Now* QUITT *goes to put the
coin into that hand but* HANS, *so as to adjust to* QUITT, *has already
stretched out his first hand again. When he notices that* QUITT *etc., he
stretches out his second hand again. But meanwhile* QUITT *has tried to
put the coin into* HANS's *first hand again. And so on until* QUITT *puts the
coin away again, walks to the piano and plays a boogie.* WIFE *takes*

HANS *and dances with him* . . . *Then* QUITT *suddenly plays a slow sad blues, singing as he plays.*

Sometimes I wake up at night
and everything I want to do next day
suddenly seems silly
How silly to button your shirt
How silly to look in your eyes
How silly the foam on the glass of beer
How silly to be loved by you.
Sometimes I lie awake
and everything I imagine
makes everything that much more unimaginable
Unimaginable the pleasure of standing at a hot-dog stand
Unimaginable New Zealand
Unimaginable thinking of sooner or later
Unimaginable to be alive or dead.

I'd like to hate you and I hate PVC
You'd like to hate me and you hate the fog
I'd like to love you and I love hilly countrysides
You'd like to love me
and have a favourite city, a favourite colour, a favourite pet.

Everyone stay away from me
It is the time after my death
and what I've just imagined, with a sigh, as my life
are only blisters on my body
which sigh when they burst. (*He stops singing.*)

But things are going well for us right now, aren't they? I simply saw a woman walking in the sun with a full shopping bag and I knew at once: nothing more can happen to me now! I hear an old lady say: 'Parsley on the stalk? I've never eaten that.' And then she says: 'Yes, and I don't think I'll indulge in it now.' Nothing can happen to me any more! Nothing can happen to me any more! (*He resumes singing.*)

No dream
could make anything seem stranger

than I've already experienced it
and there's no cure
for the peace and quiet . . .
(*He speaks again.*) . . . with which every morning I let my jack-
in-the-box out from behind my flies to dangle in the peep-hole
answering the call of nature that I could no longer imagine during
the sleepless night.

VON WULLNOW, KOERBER-KENT *and* LUTZ *appear silently.*
QUITT'S WIFE *makes to go.*

QUITT. Stay here.

She leaves. HANS *leaves too. Pause.*

So you still exist. (*Pause.*) Why don't we make ourselves
comfortable? (*Pause.*) What can I offer you? Schnapps? Cognac?

KOERBER-KENT. No thank you. It's still too early for that.

QUITT. Or fruit-juice, freshly squeezed?

KOERBER-KENT. That doesn't agree with my stomach. Hyper-
acidity.

QUITT. Then a few breadsticks. Or would you prefer cocktail
sausages?

LUTZ. Thank you, we really don't want anything. Seriously, don't
go to any trouble.

QUITT. You've got a frog in your throat. Hans will make you a
camomile tea. (LUTZ *shakes his head.*) Camomile which we picked
ourselves on the Mediterranean. The blossoms are still intact!

LUTZ (*clears his throat*). I'm over it already. I don't need anything.

QUITT. And you, Monsignore? Perhaps you'd like a peppermint
drop? One hundred per cent pure peppermint.

KOERBER-KENT. I'm perfectly happy too.

QUITT. I'd put it on your tongue myself.

KOERBER-KENT. I usually enjoy sucking peppermints, but not today.

QUITT. Why not today? It isn't Friday, is it?

KOERBER-KENT. I simply don't want to. That's all.

QUITT. You want to jilt me?

KOERBER-KENT. If that's how you want to take it.

QUITT. I'm offended.

He walks out. KOERBER-KENT *goes to make a gesture to stop him but* VON WULLNOW *makes a sign not to.*

VON WULLNOW. I know. I could cut off his head with one slash of the whip and slap the decapitated chicken on the table before you. I was grinding my teeth so fiercely just now that some must have cracked. (*He shows his teeth.*) There! You traitor, you upstart, you greasy rat! (*Raving.*) My hand even trembled briefly, which is usually the strangest of all things to happen to me. In the meantime, of course it is completely steady again. Look! (*He holds out his hand.*) But we have to be rational now, in the most economic sense of the word: at first as rational as necessary and then, when he no longer has any need for our reason, as irrational as possible. I'm already looking forward to my irrationality. (*He goes through the motions of trampling, torturing and throttling.*)

LUTZ (*interrupting him*). Yes, that's it; we have to let ourselves go for a moment. Like you just now. Perhaps that'll teach us what to do next. Let's say or do whatever comes to mind. That will determine our method. After all, that's the way he does it. So let's dream. (*Pause. They concentrate. Pause.*) Nothing is happening. I only see myself cutting a steak against the grain or playing tennis in such brief shorts that my testicles are hanging out one side. (*Pause. They concentrate.*) Do you know what I'm most afraid of about myself? (*They regard him expectantly.*) That one day I will get up in a restaurant so lost in thought that I forget to pay the bill.

Pause. KOERBER-KENT *scraches his behind and they regard him.*

KOERBER-KENT. I just happened to think of our minority share-holder . . .

Pause.

LUTZ. Don't you ever dream?

KOERBER-KENT. Ah! Monstrous dreams!

LUTZ. Well! Let's hear.

KOERBER-KENT (*powerfully*). I . . . I'm walking in the woods alone . . .

Long, embarrassed silence. VON WULLNOW *laughs.*

LUTZ. Are you laughing?

VON WULLNOW. I was remembering.

LUTZ. Was it that funny?

VON WULLNOW. Remembering it was. (*Pause.*) The grainbins in the loft, the trickling grain and the mouse droppings inside, the swirl of grain that my memory delved into like a boy's naked foot, the grains between the toes, the vacated wasp nest, still so enlivened by memories, on the underside of the roof tiles. (*Pause.*) I've got to stop. Remembering makes me a good person. Usually I would make my peace in a moment. O Quitt, O Quitt, why hast thou forsaken us?

LUTZ. Now I know what we are going to do. We have to talk about ourselves, about us as individuals . . . what we're really like. I for one sometimes feel like hopping up and down on the street and don't do it. Why not? And last summer passed by while I sat in my office with its tinted window and never experienced the summer once. Every so often I do something quite crazy: I eat the rotten part of an apple, slam a car door before everyone's got out . . .or something like that . . . and if that doesn't help, there's still – (*To* KOERBER-KENT.) – our minority shareholder.

QUITT *returns.*

He'll show him where the moon is rising.

QUITT. I do miss you. And perhaps you miss me too.

VON WULLNOW. Quitt, today I had a bag of flour in my hand. Do you know how long it has been since I've held flour in my hands? I don't even know myself. The package was so soft and heavy. This weight in my hand and at the same time the gentleness of the pressure . . . I was transported into delicious unreality. Doesn't the same thing ever happen to you?

QUITT. I find the most vicious reality more bearable than the most delicious feeling of unreality.

LUTZ (*trying to distract*). How is your wife?

QUITT. My wife? My wife is fine.

LUTZ. She looked well just now. With her cheeks all rosy as though she'd just been playing tennis. That made me think of my wife who has to rock the child all day long on the terrace. You know, we have a retarded child who screams as soon as we stop rocking. My wife stands days on end in the garden and pushes the swing, imagine that. But she's come to like doing it in the meantime. She says that it even calms her down. And she feels it makes her superior to the other women in the neighbourhood who can't think of anything to do but tell their cleaning women how to do the housework. By the way, excuse me for talking about myself.

QUITT. I like women who do nothing but give orders.

VON WULLNOW. I know you like hearing stories, I have one.

QUITT. Is it long?

VON WULLNOW. Very brief. A child walks into a shop and says: 'Six rolls, the morning paper and three white loaves!'

QUITT. Go on.

VON WULLNOW. That's the story.

Pause.

QUITT. It's beautiful.

VON WULLNOW (*suddenly embracing him vehemently*). I knew you would like it. I knew it. I'm usually too shy to touch anyone, but this time I simply must. (*He pulls* QUITT'*s cuffs out of his jacket, takes his hand.*) I've been looking at this dirty fingernail all the time . . . now I have to clean it for you. (*He does so, using his own fingernail, steps back.*) I don't know what's the matter with me. I've been quite tipsy with memories recently. Do you remember that time we dressed up as workers at the opera ball? With red bandanas, t-shirts, hoist-up trousers and muddy boots. The way we stepped on the ladies' toes? The way we scratched our crotches? Staring at everything, our mouths agape? Ordered Crimean champagne and drank out of the bottle? And at the end pushed our caps off our foreheads and sang the Internationale?

QUITT. 'Crimean champagne' is an illegal label. It should be called 'Sparkling Wine from the Crimea'. (*Pause.*) Yes, we played the part very expertly, so that we could only play ourselves.

VON WULLNOW. And now you're in league with them.

QUITT. How so?

VON WULLNOW. By thinking only of yourself. The huge share of the market which you control provides the enemies of the free enterprise system, who are our enemies too, with the welcome opportunity . . .

LUTZ (*interrupting him quickly*). Not like that. (*To* QUITT.) I've been thinking a lot about death lately. Everything I encounter looks like a sign to me. When I read in the papers: 'Next Wednesday junk collection,' then I sense at once: 'That junk, that's me.' Recently when I went into a tobacco shop somewhere out in the country I saw an obituary pinned up on the wall . . . and under the obituary lay a filthy, shrivelled-up glove: that leather glove, that'll soon be me, my heart fluttered.

QUITT. And I recently saw an empty plastic bag in a hallway with the legend 'Fresh Ham from Poland' on it. Should that have been a sign too? In any event, I suddenly felt incredibly safe when I read that.

LUTZ. Don't you ever think of death?

QUITT. I can't.

VON WULLNOW (*strikes his fist against his forehead*). And I can't any more! I'd like to open a newspaper now and read the word 'arsehole' in it. This jungle. This slime. This swamp. These will-o'-the-wisps. (LUTZ *has nudged him with his elbow and* VON WULLNOW *calms down.*) These will-o'-the-wisps above the swamp when we used to walk home in the autumn after our dancing lessons! Wanda on my arm, I could feel her goose pimples through her blouse, and a pheasant screamed in its sleep as I kissed her – an ugly word actually, kissing – only the cracks of our lips touched each other, as unfeeling as peeled bark. (*Pause.* VON WULLNOW *looks at* LUTZ *who gives him the cue by forming the word 'nature' with his lips.*) Why nature? Of course, I was about to talk about nature: it was nature that made me aware – by teaching me how to perceive. Houses, streets and I were just a daydream at first, dreamer and dreamt were in one and the same bubble where the dreamer – hypnotised by the never-changing bulge on the never-changing house wall, grown together in his sleep with the same street curve day in and day out – also considered himself part of his dream. Dark spots inside me as the only thing undefined. Then the bubble burst and the dark spots *inside* me unfolded like the forest *outside* me. Only then did I begin to define myself as well. Not the civilisation of house and street, but *nature* made me aware of myself – by making me aware of nature. So: only by perceiving nature and not in the hallucinatory monotony of the objects of civilisation can we arrive at our own history. But in the meantime most people have become so civilised that they simply dismiss rapport with nature as some kind of withdrawal into childhood – although it is children whom one keeps having to make artificially aware of nature – or, even if they pretend to have rapport with nature, cannot endure this nature without the fata morgana of civilisation: inside the forest they have no feeling for the forest; only when they look out at it from the window of a terraced house which they themselves would plan, erect and offer for sale – only then would the same forest be an experience of nature for them. You're going to ask me what I mean by all this.

QUITT. No.

VON WULLNOW. I mean to say that you, you with your ruthless over-expansion, are destroying our nature. You senselessly transform the old countryside where we could come to our senses into construction sites. Your blind department stores squat like live bombs in our old city centres. Every day a new branch goes up, differing from the others only by its tax identification number which you even set up in neon light to blink from its roof as an advertisement of your sense of public responsibility!

QUITT. A good idea, isn't it?

VON WULLNOW. You're ruining our reputation by carrying on just the way the Joneses think a businessman behaves.

QUITT. Perhaps it's not our reputation I'm ruining but you.

VON WULLNOW. You know neither honour nor shame. The manure pit behind my country house is too good for you. I'd like to choke you by stuffing blotting-paper down your throat. I damn you! Whosoever utters your name before me, there shall I reach into his mouth and rip out his tongue, and with my very own hands to boot. Wait, I'm going to step on your foot. (*He does so.* QUITT *does not react.* VON WULLNOW *blows out his cheeks and slaps them with his hands. He bites the back of his hand. He hits his head with his fist and quickly smooths down his hair.*) You've disappointed me, Quitt. It's a pity about you. I liked you best of all. We've got so much in common. I still admire you. Whenever I have to reach a decision I think of what you would do under the same circumstances. (*He screams.*) You rat, you Judas, for twenty pieces of silver . . .

QUITT. Thirty, to be exact.

VON WULLNOW. Twenty, I say.

QUITT (*to* KOERBER-KENT). But thirty is right, isn't it?

KOERBER-KENT. Yes, it was thirty pieces of silver. According to the latest findings, it's a question of . . .

VON WULLNOW (*screaming*). Pervert! Atavist! (LUTZ *places a hand on his shoulder.*) I once dreamed that we had grown old together. Every day we drove in a carriage through town, playing bridge. And now all that is supposed to remain a dream? Let's stop fighting each other, Quitt. It could be so beautiful . . . just the four of us – that is, five, counting Mrs Tax – and since all the others have thrown in the towel in the meantime, we lone wolves have become so big there's no longer any need for arrangements. Those who help us into our coats after our conferences could conduct our affairs for us. Let's not undercut each other any more.

QUITT. *I* undercut *you*.

VON WULLNOW *roars*.

Does it help?

VON WULLNOW. Like a hobnailed boot in the privates! Don't you understand me! What am I at this moment? A radical! How I'd like simply to yawn at you. Do you have a slice of bread on you?

QUITT. Are you hungry?

VON WULLNOW. I'd like to have something to crumble between my fingers. My brain is scraping against my brain-pan. Actually a pleasant sensation. So animalistic. (*To* LUTZ.) I won't say anything more now. (*To* QUITT.) I'd like to change places with you, you shark. Besides, it's time for your wife to pass through the room again, isn't it? Come on, say something, I'd like to have something to laugh about! Dear Hermann . . . (*Pause. He takes* QUITT's *arm.*) You know, I could be your father? Let's go fishing together; fathers always take their sons fishing. Up the stream before the thunderstorm hits. I'd like to be drunk now so that I could remember something. (*He lets go of* QUITT's *arm.*) Apropos streams. You ruin them with your plastic monsters, let the countryside choke on plastic still-lives stamped 'biodegradable' where no environment is even left or, at most, a multi-coloured mildew on the ground, a soot-coloured dust on a sweetly crinkling leaf, a fishbelly in the animated foam-flecked water. Do you know what children ask when they're actually shown a big ripe tomato? 'Is it made of plastic?' they ask. And I personally saw a child that didn't want to sit down in a Rolls because the seat wasn't made of plastic. Let's stop all this over-expansion, Hermann . . . or let's limit ourselves to products for environmental protection. There's still a pretty penny to be made in that field. Everything could be the way it used to be.

QUITT. But you stopped expanding a long time ago. Besides, as you so rightly say, the functional units are diminishing in size. So the number of units can continue to increase, correct? I'm not the kind of man who wants to leave everything the way it is. I can't see anything without wanting to utilise it. I want to make everything I see into something else. And so do you! Except that you can't any more.

VON WULLNOW (*steps away from* QUITT). You refuse to understand us.

QUITT. I understand you very well. You know what it means when one of us becomes human or even speaks about death. An emotion, after the first moment of fright, becomes a method for us.

VON WULLNOW. It's not that I call your behaviour treason . . . but what should I call it? Faithlessness? Treachery? Unreliability? Falseness? Bitchiness? Disloyalty?

QUITT. Those are the expressions you apply to employees. Among ourselves I would call it business behaviour.

VON WULLNOW. Now I really won't say anything more. I'll stick my finger down my throat in front of you. (*Does so and leaves, but returns immediately.*) And I really was attached to you. (*He leaves and returns.*) You with your frog's body. (*He leaves and returns.*) My spit is too good for you. All I'll do is spit from the back of my mouth to the front. (*Does so, leaves once more, returns once more, is beside himself, pulls a horrible face and leaves once and for all.*)

LUTZ *wants to say something.*

QUITT. I know what you want to say.

LUTZ. Then you say it.

QUITT. It's true. I didn't stick to our agreement.

LUTZ. But you didn't plan it that way.

QUITT. I simply forgot about it, did I?

QUITT. Not exactly forgot perhaps, but you didn't take it seriously enough.

QUITT. Why should I have taken it seriously?

LUTZ (*laughs*). Not bad. Very tricky indeed . . . (*Pause.*) Excuse me, I interrupted you. You were going to say something.

QUITT. No, that was it.

LUTZ. Why don't you defend yourself?

QUITT. Why don't you accuse me?

LUTZ. You must be very unhappy.

QUITT. Why?

LUTZ. One is completely locked up inside oneself like you only when one is miserable. I know that from my own experience.

QUITT. Don't compare me with yourself.

LUTZ. There, you see. For you there's only you, you don't even want to be compared. You must be in pretty bad shape.

He's been playing with his forefinger and thumb the whole time, unconsciously, as though he were counting money. QUITT *takes hold of his hand.*

QUITT. Why don't you admit that: that's nothing but your expression for something tangible? Anyway, you've been counting money ever since you started to talk.

LUTZ. All right. Now I'm going to tell you what I think of you.

QUITT. But watch out. Perhaps you'll think differently once you've begun to speak.

LUTZ. Once I begin to speak everything is completely thought out. I don't stutter. (*To* KOERBER-KENT.) He multiplied his share of the market at our expense. I have nothing against his methods, but he should have discussed them with us. And besides, of course I do have something against his methods: he recruits the ex-convicts away from us in the labour market and promises

them a sympathetic environment – and that means that he leaves
them entirely to themselves in a certain area of production and
pays all of them the same low wages. As he admitted just now, he
manufactures smaller and smaller amounts of his products but
without changing the size of the package, so that the buyers
believe they're getting the same amount. This way his prices
appear to remain the same while we have to raise ours. He lets
doctors buy shares in his drug firms and then they prescribe his
medicines. (*To* QUITT.) You duplicate our most expensive
products with cheap materials. Your guarantees are only valid for
Three-Star refrigerators. You print the national emblem next to
your recommended retail prices, so that it looks as though they
are government approved. Your price labels are huge – so that
people believe your things are cheaper even when they are at least
as expensive as anywhere else. The price structure has cracked,
Quitt. We are standing at the death-bed . . . at the death-bed of
the old concept of pricing and have become footsore ourselves.
We shiver in the shadow of your competition. As far as I'm
concerned, I'm still far too calm. Perhaps that is the calm before
the next breach of the agreement which will be my downfall. I
can already see the hailstorm in the distance, and panic flattens
my ears against my head. I'm afraid, Quitt, afraid of the great
storm when I won't be wearing the thick coat of capital. And yet I
tried to save the structure by means of massive redundancies.
Quitt, you've ruined our prices. You pushed them down to pre-
war level! Everything is cracking up. Every day there's one
product less on the market. The beautiful diversity of the market
is all over. Even the high consecration is for nothing. It's the end
of all our proud figures. I'm at a loss. I am at a most poodle-
befuddled loss and in utter despair. (*To* KOERBER-KENT.) I was
my parents' only child. Even my birth was a business decision: it
meant my mother's death. At the age of four I kneaded imitation
coins out of mud. At age seven I picked flowers for invalids in the
neighbourhood and sold them. At school they called me 'Moneybags'. A sensible boy, my father said. He still had respect for
material values, said my relatives. Before my first communion,
the priest said that if you wished for something afterwards and
really believed it the wish would come true. Still feeling the

pressure of the host against my gums, I walked all the way home with my head lowered: because every cell of my body believed I would find the coin I had wished for. (*To no one in particular.*) Since that time I've had my doubts about religion. (*To* KOERBER-KENT.) But I remained reasonable and became more and more reasonable. He's all business, people said of me. But now it's all over. All over. I don't want to believe anything any more. What is there left to believe in if that so and so destroys our prices and our rational system? What kind of age is that? What's still valid? I too want to be unbusinesslike at last! (*Pause.*) I dreamed that I was running and kept on running so that a huge bank-note wouldn't fall off my chest. Just the way I keep on talking now. I'd like to put my head into a bowl of water and drown myself. (*Off.*)

KOERBER-KENT *makes to follow him but turns back.* QUITT *paces up and down.*

KOERBER-KENT (*with lowered head*). I don't envy you, Quitt. I could also tell you about myself, like the others, but that's not my way. I never talk about myself. I'm proud that I eliminated myself from my own calculations long ago. I'm not interested in the fluff in my navel. I'm glad that I can be replaced. (*Pause.*) I pity you, Quitt. And I'm afraid for you. I recently saw a drawing a painter made of his dying wife: the pupils had lost almost all their colour in the fever, and the iris too had become very pale. Nothing but a dark circle separated it from the white of the eye round it, and the centrifugal force of dying had even thickened this circle. It was as if the eyes sighed towards the observer. The artist's pencil had hatched an endless sea of sighs from a mortal seeing hole, as I called it. And the following morning the woman is really supposed to have died.

A popping sound off-stage.

What was that?

QUITT. Hans is at work. He isn't very good at uncorking bottles. There's almost always a pop when he opens the cooking wine.

Pause.

KOERBER-KENT. Aren't you afraid to die?

He raises his head and wants to transfix QUITT – *but* QUITT *happens to be standing behind him.*

QUITT. Over here.

KOERBER-KENT. Don't you ever have to push everything away from you just because you are deathly afraid?

QUITT *steps away from him and comes to a halt with his back to him.* KOERBER-KENT *lowers his head again and closes his eyes.*

Someone once told me how he dreamed he was dying. He was sitting on a sled and still saying: I am dying. Then he was dead and at some point they closed the coffin-lid over him. And only then did he become deathly afraid, he didn't want to be buried. He woke up, his heart was fibrillating. Besides, he was very ill, the dream was trying to kill him. Cause of death: a dream, you could say. (*Very loudly.*) You see, dying in your sleep isn't at all peaceful, but perhaps the worst death of all.

QUITT *has kept pacing around in the meantime, absent-mindedly, and now stands in front of* KOERBER-KENT.

QUITT (*very softly*). Really.

KOERBER-KENT (*startled, he now does look up at* QUITT). I know from other stories – (*A key can be heard turning in a lock off-stage and a door-handle being pressed down.*) – that a dying person keeps looking away whenever his eye catches a specific object, as thought he could postpone death in this way . . . (*He listens.*) Someone pushed down a door-handle just now, didn't they? Why don't I hear a door opening? (*Pause.*) Once during a meal I personally sat opposite a man who suddenly started putting the table in order: put the knife and fork parallel to each other, wiped the edge of the glass with his serviette, pushed the serviette into its silver ring. Then he keeled over dead.

QUITT (*distracted*). Who kneeled on the bread?

KOERBER-KENT. He keeled over dead, I said. (*Frightened.*) You're afraid too.

QUITT (*scratching absent-mindedly at his trousers*). Damn! The cleaner didn't get that spot out either. Yes? I'm listening.

KOERBER-KENT. He was still smiling beforehand – (*Two or three distinctly audible steps off-stage.*) – but in his deathly fear he bared his *lower* teeth instead of his upper teeth as you would expect. Nothing wrong with a dead dwarf, that's still a vegetative process, almost. But a *fully grown* corpse, just imagine that! It's monstrous. (*He listens.*) Why doesn't he walk on? Wasn't there someone walking just then?

QUITT. My baby fat starts growing back when I listen to you. You and your deathly fear . . . at the moment everything seems thinkable to me and also beside the point.

KOERBER-KENT. What? What?

QUITT. It was just the floor creaking, I'm sure of it.

PAULA *appears, in a dress and with a veil in front of her face. At the sight of her,* QUITT *unzips his flies halfway down and up again. A dustbin lid bangs loudly on a hard floor off-stage.*

KOERBER-KENT. As I said, I've got an eye for those who are marked. (*He points to* QUITT.) It's that thin line on the upper lip . . . (*He notices* PAULA.) It's you! How good that you are here. Perhaps you could . . . er . . . thingamy him . . . (*He tries to find the word.*) What's the word?

QUITT. Congratulate him?

KOERBER-KENT. No.

QUITT. Work on him?

KOERBER-KENT. Something like that . . . no.

QUITT. Take him over your knees?

KOERBER-KENT (*panic-stricken*). Oh God, how did this happen? I can't find the right word any more. What are they doing to me? Come down, eclipse of the sun! Hell-fires, burst forth from the earth!

QUITT *walks up to* PAULA *and whispers in her ear.*

PAULA (*loudly*). 'Deathly afraid?' (*To* KOERBER-KENT.) You are trying to make him deathly afraid? Do you think he'll admit us back into the market?

KOERBER-KENT (*screams*). I know what I'm talking about. I've seen thousands die in the war.

QUITT *sighs*.

KOERBER-KENT (*normal tone of voice at once*). Am I keeping you from something?

QUITT. Not at all.

KOERBER-KENT (*screams*). I can read signs. I know why you hunch up your shoulders when you walk around. But soon you will shoulder the necessary weight of death, no matter what, Hermann Quitt. Even if you dangle your arms back and forth like that and scurry every which way. Even if you sit up straight like a candle in your deathly fear! (*He begins walking out backwards.*)

HANS *appears wearing his chef's hat.*

You won't even be able to imagine the moment. There will be nothing but abrupt, animalistic anxiety-ridden anticipation. You won't even dare to swallow you will be so afraid, and the spit will turn sour in your mouth. Your death will be gruesome beyond all imaginings, complete with moaning and bellowing. I know what I'm talking about. With moaning and bellowing. (*He walks backwards into* HANS *and emits a scream. He goes.*)

HANS *leaves too.* QUITT *and* PAULA *regard one another for a long time.*

QUITT. If you keep looking at me any longer I will lose the rest of my feelings.

PAULA. I won.

QUITT. Why?

PAULA. Because you were the first to talk.

QUITT. Now it's your turn.

PAULA. I love you, still. (*She laughs.*)

QUITT. Why are you laughing?

PAULA. Because I succeeded in saying that.

QUITT. I can't buy myself anything with that.

PAULA. You are so artificial. You're sacrificing the truth now for a slick cliché.

QUITT. Moreover I didn't give you any excuse for it. (*Pause.*) I keep having to get used to you all over again. (*He looks her over from head to foot.*)

PAULA. I'm not one of those.

QUITT. Who, after all, is one of those? (*Pause.*) I'm tired. When I take a step I feel as if my real body has stayed behind. I don't need you. When I saw you I was happy, but I also was a bit put off. I took that as a sign that all my desire for you is gone.

She laughs. He regards her considerately until she has finished.

PAULA. What you say is supposed to humiliate me. But the voice that I hear flatters me.

QUITT. You've changed. You're out of breath. Before you used to show your feelings you used to be much more self-assured. Why can't it be that way now? Stop playing the humble woman. I only want to touch you when you talk about business. (*Spitefully.*) Incidentally, why are you by yourself and not with the team? Do you call that creative? My head hurts. Besides, I like you better when you wear slacks.

PAULA. Your head is also hurting me, yes, your whole life . . . (QUITT *pats her arm.*) You pat me the way a conductor raps his baton . . . (*She caresses him.*)

QUITT. Your caresses tickle me.

PAULA. Yes, because you don't want to enjoy them.

QUITT'S WIFE *enters. She is wearing the same dress as* PAULA. *She notices, stops and leaves again.*

Now caress me too. (QUITT *caresses her and steps away from her.*) That was one too few. (QUITT *returns and caresses her once more.*) Oh yes. (*Pause.*) Tell me about yourself.

QUITT (*animatedly*). I was thirsty a few days ago. (*Pause.*) It just occurred to me.

PAULA. Look at me, please.

QUITT. I don't like to look at you.

PAULA. Well, what am I like?

QUITT. Unchanged.

PAULA. Before I got to know you better I thought you were unfeeling and tough. I once heard you say of me: 'that brunette there', as if you were talking about a whore.

QUITT. You always tell yourself stories like that afterwards.

PAULA. What would you say I would say now? Mr Quitt?

QUITT. Don't call me that.

She puts her hand on his shoulder. Suddenly she begins to choke him. He lets her do so for some time then shakes her off. QUITT'S WIFE *has returned in a different dress. She watches, giggling inaudibly, sucking her thumb.* QUITT *seats himself in the deck-chair and lowers his head.* PAULA *squats down and wants to take his head in her hands. He gives her a kick. She falls down and gets up, warbling. He kicks her again. She gets up, warbling. He makes to kick her again, but she eludes him, warbling.*

Your slimy tongue. Your absurd hips.

PAULA (*lifts her dress*). Look at the way my thigh is twitching. Can you see it? Why don't you come closer?

QUITT *grunts.*

Come on.

QUITT *puts his hand on her thigh.* PAULA *presses her head close to him. Pause.*

QUITT. All right, clear off now. (*He steps back. Pause.*) The saliva in your mouth is going to run over in a moment. And the way your eye-balls are jerking about! (*He turns away.*)

Pause.

PAULA. I'm going already. It's no use. I'll sell.

QUITT (*looking at her*). And I'll determine the fine print.

PAULA. Only promise me that you won't clean up the moment after
I've left.

QUITT. Buying yourself a hat can be very comforting.

PAULA. Now I know why I like you. It's so easy to think of
something else when you're talking.

QUITT. Tomorrow at this time it will already be lighter, or darker.
Perhaps that will comfort you too.

PAULA *suddenly embraces* QUITT'S WIFE, *releases her and tosses*
QUITT *a friendly as well as serious kiss as she walks out.*

PAULA. 'No hard feelings . . .'

QUITT *throws a stool after her.* PAULA *goes.* QUITT'S WIFE *comes
closer. They stand opposite each other, not saying anything. The lighting
on stage changes after some time. First sunshine, then cloud shadows
moving across the two of them. Crickets chirp. Far off in the distance a
dog barks. The sound of the ocean. A child shouts something into the
wind. Distant church bells. Woolly tree blossoms blow across the stage.
Both of them as silhouettes in the dusk against the backdrop of city lights
which are just coming on. The noise of an aeroplane engine, very close,
slowly receding – while the previous stage lighting comes back on.
Silence.*

WIFE (*softly*). You look so unapproachable.

QUITT. Remembering does that. I'm just remembering. Let me be.
I've got to remember to the end.

QUITT *sits down on the deck-chair. She steps closer. He touches her
lightly with his foot.*

WIFE. Yes?

QUITT. Nothing, nothing. (*He leans back and closes his eyes.*)

WIFE (*sighs*). Oh.

QUITT (*to himself*). So that it crashes and splinters . . .

WIFE. What will you do?

QUITT (*to himself*). Stop. Destroy. (*He looks back at her.*) Strange: when I look at you my thoughts skip a beat.

WIFE. I'd like to speak about myself for once, too.

QUITT. Not again!

WIFE. Why, are you listening to me?

QUITT. You could have been talking about yourself while you asked that. Did you wash your hair?

WIFE. Yes, but not for you. I am not well.

QUITT. Then scream for help.

WIFE. When I scream for help you reply by telling me a story of how you once needed help.

Pause. She laughs a few times in quick succession as though about something funny. QUITT *doesn't react.*

WIFE. Help!

QUITT. You have to shout at least twice.

WIFE. I can't any more.

QUITT (*gets up*). Then do away with yourself. (*He turns away.*)

WIFE (*mechanically wipes the dandruff off his shoulders*). You've got something up your sleeve. I can't look at you for too long, otherwise I'll find out what.

QUITT. What do you want? I have a pink face, my body is warm, pulse eighty.

Pause.

WIFE. My eyes are burning. I'm so sad I forgot to blink.

QUITT. What's there to eat today?

WIFE. Fillet of veal with truffles.

QUITT. I see. Well, well. Interesting. *What* is there to eat today?

WIFE. But you've just asked that. Why are you so distracted?

QUITT (*to himself*). Because every possibility has been tried except the very last one, and that one shouldn't turn into just another idle mental exercise! Of course, fillet of veal with truffles, you said so – I hear it only now. Why am I so distracted? I have to tell you something, my dear.

Pause. She looks at him.

WIFE. No, please don't say it. (*She shies away.*)

QUITT. I have to tell someone.

WIFE (*shies away and holds her ears shut*). I don't want to hear it.

QUITT (*follows her*). You'll know it in a moment.

WIFE. Don't say it, please don't.

She runs away and he follows her. Silence. Pause. She returns, slowly walking backwards, and goes off again, without letting her face be seen. KILB storms in. HANS appears behind him wearing the chef's hat. KILB is holding a knife and runs back and forth.

KILB. You have to die now. It's no use. I'm alone. No one pays me. Not even them. It's our last way out. Don't contradict me. (*He notices that there's no one present, and puts the knife back in his pocket.*) He isn't even here! And I rehearsed it so well! Into the room and right at him! One, two. A picture without words, only dashes for the caption underneath.

HANS. You'll have to try again.

KILB. I'll have to concentrate once more for that. If I'm as unconcentrated as I am now, everything could just as easily be something else, I think, even I myself. And that is a hideous feeling. Leave me alone.

HANS. But look at me first: because it's really me now. People used to say about me: that bloke it's eating him up inside but one day he'll blow his top and the walls will come tumbling down. That moment has come. So I will leave the room and cook the truffle fillet with special tenderness, thinking how it will be left over for me. I leave Mr Quitt to his fate, he believes in things like that.

First of all I'm going to stick to myself and I'm curious what that will bring. My big toe is already itching, a good sign; I'm becoming human.

KILB. How?

HANS. Because an itching big toe means that you should remember something, and someone who remembers becomes a human being. So all I need to do is remember.

There was a time something inside me wanted to scream
At the mere thought that I might dream.
Now I want to learn dreaming
So as to leave the floor of facts incomplete.
My eyes I want to learn to close
So as to know more of the little that I knows.
In my youth someone read in my palm
That I was able
To change the world's plan.
With this I announce at least the replanifications of *my* world.

He quickly punches the balloon punch bag fashion. The balloon bursts. HANS *off.* KILB *concentrates, stands the stool on its legs, gently closes the lid of the piano, puts in order what needs putting in order.* QUITT *returns.*

KILB. Not yet!

QUITT. You again.

KILB. But we haven't seen each other in ages.

QUITT. Not ages enough. Recently I thought of a mistake I once made. I couldn't remember what kind of mistake it had been – but I was sure at once that it was not an important mistake. Later on I remembered more distinctly: it had been an important mistake after all. It occurred to me only when I was dealing with you.

KILB. Please stay like that.

Pause.

QUITT. Kilb, I'm happy that you came. And please note that I said 'I'm happy' and not 'it makes me happy'.

KILB. Please don't become too friendly now.

Pause. QUITT *regards him for a long time.*

Why are you looking at me?

QUITT. I'm only too tired to look elsewhere. Why don't *you* at least sit down, so that I won't become even more tired. (*He points to the deck-chair.*)

KILB. No, that's too low for me, I'll never be able to get out of it.

QUITT *sits down in it.*

Particularly if you keep your hands in your pockets the way you do. I always keep my hands out of my pockets in moments of danger.

QUITT. Kilb, nothing is possible any longer. I feel as though I'm the sole survivor, and I find it unappetising that there's nothing left beside me. If only there were an appetising explanation for this state of affairs . . . but my awareness is the awareness of a pile of garbage in an infinite empty space. Imagine: the telephone no longer rings, the postman doesn't come any more, all street noises have ceased, only the wind is rustling one dream further away . . . the world has already died. I'm the only one who hasn't heard of the catastrophe. I'm actually only a phantom of myself. What I see are after-images, what I think are after-thoughts. A hair bends over on my head and I'm frightened to death. The next moment will be the last and untime will begin. Just a moment ago there was still a bubble where I was, but not any more. I know that my time is over. You were right, Paula.

KILB. Absolutely right. You're an anachronism, Mr Quitt. Like the goose-step of your soul.

QUITT. Be quiet. No one but me can say that. (*He bounces a little ball and looks at* KILB.) Now that it's just the two of us, instead of

becoming different you only become afraid that you might
become different. (*Pause.*) There is nothing unthought-of any
more. Even the Freudian slip has already become a management
method. Even dreams are dreamed from the beginning so as to be
interpretable. For example, I no longer dream anything that isn't
articulated, and the pictures of the dream follow each other
logically like the sequence of days in a diary. I wake up in the
morning and am paralysed with all the speeches I've made in the
dream. There's no longer the 'and suddenly' of the old dreams.
(*The ball escapes him and rolls away*.) Oh too bad . . . (*He gets up.*
KILB *has approached*.) That chair really is too low you're right.
When I think of myself, using hard concepts, I have one attack of
nausea after the other. This businessman with his breast pocket
handkerchief and his Savile Row suit full of *weltschmerz*, on
board his private plane, the soot from whose jets drift down on
the workers' housing estates, with organ music of the old masters
oozing from the in-built loud-speakers . . . stop it, get rid of it,
bomb it, it's logical. But: every logical conclusion is immediately
contradicted within me by this totally indecisive yet totally self-
assured *feeling*.

KILB. It's logical. You want to go on living.

QUITT. The little man is trying to put on airs.

KILB. Why not. What else has the little man left to put on?

QUITT. You're right. Why not. A good cue. I'm still stuck too deep
in my role. At the hospital I walk past the overcrowded National
Health Service wards and enjoy a certain *schadenfreude*. I look
away if a stranger stands in front of my table in the dining-car.
Why do I do it, actually? There's scarcely anyone who looks as if
he could still fall out of his role. Once I was walking along the
street and suddenly noticed that I didn't have anything to do with
my face any more . . .

KILB. The old story with the masks.

QUITT. Yes, but now someone who experienced it is telling about it.
Outside, the muscles clung to the dead skin, then one dead layer

on top of the other, only inside, in the deepest centre, where I should have been, there was still a little twitching and something wet. A car would have to crash into me at once! . . . Only then would I stop making a face. And not merely show my true face when I can't avoid that onrushing car any more, I thought. But this dead skin, that actually was my true face.

KILB. Nothing but stories. Where's the connection?

QUITT. I don't know anything about myself ahead of time. My experiences only occur to me in the telling. That establishes the connection. I'm now going to tell you what is hell for me: hell for me is the so called 'bargain', what's cheap. In a dark hour I happened into a restaurant which had the same menu that people like me usually eat, only half as expensive – but this wasn't the same food: the meat deep-frozen, thrown into the pan and fried to death, the potatoes water-logged, the vegetables something slopped into the pot with the liquid from the tin can, the paper napkin shredding after one wipe, and, tossed in for good measure, a table cloth with static which made the hairs on my fingers stand on end. Pressed against the table by other people sitting behind and beside me, the only view the frosted window-pane in front of which the potted flowers flapped in the air from the heating vent. Only a luxurious existence isn't a punishment, I thought. Only the greatest luxury is worthy of a human being. What's cheap is inhuman.

KILB. That's why your products are always the cheapest.

QUITT. How much do you want for your answer? For once couldn't I be the topic? Me – that's what makes me shy back, that's what I've had enough of, that's what still sits on the tip of my tongue all the time – something as rare and ridiculous as a living mole. I feel watched from all sides like the dead flesh from a wound that has long since healed and still I dance on the inside with self-awareness. Yes, inside I'm dancing! I once sat in the sun in actual shock, the sun was shining on me, not that I felt it, and I really felt like the outline of suffocating nothingness in the airy space around me. But even that was still me, me, me. I was in despair, could neither think back nor forward . . . had no sense of history left. Each recollection came in dribs and drabs, unharmonically, like the recollection of a sex act. This aching lack of feeling, that was myself, and I was not only I but also an attribute of the world. Of course I asked about the terms. Why? Why this condition? These conditions . . . why no history but only these conditions? But all the conditional requirements were fulfilled. No 'whys' helped any more. Only the unconditional require-ments remained. 'I'm bored', a child once said. 'Then play at something. Paint something. Read something. Do something,' it was told. 'But I can't, I'm bored,' it said. (*He keeps taking objects from his pockets, looking at them and putting them back again.*) The goose-step of my soul, you said? I want to speak about – (*Laughs.*) – myself without using categories. I don't want to mean anything any more, please, not be a character in the plot any more. I want to freeze at night in May. Look, these are photos of me: I look happy on all of them and yet I never was. Do you know the feeling when one has put a pair of trousers on backwards? One time I was happy: when I visited someone in a tenement and during a long pause in the conversation I could hear the lavatory flushing in the flat next door. I became musical with happiness! Oh my envy of your sleepy afternoons in those tenements with their mysteriously gargling lavatory bowls! Those are the places I long for: the tower blocks at the edge of the city where the telephone booths are lit up at night. To go into airport hotels and simply check oneself in for safe-keeping. Why are there no depersonification institutes? How beautiful it used to be when you opened a new tin of shoe-polish! And I could still imagine buying a ham sandwich, looking at cemeteries, having something in common with someone. Sometimes one thing simply led exhilaratingly to the other – that's what it meant to feel alive! Now I'm heavy and sore and bulky with myself. (*He punches himself under his chin while talking, kicks his calf.*) One wrong breath and I disintegrate. Do you know that I hear voices? But not the kind of voices that madmen hear: no religious claptrap, or poetry regurgitated from schooldays or one-line philosophies, none of the traditional formulas – but film titles, pop songs, advertising slogans. 'Raindrops are falling on my head' frequently resounds in a whisper in the echo chamber of my head, and in the middle of an embrace a voice interrupts me with 'Guess who's coming to dinner?' or 'Please refrain from smoking in this section of the building . . .' And I am positive that in the future even madmen will only hear voices like that . . . no longer 'know thyself' or 'thou shalt honour thy father and mother . . .', the super-ego voices of our culture. While one set of monsters is being exorcised the next ones are already burping outside the window. (*He interrupts himself.*) How odd: while I go on talking logically like this I simultaneously see, for example, a wintry lake at dusk which is just beginning to freeze over, a small tree with a bottle stuck on its top, and an unshaven Chinaman peering round a doorway – now he's gone again – and, moreover, during the whole time keep humming a certain moronic melody inside myself. (*He hums.* KILB *wants to say something.*) No, *I* am speaking now. I am blowing my horn! The goose-step of my soul. You should try it too. At least try . . . Stand still, why don't you! Do I spit when I talk? Yes, I can feel the spit bubbles on my teeth. But my time to speak isn't over yet. At one time I used to drink, let's hope the next world war doesn't start before my new suit is ready. By talking I want to have the transmission of consciousness, now, before you are finished with me. For too long my lips have held themselves joylessly shut. (*He suddenly embraces* KILB *and holds on to him.*) Why am I talking so fluently? Whereas I actually feel the need to stutter. (*He bends over and therefore presses* KILB *more tightly.* KILB *is writhing.*) I w . . . want to s . . . stutter . . . And why do I see everything so distinctly? I don't want to see the grain in the wood floor so distinctly. I'd like to be short-sighted. I'd like to tremble. Why am I not trembling? Why am I not stuttering? (*He bends over vehemently and* KILB *writhes.*) I once wanted to sleep. But the room was so big. Wherever I lay down I created spots of sleeplessness. The room was too big for me alone. Where is the place to sleep here? Smaller! Smaller! (*He bends over so firmly that* KILB *groans. He bends even more and the groaning ceases.* KILB *falls to the floor and doesn't move.* QUITT *crosses his arms. Pause.*) I can smell the cologne he smelled of. (*Pause.*) How happy I became once when I put on a shirt one of whose buttons had just been sewn on. My shirt is torn. How beautiful! I have already worn it for so long that it has become brittle.

Pause.

A tremendous burping pervades the entire room.

Long pause.

The burping.

QUITT *runs his head against the rock. After some time he gets up and runs against the rock again. He gets up once more and runs against the rock. Then he just lies there. The stage light has been extinguished. Only the trough with the risen dough, the melting block of ice, the shrivelled balloon and the rock are lit. A fruit crate trundles down, as though down several steps, and comes to rest in front of the rock. A long grey carpet rolls out from behind the rock: snakes writhe on the rolled-out carpet and in the fruit crate.*

Notes by Handke

A MANIFESTO

1   Refuse to make any statements.
2   Don't let the truth slip out.
3   Lie through your teeth.
4   Turns things upside-down.
5   Don't let reality become language, let language become reality.
6   Don't talk about language.
7   Get tied up in contradictions.
8   Don't write for today.
9   Don't write for eternity.
10   Keep everything in the balance.
11   Don't face the facts.
12   Don't keep both feet on the ground.
13   Don't set up rules for other people.
14   Stress the importance of conversation as first and last aid.
15   Learn how to die from wildwest films.
16   Recognise in even the smallest gut-spilled frog the absence of God.
17   Overshoot the mark in youthful exuberance.
18   Put your self first.
19   Don't try to put yourself in anyone else's position.
20   Write only about yourself.
21   Always act premeditatedly.
22   Don't exchange thoughts with anyone.
23   Distance yourself from all things human.
24   Seek to talk your way out by writing.
25   Go to the movies.
26   Lie in the grass.
27   Don't compose manifestos.
28   Buy black shoe-polish.
29   Get to be world famous.

NOTE ON THE 'SPRECHSTÜCKE'

The speak-ins (*Sprechstücke*) are spectacles without pictures, inasmuch as they give no picture of the world. They point to the world not by way of pictures but by way of words; the words of the speak-ins don't point at the world as something lying outside the words but to the world in the words themselves. The words that make up the speak-ins give no picture of the world but a concept of it. The speak-ins are theatrical inasmuch as they employ natural forms of expression found in reality. They employ only such expressions as are natural in real speech; that is, they employ the speech forms that are uttered *orally* in real life. The speak-ins employ natural examples of swearing, of self-indictment, of confession, of testimony, of interrogation, of justification, of evasion, of prophecy, of calls for help. Therefore they need a vis-à-vis, at least *one* person who listens; otherwise, they would not be natural but extorted by the author. It is to that extent that my speak-ins are pieces for the theatre. Ironically, they imitate the gestures of all the given devices natural to the theatre.

The speak-ins have no action, since every action on stage would only be the picture of another action. The speak-ins confine themselves, by obeying their natural form, to words. They give no pictures, not even pictures in word form, which would only be pictures the author extorted to represent an internal, unexpressed, wordless circumstance and not a *natural* expression.

Speak-ins are autonomous prologues to the old plays. They do not want to revolutionize, but to make aware.

NOTE ON *Offending the Audience*

Offending the Audience is not a play against the theatre. It's a play against the theatre as it is. It's not even a play against the theatre as it is, it's just a play. *Offending the Audience* is a play against the theatre as it is, and a play for the theatre as it is and was. It's a play against the theatre as it is, only insofar as it requires no story as an excuse for making theatre. It doesn't make use of the mediation of a story in order to create theatre, it is unmediated theatre. The spectator doesn't need to get into a story first, he doesn't need to have pre-histories or post-histories related to him: on stage there is only now, and this is the spectator's now too. If the spectator can bring himself to listen, this now will become comprehensible. That is why it is ultimately not a question of the physical reaction of the spectator, but of his reflection.

Offending the Audience is not a play against the spectator. Or it's only a play against the spectator in order that it may become a play for the spectator. The spectator is alienated, so that he gets to think. The play is not directed against a particular audience either, say against an audience that's sitting back comfortably in their seats. (On the contrary, the audience should sit back as comfortably as they can, or anyway comfortably enough so they can listen attentively.) The play is not written so that the usual audience should make way for another audience, but so that the usual audience should become another audience. The play may serve to make the spectator conscious of his own presence, comfortably or uncomfortably, to make him conscious of himself. It can make him conscious that he's there, that he's present, that he exists. At best it won't affect him, but concern him. It can make him attentive, keen-eared, keen-eyed, not just as a theatre-goer.

KASPAR'S SIXTEEN PHASES

1 phase   Can Kaspar, the owner of one sentence, begin and begin to do something with this sentence?

2 phase   Can Kaspar do something against other sentences with his sentence?

3 phase   Can Kaspar at least hold his own against other sentences with his sentence?

4 phase   Can Kaspar defend himself from other sentences and keep quiet even though other sentences prod him to speak?

5 phase   Can Kaspar only become aware of what he speaks through speaking?

6 phase   Can Kaspar, the owner of sentences, do something with these sentences, not only to other sentences but also to the objects of the other sentences?

7 phase   Can Kaspar bring himself into order with sentences about order, or rather, with ordered sentences?

8 phase   Can Kaspar, from the order of a single sentence, derive a whole series of sentences, a series that represents a comprehensive order?

9 phase   Can Kaspar learn what, in each instance, is the model upon which an infinite number of sentences about order can be based?

10 phase   Can Kaspar, with the sentence model he has learned, make the objects accessible to himself or become himself accessible to the objects?

11 phase   Can Kaspar, by means of sentences, make his contribution to the great community of sentences?

12 phase   Can Kaspar be brought to the point where, with rhyming sentences, he will find rhyme and reason in the objects?

13 phase   Can Kaspar put questions to himself?

14 phase   Can Kaspar, with uninhibited sentences which he applies to his old inhibited sentences, reverse the inverted world of these sentences?

15 phase   Can Kaspar defend himself at least with an inverted world of sentences against inverted sentences about the world?

Or: Can Kaspar, by inverting inverted sentences, at least avoid the false appearance of rightness?

16 phase Who is Kaspar now? Kaspar, who is now Kaspar? What is now, Kaspar? What is now Kaspar, Kaspar?